Cultural Diversity
in the
Workplace

Cultural Diversity in the Workplace

ISSUES AND STRATEGIES

George Henderson

Q

Quorum Books

WESTPORT, CONNECTICUT • LONDON

Library of Congress Cataloging-in-Publication Data

Henderson, George.
  Cultural diversity in the workplace : issues and strategies /
George Henderson.
    p. cm.
  Includes bibliographical references and index.
  ISBN 0–89930–888–0 (alk. paper)
    1. Minorities—Employment—United States. 2. Multiculturalism—
United States. 3. Personnel management—United States. I. Title.
  HF5549.5.M5H46 1994
  658.3′041—dc20   94–2991

British Library Cataloguing in Publication Data is available.

A paperback edition of *Cultural Diversity in the Workplace*
is available from Praeger Publishers, an imprint of
Greenwood Publishing Group, Inc. (ISBN 0–275–95095–6).

Library of Congress Catalog Card Number: 94–2991
ISBN: 0–89930–888–0

First published in 1994

Quorum Books, 88 Post Road West, Westport, CT 06881
An imprint of Greenwood Publishing Group, Inc.

Printed in the United States of America

The paper used in this book complies with the
Permanent Paper Standard issued by the National
Information Standards Organization (Z39.48–1984).

10 9 8 7 6 5 4

This book is dedicated to readers
who embrace the theories and intervention
strategies presented in this book and
become more effective in managing
culturally diverse workers.

Contents

Tables and Figures   ix

Preface   xi

Acknowledgments   xiii

Part One: People

  1. Introduction   3

  2. Ethnic Minorities   19

  3. Women   47

  4. Older Workers   73

  5. Workers with Disabilities   91

  6. Foreign Workers   111

Part Two: Workplace Issues and Interventions

  7. Barriers to Cultural Diversity   133

  8. Communication in Organizations   151

  9. Words That Hurt   177

 10. Cross-Cultural Conflict   195

 11. Epilogue   217

Appendix   231

References   233

Index   253

Tables and Figures

TABLES

1.1 Comparing Affirmative Action, Valuing Differences, and Managing Diversity   7

2.1 Cultural Value Preferences of Middle-Class White Americans and Ethnic Minorities: A Comparative Summary   25

2.2 Occupational Employment in U.S. Private Industry by Race/Ethnic Group/Sex and by Industry, 1990   36

2.3 State and Local Government Employment: Full-Time, 1991—6,080 Reporting Units   37

3.1 How to Tell a Businessman from a Businesswoman   52

6.1 Occupations of Applicants for Legalization   118

8.1 Contrasting Values, Beliefs, and Behaviors   165

11.1 Technical Training versus Diversity Training   219

FIGURES

3.1 Private Sector Employment Participation Rates of Minority Men and Women: U.S. Summary, 1966–1990   56

3.2 State and Local Government Full-Time Employment Participation Rates of Minority Men and Women: U.S. Summary, 1974–1990   57

Preface

I have combined data from several areas of study to capture some of the salient aspects of managing cultural diversity. It is fair for me to warn the reader that this book is not value free or completely objective—if any book can be. A lifetime of living as an African American has too deeply etched in my mind the need for equal opportunity, affirmative action, and cultural diversity in the workplace. Like countless other people of color, I can verify from personal experiences that diversity training at its best helps bring about organization transformation; but when done poorly, people—disproportionately, ethnic minorities and women—are economically, emotionally, and socially hurt. Hopefully, I have written a book that will help administrators facilitate better human relations among *all* employees.

My intended audience consists of managers who currently are trying to effectively and humanely manage culturally diverse employees; college students who may some day have to manage diversity; and consultants who themselves need additional knowledge in their diversity armamentarium. Equally important, I offer a challenge to the employees who bear the brunt of diversity program failures—ethnic minorities, women, older workers, people with disabilities, and immigrants. I encourage them to tell their stories, offer their suggestions, and stay the course until diversity is celebrated and perpetuated.

The cultural diversity problems I discuss in this book exist in some form in all organizations—private and public. In an attempt to seek solutions, rather than assess blame, I have drawn my strategies and recommendations from a variety of sources, including case studies, relevant literature, and my own personal experiences. For CEOs, managers, supervisors, and other people concerned about effectively managing diversity, I have tried to dispel the myth that diversity-related problems will disappear if they are ignored. In the process of managing diversity, an important theme, one many employers have difficulty identifying with and finding comfort in, is the notion that we are people.

The world is made up of people, but the people of the world forget this. It is hard to believe that, like ourselves, other people are born of women, reared by parents, teased by brothers, . . . consoled by wives, . . . flattered by grandchildren, and buried by parsons and priests with the blessing of the church and the tears of those left behind. (Menninger, 1942, p. 114)

The collective attempt of organizational leaders to understand and optimally utilize their diverse workforce is a classical study in frustration. Within most organizations, laughter and incessant chatter frequently hide serious diversity-related problems. In many instances, those problems fester like a cancerous sore and erupt into personnel grievances.

Acknowledgments

I am grateful to Marcy Weiner, acquisitions editor, who not only took a personal interest in the manuscript but also helped me to polish the final draft. Maria denBoer, copy editor, and Karen Davis, production editor, ensured quality editing and production. My special thanks go to Shirley Marshall and Maria Wilson, who typed the manuscript.

Part One

People

CHAPTER 1

Introduction

Based on the most reliable studies, America's workplace will undergo a dramatic metamorphosis within the next decade. That is, during the next ten years, our workforce will be reshaped with respect to race, ethnicity, gender, national origin, and age. Consider, for example, the projections in the Hudson Institute's (1987) *Workforce 2000:*

- Throughout the 1990s, immigrants, women, and minorities will account for 85 percent of the net growth in the labor force.
- By the year 2000, women will account for more than 47 percent of the total workforce, and 61 percent of all American women will be employed.
- By the end of the 1990s, African Americans will make up 12 percent of the labor force; Hispanics, 10 percent; and Asians, Pacific Islanders, and Native Americans, 4 percent. More than 25 percent of the workforce will be comprised of Third World peoples.
- By the year 2000, people aged thirty-five to fifty-four will make up 51 percent of the workforce. But those aged sixteen to twenty-four will decline to about 8 percent.

"Managing diversity" is fast becoming the corporate watchword of the decade—not because corporations are becoming kinder and gentler toward culturally diverse groups but because they want to survive (Edwards, 1991). And in order to survive a growing number of U.S. organizations will have to recruit, train, and promote culturally diverse employees. In essence, this is nothing more than developing additional human resources (Riche, 1991).

THE HUMAN RESOURCE APPROACH

The human resource approach focuses on the interplay between people and the organization, and recognizes that cultural diversity includes every employee. This frame of reference starts with the premise that people are the most important resource in an organization. The challenge is to successfully apply skills, insight, energy, and commitment to make an organization better (Bolman & Deal, 1984). The following major assumptions provide the foundation of this approach: (1) organizations exist to serve human needs; (2) organizations and people need each other; (3) when the fit between the individual and the organization is poor, one or both will suffer; (4) when the fit between the individual and the organization is good, both benefit. The concept of need is very important. And needs are hard to define and difficult to measure.

Of primary importance for effectively managing diversity is the manager's understanding of the cultural beliefs and values of his or her organization. These beliefs and values coalesce to create an environment that employees perceive as supportive or not supportive of diversity. Within all organizations there are culturally supportive and nonsupportive people, policies, and informal structures. This is sometimes referred to as the *organizational climate*—the propensity to perpetuate particular behaviors. The process of change requires skillful interventions. Richard Beckhard (1969) made the following relevant observations about organizations:

1. The basic foundation of an organization is its people, and the basic unit of change is its people.
2. A necessary change goal is the reduction of inappropriate competition among parts of the organization and the development of cooperation.
3. Decision-making in a healthy organization is best delegated to the sources of information rather than being made a function of a set role in a rigid hierarchy.
4. The subunits of an organization tend to manage their affairs in terms of predetermined goals. Controls are set in terms of production measurements, not human relations.
5. One goal of a healthy organization is to develop open communication, mutual trust, and confidence in management.
6. People support what they help create. Ideally, individuals to be affected by a change should be given an opportunity to participate in the planning and implementation of that change.

An organization is only as effective as the people who operate it. Too many public and private organizations are similar to a malnourished body. They look healthy to untrained eyes, but in reality they are sick and decaying inside. The laughter and incessant chatter frequently hide a series of disruptive cultural problems. Like vaudevillian actors, personnel in need of help typically push aside their own problems as they try to perform their jobs. In most instances, there is little or no help for disgruntled minority and female employees. This is not because none of the other personnel want to help. Many of them do, but few of them know how to help their colleagues and subordinates who are culturally different.

A major impetus for diversity lies in the principle upon which the United States was founded: the belief that "all men are created equal." Further, U.S. culture and character have been built on concepts such as "one nation under God, indivisible, with liberty and justice for all." While created by culturally diverse peoples, "one of the hidden rules in American culture is that you don't comment on differences because it is assumed differences mean deficiency" (Edwards, 1991, p. 46). The denial of difference is illustrated in the following situation: An unknown African-American male walked into a room full of white executives and they ignored him. Yet each of them frantically tried to find out "Why is *he* here?" During the same period, two unknown white males also entered the room. They were greeted and quickly incorporated into the group. Sue Schellenbarger (1993) cited data to show that employees who have experiences living or working with people of other races, ethnic groups, and ages exhibit greater preference for diversity in the workplace. But few employees—even those under twenty-five years of age—have this kind of experience.

THE CHALLENGE OF DIVERSITY

The challenge of getting women and minorities into senior-level management positions is difficult. While the proportion of women and minorities in the workforce has increased significantly during the past decade, few of them have made it to the top. Specifically, women and minorities account for more than 50 percent of the American workforce but they comprise less than 5 percent of senior management positions (Nelton, 1991). Gains have been slow. For example, in 1983 there were 482,000 (4.5%) black Americans in executive, administrative, and managerial positions; in 1991 there were 858,000 (5.7%). This was a modest gain of 1.2 percent. Also in 1991, only three out of every one hundred top executive positions in Fortune 500 corporations were held by women (Saltzman, 1991). There is indeed a *glass ceiling*—an invisible barrier that prevents a disproportionate number of women and minorities from rising to top corporate positions (Combs & Gruhl, 1986; Cox, 1991; Gunsch & Filipowski, 1991; Morrison, White & Velsor, 1982). For this reason, diversity must be valued, nurtured, and effectively managed.

Along with shifts in organization demographics come additional competition. Some white male employees must now compete against people they did not consider rivals before—mainly women, blacks, Hispanics, and Asians. Even though they still control most of the managerial positions, many white males sense an impending loss of job entitlements. They are,

Thomas Kochman observed, "like the firstborn in the family, the ones who have had the best love of both parents and never forgave the second child for being born" (Galen & Palmer, 1994, p. 52). The transition from a workplace dominated by white males to one in which managerial and supervisory jobs are shared with representatives of other groups usually precipitates tension and conflict. The issue is further complicated by organization downsizing and restructuring—activities that add to the fear of lost opportunities.

For many white male employees the central measure of diversity is "ability" or "merit." Numerous surveys document that most white males do not object to women, minorities, and other underrepresented people being hired or promoted if they are the best qualified people. Unfortunately, when women and minorities in particular are appointed, some white males are quick to cry "tokenism" or "reverse discrimination." Often, in these instances, white males project a higher standard of "best qualified" for women and minorities than themselves. That is, women and minorities are expected to be better than best—a contradiction of qualifications.

Andrew Brimmer (1993) put employment discrimination against blacks into a national perspective:

Such discrimination doesn't hurt only blacks. In 1991, racial bias deprived the American economy of about $215 billion and was equal to roughly 3.8% of the gross domestic product (GDP). While part of the loss can be traced to the lag in black educational achievement, the bulk is related to bias that hampers access to higher paying jobs. (p. 27)

Contrary to some critics, black workers are still the last hired and the first fired. There is no conclusive evidence to support the assumption that white males are more productive workers than minorities and women. Qualified minorities and women are routinely passed over for jobs and promotions in favor of less qualified white males (McCoy, 1994). If equal opportunity is a worthwhile goal, as most Americans believe, it will be achieved through structured outreach, recruitment, training, retention, and promotion—affirmative action, valuing diversity, and managing diversity.

Words and Action

It is important for employers to know the difference among affirmative action, valuing diversity, and managing diversity. (See Table 1.1.) *Affirmative action* refers to legally mandated written plans and statistical goals for recruiting, training, and promoting specific underutilized groups. This quantitative, compliance-oriented approach is remedial in that it attempts to right previous wrongs. The major focus is to assimilate qualified, underrepresented people into the organization. It is assumed that difference is

Table 1.1

Comparing Affirmative Action, Valuing Differences, and Managing Diversity

Affirmative Action	Valuing Differences	Managing Diversity
Quantitative. Emphasis is on achieving equality of opportunity in the work environment through the changing of organizational demographics. Progress is monitored by statistical reports and analyses.	**Qualitative.** Emphasis is on the appreciation of differences and the creation of an environment in which everyone feels valued and accepted. Progress is monitored by organizational surveys focused on attitudes and perceptions.	**Behavioral.** Emphasis is on building specific skills and creating policies that get the best from every employee. Efforts are monitored by progress toward achieving goals and objectives.
Legally driven. Written plans and statistical goals for specific groups are utilized. Reports are mandated by EEO laws and consent decrees.	**Ethically driven.** Moral and ethical imperatives drive this culture change.	**Strategically driven.** Behaviors and policies are seen as contributing to organizational goals and objectives such as profit and productivity, and are tied to rewards and results.
Remedial. Specific target groups benefit as past wrongs are remedied. Previously excluded groups have an advantage.	**Idealistic.** Everyone benefits. Everyone feels valued and accepted in an inclusive environment.	**Pragmatic.** The organization benefits: morale, profits and productivity increase.
Assimilation Model. Model assumes that groups brought into the system will adapt to existing organizational norms.	**Diversity model.** Model assumes that groups will retain their own characteristics and shape the organization as well as be shaped by it, creating a common set of values.	**Synergy model.** Model assumes that diverse groups will create new ways of working together effectively in a pluralistic environment.
Opens doors. Efforts affect hiring and promotion decisions in the organization.	**Opens attitudes, minds and the culture.** Efforts affect attitudes of employees.	**Opens the system.** Efforts affect managerial practices and policies.
Resistance. Resistance is due to perceived limits to autonomy in decision making and perceived fears of reverse discrimination.	**Resistance.** Resistance is due to a fear of change, discomfort with differences, and a desire to return to the "good old days."	**Resistance.** Resistance is due to denial of demographic realities, of the need for alternative approaches, and of the benefits of change. It also arises from the difficulty of learning new skills, altering existing systems, and finding the time to work toward synergistic solutions.

Source: Adapted from *Managing Diversity: A Complete Desk Reference and Planning Guide,* by Lee Gardenswartz and Anita Rowe. Copyright 1993, Business One Irwin.

synonymous with deficit. In this instance, majority-group employees tend to describe selective "minority" or "affirmative action" hires as evidence of reverse discrimination. While generally effective, affirmative action may inadvertently be analogous to a cloud over the careers of protected class employees, especially minorities and women. Frequently, there is speculation that some of them are not the best qualified people for the jobs.

Valuing diversity evolves around moral and ethical imperatives to recognize and appreciate culturally diverse peoples (Broadnax, 1992). Theoretically, every member of an organization is to be valued. This is a pluralistic approach that does not seek assimilation: difference is better. Like salads or flowers, people have value for their own unique contributions to the organization. The focus is mainly on changing employees' perceptions and attitudes about minorities and women. In many instances this approach results in white male bashing, which magnifies rather than lessens intergroup conflict.

Managing diversity emphasizes managerial skills and policies needed to optimize every employee's contribution to the organizational goals. Initiatives are taken not because of legal mandates or moral and ethical imperatives but instead to enhance organization morale, productivity, and benefits. After underrepresented people are hired and employee consciousness had been raised, appropriate policies, procedures, and managerial interventions are needed to operationalize a culturally diverse workplace. Edward Jones (1986) offered this advice: "Corporations cannot manage attitudes, but they can manage behavior with accountability, rewards, and punishment, as in all other important areas of concern. What gets measured in business gets done, what is not measured is ignored" (p. 93).

The Bottom Line

Some managers and supervisors deal with hundreds of cross-cultural employee problems as well as millions of dollars worth of business capital. Regardless of the number of employees and capital involved, the task of managing diversity in the workplace is enormous. Most employers do not question the assumption that human resources are their most valuable asset (Peters & Waterman, 1982). The dimensions of cross-cultural problems, however, are seldom adequately covered in college courses or inservice training programs (Hill, 1981; Steinmetz, 1969). The gravity of unresolved employee problems was vividly underscored by Dale Masi (1984), who speculated that only 18 percent of any workforce population is working at 75 percent capacity; the others are working below capacity.

Masi's estimate may be too low because it includes only measurable things such as absenteeism, sick leave, accidents, and rising health costs. He did not factor in other costs associated with employee personal problems: poor job-related decisions, decreased work quality, early retirement, and workers' compensation claims. Nor did he consider the fact that "The incidence of mental, emotional, and personality disorders in the work force and the economic costs of such disorders to places of employment are of such proportions that they cannot be ignored" (Follman, 1978, p. 138). Problems centering on diversity issues almost always impact economic costs. The most incriminating costs are legal fees and plaintiff awards in discrimination and sexual harassment cases. Employees who believe they have little opportunity for career advancement tend to be less loyal, less committed, and less satisfied on the job than their co-workers who project career advancement.

James Greiff (1989) postulated that 10 percent to 15 percent of American adults develop problems that interfere with their job effectiveness. This includes diversity-related problems such as racial and sexual harassment that culminate in worker alienation. Joseph Follman estimated that 80 percent to 90 percent of industrial accidents are due to emotional problems. The major reason most employers try to prevent or abate these problems is cost. Further, Frink (1992) calculated that the national average cost of replacing an employee is $7,000, which includes only recruitment and hiring processes. From this perspective, Thomas Peters and Robert Waterman (1982) were correct to caution CEOs to treat their employees as the primary source or productivity gains, not as capital spending. A satisfied, healthy, diverse workforce is a requisite to a productive workforce.

Contrary to popular opinion, managing a diverse workforce is not a new concept. The more effective managers have always been aware of the cultural differences in their employees. But awareness is not enough. Managers must be able to utilize the skills of each employee and do so in a way that maximizes his or her unique contributions. For people who are concerned mainly with the "bottom line" of effectively managing diversity, Jack Gordon (1992) cited several large discrimination lawsuit awards that the companies probably would have avoided if managers and supervisors had valued and sensitively managed their culturally diverse employees: State Farm Insurance, $300 million; General Motors, $40 million; USX Corporation, $42 million; K Mart, $3 million; Pillsbury, $1.8 million; Northwest Airlines, $1.2 million. The average discrimination suit that is litigated costs a company about $75,000.

In a more positive vein, Rosabeth Kanter (1983) cited a study that showed that companies with progressive affirmative action and equal opportunity programs had unusually high profitability and financial growth over a twenty-five-year period. Diversity benefits organizations in the following ways: (1) CEOs who value diversity promote a harmonious workforce and better serve customers and clients who are culturally diverse; (2) managers and supervisors skilled in managing culturally diverse subordinates run productive departments; (3) managers and supervisors who are comfortable with culturally diverse employees facilitate less worker turnover and greater work efficiency; and (4) employees who value diversity interact more effectively with each other, thereby enhancing productivity and job satisfaction.

Even with the rash of diversity workshops and in-service training programs, most managers and supervisors do not adequately understand the cultural backgrounds or skills of their employees. Few college courses focusing on business law, accounting, and organizational behavior adequately address problems and strategies for change that center on culturally diverse workers. Relatedly, quick-fix on-the-job training activities merely scratch the surface and, in some instances, do more harm than good (Mobley & Payne, 1992). The typical approach of such training is to try to homogenize the employees. Although most organizations have a rich heritage of creating sameness out of differences in order to achieve "organization effectiveness," managerial tactics and behaviors that worked in previous years are becoming increasingly dysfunctional in the global marketplace. John McConnell's approach epitomizes a philosophy that is becoming archaic:

The time has come when if you give me any normal being and a couple of weeks I can change his behavior from what it is now to whatever you want it to be, if it's physically possible. I can't make him fly by flapping his wings, but I can turn him from Christian into a Communist and vice versa. (Quoted in Flanders, 1976, p. 121)

In order to be effective in relating to culturally diverse workers, a manager must possess a degree of sophistication in understanding their beliefs and values (Huber & Williams, 1986). That is, managers must: (1) recognize individual differences, (2) allow for ego defensiveness, and (3) accept rather than merely tolerate culturally diverse workers. In addition, four other areas require attention: (1) stereotypes and their associated assumptions, (2) actual cultural differences, (3) the exclusivity of the "white male club" and its associated access to important organization information and relationships, and (4) unwritten rules and double standards for success that are often unknown to minorities and women.

Among human beings, being different is normal. Each person has an individual history and a unique socially constructed reality that sets him or her apart from other people. Yet there is the tendency for managers to pay more attention to employees' cultural differences than individual similarities. James Anderson (1993) cautioned managers to be aware that "Different types of employees have different perceptions about instructions, problem solving tasks, and so forth. . . . Some workers need nurturing, affiliation, and cooperation to be at their most productive. Others perceive the role of manager as one of rigid, authoritarian ways. . . . Some people value intrinsic motivation; others prefer extrinsic rewards" (p. 60). These differences cut across cultural boundaries.

THROUGH THE LOOKING GLASS

If the United States is to continue to be economically competitive, it must reverse the low-skill, high-wage workforce trend. Skills deficiencies in the workplace cost in waste, lost productivity, increased worker remediation expenses, reduced product quality, and, ultimately, a loss in competitiveness. The United States can compete globally with other industrial nations if it correctly utilizes its culturally diverse workforce. This means that talents are not wasted because of irrelevant job criteria such as race, gender, religion, or country of origin (Hasan, 1992). Two basic ways to improve the quality of the American workforce are to invest in creating additional labor market skills and to use the skills that currently exist more efficiently (Nelton, 1992).

In 1989 the Department of Labor launched a program called the "Glass Ceiling Initiative," which examined the issue of a glass ceiling in nine Fortune 500 companies (Dominquez, 1992). The results of this study are as follows:

- There was a glass ceiling or level beyond which very few minorities and women advanced. In fact, the level was lower than the researchers had expected. Much of the glass ceiling literature focuses on the executive suite. The critical mass of minorities and women were employed well below that level. Furthermore, the study found that minorities plateaued at levels lower than women.

- There was a lack of corporate strategies to achieve equal employment opportunity practices. Relatedly, monitoring for equal access and opportunity was more frequently perceived as the responsibility of someone in the human resources office than as a collective corporate responsibility.

- Minorities and women were largely employed in staff positions instead of line positions where there was more of a career track to the executive suite and greater bonus and reward eligibility.

- Minorities and women did not have as much access as other employees to career development practices and credential-building experiences, including advanced education and career-enhancing assignments such as membership on corporate committees, task forces, and special projects.

- Recruitment practices prevented a disproportionately large number of qualified minorities and women from being considered for management positions. Nor were all of the executive search firms employed by the companies aware of their equal employment opportunity responsibilities as agents of companies. Also, recruitment practices such as word-of-mouth announcements and employee referrals resulted in a paucity of qualified minority and female applicants.

- There were inadequate provisions within the companies for monitoring the total compensation systems that determined salaries, bonuses, incentives, and perks to ensure nondiscriminatory practices.

A challenge that must be met by many organizations is to devise ways for employees to expand their individual comfort zones. It is no secret that most employees tend to associate or bond with people who are most like them (Thomas, 1990). This tendency makes it much more difficult for relative newcomers in the workplace (women, minorities, immigrants, and individuals with disabilities) to move up the organization ladder. Lacking access to networking opportunities and seeing few, if any, role models to emulate, minorities, women, and other protected class people are often alienated in the workplace. This suggests the need for organizations to involve all employees in culture creation, to endorse a "different but equal" operating philosophy, and to have flexible definitions of effective job performances.

Because valuing diversity represents a major change in the management of human resources, it cannot succeed without commitment at all levels. Within leading-edge organizations, this realization has mobilized senior executives to become visibly and philosophically identified with diversity efforts. They are not shadow supporters. Rather, these executives seek additional knowledge about the issues, speak the language of diversity, and attempt to practice what they mandate as they set policy and provide guidance (Flower, 1989; Morrison, 1992). Rather than position themselves as "experts," they tend to present themselves as "motivated learners" with a personal and professional interest in acquiring more knowledge (Cox, 1991; Loden & Loeser, 1991).

In most leading-edge organizations, managers recognize the difference between equal treatment and treating everyone the same. They do not expect all employees to adapt their personal styles of working in order to "fit" an amorphous, homogeneous standard. Instead, they recognize and respect the different perspectives, talents, and communication styles of diverse employees. In evaluating performances, these managers try to distinguish *style* from *substance,* so that many styles and approaches can be accommodated without sacrificing effectiveness within the organization. As the homogeneous ideal fades, new standards of effective performances are incorporated. And these standards are now being developed with the active involvement of diverse employee groups.

Assumptions

Once diversity is accepted as an organizational value, new assumptions about its positive benefits surface. While they may not be written down or well-articulated, the following assumptions influence the day-to-day actions within leading-edge organizations.

There is the belief that employee diversity is a competitive advantage. Little time is spent debating the importance of diversity or the need for change. Instead, most managers and subordinates understand that diversity is a reality and they assume that it can provide an important competitive advantage in the workplace and the marketplace. For example, members of profit organizations see diversity as a means of enhancing recruitment, expanding markets, and improving customer satisfaction. As one corporate recruiter stated, "If we can create a culture of diversity, we'll be able to beat our competitors in campus recruiting. Women and people of color will be more receptive to us. They will know that there is more opportunity for them in our company than our competitors."

There is a goal to change the organization culture, not the people. The most common assumption within leading-edge organizations is the belief that valuing diversity requires the organization culture to change and not employees who already have relevant job skills (Hammond & Kleiner, 1992). Unlike traditional organizations that attempt to train, coach, and coerce diverse employees to "fit" within the cultural mainstream, leading-edge organizations focus on modifying policies and systems to optimize employee self-actualization. These organizations abolish standards that are no longer appropriate in order to make room for new ways of doing things. This focus on culture change rather than individual change frequently results in innovative ways of doing business. Instead of blaming employees who have culturally different ways of doing work, managers take responsibility for the "poor chemistry" and, when prudent, alter the work climate.

It is acknowledged that conflict is inevitable. As cultural awareness builds and the culture changes, conflict is viewed as part of the change process. The more effective managers are able to tolerate conflict, and they identify potential conflict situations. Relatedly, culturally diverse employees in these organizations are generally patient with the pace of change as long as the organization makes good faith efforts. Most employees understand and accept the fact that creating an optimally diversified culture requires long-term strategies that embody ongoing discussion, debate, and modification. Because all members of the organization are affected by the change process as they move closer to creating a more viable heterogeneous culture, all employees experience varying degrees of the pain inherent in discarding traditions, practices, and embedded biases that characterize the status quo. The emerging culture typically has the following characteristics:

• executives are responsible for setting the organization climate
• systems and procedures are established that support diversity
• recruitment, promotion, and employee development are closely monitored
• culture awareness education is an organizational priority
• rewards are based on job performance

LEADERSHIP CONSTRAINTS

A number of constraints act on managers and supervisors during the course of their jobs that inhibit them from being supportive of new initiatives. A major constraint inherent in most organizations is the CEO expectation of financial prudence by his or her managers and supervisors. This leads many administrators to fire, lay off, or seek the early retirement of employees who need equity adjustments or medical care. When forced to choose between saving people or saving money, many administrators opt for the latter. Thus, in those organizations, particularly those that have undergone downsizing, administrators who have fired, laid off, or retired majority-group employees are uneasy with mandates to hire minority and women workers. Even the most socially sensitive manager is vulnerable to this kind of Hobson's choice. It is, in short, a moral consternation in which one group wins at the expense of another group.

Basically, two terms are paramount in analyzing diversity-related leadership styles: consideration and initiating structure. *Consideration* means administrators will take care of their subordinates, who in turn want supervisors to reward them for good job performance, to stand up for them, to be approachable, and to assist them in the solution of personal problems. Above all else, employees want their supervisor to protect their jobs. This is a major reason it is difficult to recruit or retain new employees during downsizing.

Initiating structure is another way of saying "getting the job done with people in mind." Specifically, it involves defining a mission, organizing the tasks to be accomplished, and devising methods to perform them. It includes such specifics as establishing organization patterns, developing two-way channels of communication, and assigning specific tasks to individuals. One common error some organizations make when initiating diversity programs is the belief that concern for mission achievement and concern for cultural diversity are mutually contradictory. There is no plausible yardstick of organization effectiveness that has productivity goals at the one end and accomplishment of diversity at the other. The effective organization will satisfy both. Again, using the downsizing illustration, frequently friends of individuals who lost their job view the new employees as impeding productivity goals.

If administrators are to be mediators between their organization and culturally diverse employees, this function must be recognized at all levels of the hierarchical structure. It must be translated into general policy guidelines. Unrealistic policies and regulations only serve to alienate employees. The diversity climate of an organization can be measured by the following:

1. *Structure:* the beliefs all workers have about the freedom or constraints of their work situation
2. *Responsibility:* the feeling supervisors have of being in control and not having to "run upstairs" every time a culturally related decision must be made
3. *Risk:* the degree to which employees believe they can initiate job improvement
4. *Standards:* the extent to which challenging goals are set for each employee; that is, the emphasis employees believe is placed on doing the best possible job
5. *Reward:* the degree to which employees are rewarded for good work and not discriminated against

6. *Support:* the perceived amount of helpfulness from managers and supervisors in accomplishing tasks

7. *Conflict:* the belief of employees that administrators do or do not want to hear different opinions in order to get internal problems out in the open where they can be dealt with

8. *Warmth:* the feeling of "fellowship" or lack of it that prevails in the organization

9. *Identity:* the degree to which individual employees feel that they are members of the organization "family"

It should be clear by now that regardless of how much power or formal authority an organization confers on its administrators, *usable* power and authority are granted by their subordinates. A human relations approach to leadership is gaining acceptance in private and public organizations. Indeed, such an approach is being implemented in some places to winnow common goals from contradictory points of view. Cultural sensitivity sessions, films, speakers with well-defined messages, and carefully controlled role-playing are but a few of many in-service activities available to administrators endeavoring to create culturally viable organizations characterized as having intercultural conflict.

There is a new spirit among administrators who dare to innovate and deviate from tradition in order to solve diversity problems that sometimes have no guiding precedent. The rigid conformist and the technocratic midget are on the way out, as is the empathy distance between supervisors and subordinates. Leadership in the diversity game is not a spectator sport; the best and the worst of persons enter the arena. Albert Schweitzer's (1961) message is appropriate: "Let those who hold the fates of people in their hands be careful to avoid everything which may worsen our situation or make it more perilous. Let them take to heart the marvelous words of the Apostle Paul: As much as lies in you, be at peace with all men. They have meaning, not only for individuals, but also for nations" (p. 100).

Sometimes organizations undergoing cultural diversity training resemble nations whose citizens are at war with each other. The wounded become alcoholics, develop ulcers, acquire mental problems, or burn out. Those fatally injured lose their jobs or die on the job. Organizations of this kind desperately need to be at peace with themselves. No organization should be a battlefield, but many of them are perceived that way by their employees. These organizations need the best possible administrators.

PRELUDE TO DIVERSITY

Most diversity problems are rooted in the organization culture. Certainly group therapy is an alternative. Another alternative is affirmative action designed to change jobs. One of the reasons managers and supervisors are continually frustrated is because the social problems they are called upon to solve are themselves the products of a larger social environment. Frequently, for example, an alienated worker's problem resolution depends not on his or her adjustment to an existing situation but instead on being moved to another job or another company. This kind of environmental change is modeled after milieu therapy. It is clear that many minorities and women do not get the help they need because company resources are not attuned to their needs. The more effective employers behave in the following manner:

1. They regard each employee as a vital part of the organization.
2. They view all personnel positively, because whatever diminishes anyone's self (e.g., humiliation, discrimination, degradation, failure) has no place in a culturally sensitive organization.
3. They allow and provide for individual and cultural differences.
4. They learn how employees see things.

Since sensitivity to their own feelings is a prerequisite to effective leadership, it is beneficial for administrators to have maximum self-insight. For some administrators, this is an integral part of their personality; for others it must be learned. A growing number of administrators are participating in some type of sensitivity training. If it is true that helping across cultures can be accomplished only with the assistance of a healthier person, then it is imperative that administrators "have themselves together." An ethnic minority worker does not need guidance from an administrator who is a racist. Nor does a female employee need a sexist supervisor. The more effective administrator is a mature person who functions with compassionate efficiency, who is able to assist his or her subordinates to solve their problems without resorting to pity, panic, or resignation. This type of administrator maintains professional balance and keeps his or her perspective through the use of self-insight and humor.

Once diversity-related problems are identified, managers should move with great care when implementing change. Some actions, although well-intentioned, will only exacerbate the problems. Anything that disrupts the existing flow of work activities can cause additional complaints and stress. This is especially true when the following conditions occur:

1. When the purpose of the diversity activities are not made clear. Suspense and anxiety are caused by mystery and ambiguity. Fear of change can be as disruptive as change itself. Administrators trying to help employees who have been discriminated against must make their reasons and intentions clear. Otherwise, all employees may see a Machiavellian plot where none is intended.
2. When persons affected by the change are not involved in the planning. People tend to support what they help plan and to resist what is imposed by others.

Involving all appropriate personnel in plans to assist a co-worker will be better received than telling them what has been decided for them to do.

3. When the habit patterns of work groups are ignored. Every work situation develops unique ways of doing things. The administrator who ignores institutionalized patterns of work and abruptly attempts to restructure them is likely to run into resistance. This is true even when reordering work patterns of an underutilized employee to prolong or increase that employee's job usefulness.

4. When there is poor communication regarding the change. All personnel expect, need, and want to be informed about changes *before* they occur.

5. When excessive work pressure is involved. Frequently, such pressure results when managers do not plan changes far enough in advance or are uneasy about these changes themselves.

6. When anxiety over job security is not relieved. Aggrieved employees, as well as those who are not, need to know what is going to happen to them. Individuals or subunits of an organization will try to protect themselves and their "empires."

The issues and change strategies introduced in this chapter are elaborated upon in subsequent ones. In this way diversity strategies are covered in a spiral approach.

CHAPTER 2

Ethnic Minorities

Most Americans can trace their ancestry back to some country across the oceans or the Mexican-American or Canadian-American borders. Each ethnic group has enriched our culture with its own particular types of music, food, customs, and dress. It usually takes two or more generations for the members of a new immigrant group to become sufficiently absorbed into the life of a community that they lose their separate identity. Some ethnic groups—mainly those of dark skin colors—never achieve total assimilation.

People concerned about and committed to improving intergroup relations must guard against such clichés as "I'm not prejudiced" and "I treat all people the same." Even the most "liberal" individuals do not treat all people the same. And, as shall be discussed in detail, they should not. All people are prejudiced *for* or *against* other people. However, *it is behaviors, not attitudes, which comprise the major intergroup problems confronting managers and supervisors.* There are many laws against discriminatory behaviors, but there are none against prejudicial attitudes. The ethnic prejudices found in neighborhoods, schools, and jobs come from two main sources: (1) the values and beliefs individuals learn from others, and (2) the tensions and frustrations all people experience while competing with other people, especially those who are culturally different. Race and racism, outgrowths of prejudice, disrupt organization behaviors (Shepherd & Penna, 1991).

DEFINITIONS

Although outmoded geography books, using color as a criterion, once divided people neatly into five races—white, yellow, brown, black, and red—these arbitrary divisions have no validity because there is no defensible means by which world populations can be precisely categorized: "Races, however defined, are not fixed entities with precise boundaries. Topologically defined races based on phenotypical likenesses do not correspond to genetic reality. In the light of modern genetics, races can best be defined as inter-breeding populations sharing a common gene pool" (Brown, 1973, p. 44). In a consideration of racial matters, a much more practical dictum, and one too often unobserved, is that all people belong to one and the same species and that the similar characteristics within the species are much greater than any differences that may be called "racial."

Regardless of the manner chosen to define race, researchers have found that the individual differences *within* races are greater than the differences *between* them, and that all individuals vary to some degree in nearly every factor that combines to constitute human beings. Of far greater importance than the variations among humans are the similarities that inextricably lead to defining the human condition. Acknowledging this truth, many writers believe that incumbent upon *Homo sapiens* is the collective responsibility of creating a world in which all human beings are accorded the status of "persons" and are not regarded as "things" or "objects" to be exploited.

The term *racism* derives from credence placed on the concept of race, for inherent in the concept is an acceptance of the validity of racial distinctions. Racism, in fact, implies that superior or inferior behavior is determined by race. In scholarly works, the term *scientific racism* is employed to describe a racial interpretation of history, or the belief that peoples of different races have different histories and cultures as a result of their race. However, the vast majority of anthropologists who study both race and culture conclude that culture affects race much more than race affects culture. Despite this, in common parlance, the term *racism* connotes discrimination and prejudice. Commenting on this, Whitney Young (1969) defined racism as "the assumption of superiority and the arrogance that goes with it" (p. 73). Almost one hundred years earlier, Benjamin Disraeli (1849) warned the British Parliament: "The difference of race is one of the reasons why I fear war may always exist; because race implies difference, difference implies superiority, and superiority leads to predominance" (p. 111).

In any attempt to understand racism in the workplace, distinctions need to be made among: (1) institutional structures and personal behavior, and the relationship between the two; (2) the variation in both degree and form of expression of individual prejudice; and (3) the fact that racism is but one form of a larger and more inclusive pattern of ethnocentrism that may be based on any number of factors, many of which are nonracial in character. A review of American cultures clearly shows that the historical sources of American race relations are infinitely complex, and there is little doubt that racial bias and discrimination have been built into most American institutions. Corrine Brown (1973) concluded: "The United States thus can be called a racist society in that it is racially divided and its whole organization is such as to promote racial distinctions" (p. 8). In this frame of reference, every citizen is necessarily a product of institutional racism, but expressions vary from person to person, in both degree and kind. It is also well to remember that what is commonly called racism is part of the larger problem of ethnic identification, of power and powerlessness, and of the exploitation of the weak by the strong.

To relegate employees to less than full human status on the basis of their membership in a particular group, whether the group is based on race, class, or religion, is a phenomenon that has become increasingly intolerable to those who are oppressed. To abolish the dilemmas within organizations that stem from racism, institutional arrangements as well as personal behaviors must sometimes be drastically revised.

What most writers commonly call *race relations* should be properly understood in the larger context of *human relations*. Of particular concern should be the expression of negative attitudes and behavior by people toward others according to their identification as members of a particular group. The expression of these attitudes and behavioral patterns is not innate but is learned as a part of the cultural process. Because of this, hope that they can be modified is justified. Negative group attitudes and destructive group conflicts are less likely to arise when employees treat each other as individuals and respond to each other on the basis of individual characteristics and behavior. It is a truism that race-relations patterns are learned behaviors or cultural patterns. And cultural patterns are but the sum of a given people's way of thinking, feeling, and acting. These patterns are not unalterable, however, and with proper interventions and patience lend themselves to modification.

Today with rapid communication and increased mobility, with the findings of science and the events of history generally made known, people everywhere are becoming aware of the alternatives to old ways. They have access to facts of history and interpretations of science that were previously unknown or unavailable to them. There have thus been opened up to them new conceptions of themselves and of other people. Much of the turmoil of the world today can be traced to the fact that modern communications and mobility have made people everywhere aware of cultural alternatives. All of these things are of the greatest significance in our changing patterns of race relations. (Brown, 1973, p. 22)

In understanding racism, an important variable is the presence of *power*. It is the power to enforce the "prejudgment" of superiority or inferiority that leads to racism. Judy Katz (1978) wrote: "Racism is perpetuated by whites through their conscious and/or unconscious support of a culture and institutions that are founded on racist policies and practices. The racial prejudice of white people coupled with political, economic, and social power to enforce discriminatory practices on every level of life—cultural, institutional, and individual—is the gestalt of white racism" (p. 10). This perspective, while intriguing, is too simplistic. It relegates African Americans, for instance, to the role of passive recipients or hosts of white racists. Another important concept in understanding racism is the idea of *ownership of the problem*. Numerous writers define racism in the United States as a national problem perpetuated in some manner by all citizens, and therefore all citizens own the problem and can help end it. Of course there is credence in the proposition that the white American majority is in the best position to combat racism (Atkinson et al., 1979). But if there is to be a successful war on racism, it will be won with the concerted efforts of representatives from all ethnic groups.

Aggregation of Third World peoples in categories (African, Asian, Hispanic, etc.) is not an adequate substitute for knowing the individual ethnic groups within such categories. However, most Americans also aggregate Euro-Americans into an amorphous "white people" group. Consider the distortions inherent in the generic term *Asian Americans* or the more inclusive term *Asian and Pacific Americans*. They are comprised of population groups from four geographic areas: (1) East Asia—China, Japan, Korea; (2) South Asia—India, Pakistan, Sri Lanka; (3) Southeast Asia—Burma, Cambodia, Indonesia, Laos, Malaysia, the Philippines, Thailand, Vietnam; (4) the Pacific Islands—Guam, Hawaii, Samoa, and Tonga. These peoples have different historical, linguistic, and sociocultural identities. But they also share common folkways and mores. Therefore, nothing short of finding out as much as one can about a particular group and, of course, the individuals within it will suffice as adequate for planning social interventions.

The term *Hispanic,* a generic name for all Spanish-surnamed peoples who reside in the United States or Puerto Rico, has generated considerable differences of opinion among its three major groups—Mexican Americans, Puerto Ricans, and Cubans—about whether they should be called something else. For example, on the East Coast the term *Hispanic* is preferred by most Puerto Ricans and Cubans; on the West Coast, the terms *Latino* (a Spanish word for people of Latin-American origins) and *Chicano* (Mexican Americans and people of Mexican heritage born in the United States) are preferred. Further, *La Raza* refers to all the peoples of the Western Hemisphere who share a cultural heritage of Spanish conquistadors, native Indians, and Africans.

Ethnicity and race are often confused in the United States. For example, Hispanics from the Americas and Puerto Rico with African ancestors, even though they tend to identify with their native country, are frequently and erroneously labeled *African Americans* in the U.S. workplace. The terms *blacks, African Americans,* and *people of color* are popular. Some writers use them interchangeably without understanding that African Americans do not include peoples of African descent who are not American citizens; and people of color refers to minorities with darker skin tone—blacks, Hispanics, Asians, Native Americans, and the like—not just African Americans.

Also of popular use are the terms *American Indians* and *Native Americans.* Some people who prefer the term *American Indians* do not favor Native Americans as their designation because it is also used for Alaskan natives. Even so, the terms are commonly used interchangeably.

Myths and Stereotypes

The United States is a nation founded on principles that affirm the supreme worth of each human being. From this idea comes the basis for the common bond of all citizens. Even so, relatively few people live by such egalitarian tenets (Farley & Allen, 1987). Although public opinion research has consistently documented a steady decline in race prejudice among Americans, reports released by the National Opinion Research Center note that a majority of white respondents believe that African Americans and Hispanics are more inclined than Caucasians to prefer welfare and to be lazier, more prone to violence, less intelligent, and less patriotic (Schuman, Steeth & Bobo, 1985). There are no substantial empirical data to support the belief that racial discrimination has been eliminated in the United States in general and in the workplace in particular (Stuart, 1992; Van Horn, 1985). Now, let us look at some erroneous beliefs pertaining to ethnic minorities in the United States.

Myth 1: Every individual is not entitled to equal rights and dignity.
   Reality: We cannot "grant" dignity to others. They are entitled to it by virtue of being human. This principle is embodied in the Golden Rule: "Do unto others as you would have others do unto you." Little dignity accrues to people called niggers, dagos, honkies, greasers, wops, Christ killers, red savages, and so forth. Nor is it likely that recipients of such epithets will receive equal rights.

Myth 2: The right to be free does not imply the right to be different.
   Reality: The American Revolution was fought to free the colonists from the tyranny of the British Empire, which limited their political thoughts and actions. A basic point of contention was the right to be different. Reminiscent of the English tyranny that led to the Revolution are the restrictive acts of the superpatriots who would silence individuals desiring to exercise *their* right to be different.

Myth 3: Democracy can work for some citizens without working for all. *Reality:* This premise contradicts: "One nation under God, indivisible, with liberty and justice for all"—another way of saying that until all citizens are free, no one is free. Americans form a human chain that is only as free or as enslaved as the individuals who make up its links. Racial discrimination is pulling the United States apart as a nation, and economic discrimination is keeping it apart as groups.

Myth 4: Minority employees are happier with their own kind. *Reality:* In the world of work, only a few high-status minority employees take an active part in the informal activities related to their jobs, while most low-status employees share in none at all. Acting as gatekeepers of informal job-related activities, some high-status workers—majority- and minority-group employees—resist broadening the base of participation to include low-status minority employees. "They need the time to improve their job skills" and "They wouldn't be happy with *our* crowd" are reasons frequently given for restricting the base of participation. When this happens, minority employees are forced to form their own social cliques.

Myth 5: All we have to do to achieve equality in the workplace is put people together. *Reality:* Heterogeneous work groups have greater potential for fostering ethnic equality than homogeneous groupings, but putting the bodies together does not ensure equity. It takes considerable work and planning to make democracy in the workplace a reality. "There's no need to waste our time working with those people," a white supervisor concluded. "Once a nigger always a nigger." He was talking about African-American workers, but in terms of sentiment he could just as well have been referring to Native Americans, Hispanics, Puerto Ricans, or any other minority group. In a democratic society, it is imperative that formal and informal job activities do not become racially determined.

Myth 6: Members of a particular minority group are all alike. *Reality:* Individuals who do not know the various social class dimensions of ethnic minorities are also unlikely to know that despite common language, color, and historical backgrounds, all members of a particular racial or ethnic group are not alike. And it is erroneous to believe they require the same treatment. Further, it is presumptuous and counterproductive to talk about *the* white workers or *the* blacks or *the* Indians or *the* Chinese as if members of these and other groups have only one set of behavior characteristics. While this text will

Table 2.1
Cultural Value Preferences of Middle-Class White Americans and Ethnic
Minorities: A Comparative Summary

Area of Relationships	Middle-Class White Americans	Asian Americans	American Indians	Black Americans	Hispanic Americans
People to nature/ environment	Mastery over	Harmony with	Harmony with	Harmony with	Harmony with
Time orientation	Future	Past-present	Present	Present	Past-present
People relations	Individual	Collateral	Collateral	Collateral	Collateral
Preferred mode of activity	Doing	Doing	Being-in-becoming	Doing	Being-in-becoming
Nature of man	Good and bad	Good	Good	Good and bad	Good

Source: From *Family Therapy with Ethnic Minorities* by M. K. Ho, Newbury Park, CA:
Sage, 1987. Copyright 1987 by Sage Publications. Reprinted by permission.

focus on ethnic group characteristics, the reader is reminded
that social class differences often are more determinant of a
worker's behavior than his or her ethnic background.

THOSE WHO ARE AFFECTED

Blacks, Hispanics, Asians, and Native Americans make up a collective
majority in 17 percent of the U.S. cities with fifty thousand residents or
more. Further, the addition of almost 10 million immigrants in the 1980s
increased the diversity in American cities and small towns. Most of the
immigrants came from Latin America and Asia. The white flight, triggered
by the influx of minorities, has dramatically changed the demographics of
cities and small towns. The 1990 U.S. population of 248.7 million people
included:

• 199.7 million whites who comprised 80.3 percent of the total.
• Nearly 30 million black Americans comprised 12.1 percent.
• 22.4 million Hispanics comprised 9 percent.
• 7.3 million Asian and Pacific Islanders comprised 2.9 percent.
• Nearly 2 million American Indians, Eskimos, and Aleut Americans comprised
  0.8 percent.

Currently, one of every four Americans is an ethnic minority. (See Table
2.1.) But these statistics are only a small part of the changing demographic

picture. Consider for a moment the fact that the white population grew 6 percent from 1980 to 1990; the black population grew 13.2 percent; the American Indian population grew 37.9 percent; the Hispanic population grew 53 percent; and the Asian population grew 107.8 percent.

The demographic shift in favor of minorities over whites of European origin is already seen in the composition of public school students. By the year 2000, one of every three Americans and half of all school-age children will be a member of an ethnic minority group. This will result in a large number of workers in the twenty-first century for whom English will not be their primary language. Workplaces will be noticeably punctuated with Spanish, Vietnamese, Khymer, and other "foreign" languages. Thus cultural diversity will be seen in the living colors of the workers and heard in their speech. For the first time, the United States will reflect the diversity commonplace throughout most of the other nations of the world. Even so, our school curriculums and businesses will probably remain primarily Eurocentric.

African Americans

Black children begin life facing higher survival odds than white children. They are more likely to die in infancy than white babies (Dewart, 1991; Sigelman & Welch, 1991). If a black baby lives, the chances of losing his or her mother in childbirth is four times as high as the white baby. The black baby is usually born into a family that lives in the inner city. (Over 75 percent of the 30 million African-American population does.) It is a family that is larger than its white counterpart, and it is crowded into dilapidated housing—quarters structurally unsound or unable to keep out cold, rain, snow, rats, or pests (Glasgow, 1980; Pickney, 1984; Wilson, 1987).

With more mouths to feed, more babies to clothe, and more needs to satisfy, the black family is forced to exist on a median family income that is barely half the median white family income. When the black youngster goes to school, he or she usually finds it no avenue to adequate living, much less to fame or fortune. And because black children are generally taught in slum schools, with inferior equipment and facilities, the education gap between black and white employees of the same age often approaches two to three years.

In most communities heavily populated by black Americans, low-income and middle-income groups live in extremely close proximity to each other (Blackwell, 1991). This situation is not caused primarily by a "natural selection" process but rather by de facto housing segregation. Consequently, the plight of poverty-stricken black Americans is distorted if only census tract data are examined. Black "haves" appear less affluent and black "have nots" seem less disadvantaged than they actually are. There is, in short, a much wider gap between the black middle and lower classes than is statistically apparent. Both groups closely approximate their white counterparts in income and living styles. Low-income African Americans are a minority within a minority (Banerji, 1987; Fisher, 1982; Landry, 1987).

African Americans are the most difficult ethnic group to categorize. The difficulty stems mainly from slavery, in which African heritages were almost entirely lost through assimilation with non-African cultures. Even so, the following generalizations typify traditional African-American cultural conditioning:

1. *Extended family.* The African-American family is sometimes extended bilaterally, but often it is maternally oriented. The family is a closely knit group, frequently consisting of grandparents, aunts, uncles, nieces, nephews, and cousins. Within the black family, roles are interchanged more frequently than in most nonblack families. This sharing of decisions and jobs in the home stabilizes the family during crisis situations.

2. *Kinship bonds.* Children born in and out of wedlock are loved. Legitimacy refers to parents; it has little to do with black children being accepted in the community. When children marry or otherwise reach adulthood, they leave home but often settle close to their parents or other relatives. Family unity, loyalty, and cooperation are part of the African-American lifestyle. (These values are also strongly held by the other ethnic groups discussed in this book.)

3. *Authority and discipline.* Childhood in the tradition-oriented African-American community revolves around assertive behavior and challenging authority. There is a constant crossing of wills. Through this process, black children learn the acceptable limits of their behavior. Discipline tends to be harsh, strict, and preoccupied with teaching children respect for their elders, respect for authority, responsibility for themselves, and an understanding of what it means to be black in America.

4. *Religious orientation.* On the whole, African Americans are highly religious. Most of them are Protestant. The church offers spiritual hope to many persons who live in oppressive environments.

5. *Achievement and work orientations.* Contrary to popular notion, most African-American parents pass on to their children high achievement aspirations. However, many black homes lack middle-class role models for children to emulate. The desire to achieve economic success has caused many African-American families to internalize a strong work orientation.

6. *Folk medicine.* African health practices make little distinction between physicians and nurses; both attend to the physical, emotional, and spiritual health of the patient. According to traditional African beliefs, both living and dead things influence an individual's health. In addition, health is directly related to nature. To be in harmony with nature is to have good health, whereas illness reflects being out of harmony with nature.

Mexican Americans

The 13.5 million Mexican Americans reflect a variety of cultural patterns that are influenced by their parental heritage and the length of time their families have been American citizens (Stoddard, 1973). Descendants of early Spanish settlers are, as a group, usually affluent, but descendants of Latin American agricultural workers tend to be poor (Amott & Matthaei, 1991). A third group is formed by *braceros*—farm workers who have migrated recently to the United States from Mexico. They speak fluent Spanish and hold tightly to Mexican customs and traditions (Feagin & Feagin, 1993; Meniendez, Rodriguez & Figueroa, 1991). In some communities Mexican Americans are the victims of more job discrimination than African Americans (Mizell, 1992).

Census projections indicate that the total Hispanic-American population may soon exceed the African-American population. Currently there are 22.4 million Hispanics. In addition to Mexicans and Puerto Ricans, a sizable number of legal and illegal immigrants come from Argentina, Cuba, Peru, and Venezuela. Part of the difficulty in accurately counting and classifying Hispanic immigrants is due to the tendency of non-Puerto Rican Hispanics to list themselves as Puerto Rican to gain full rights as American citizens. In Texas and California it is estimated that one million illegal immigrants have entered from Mexico. The Mexican-American *barrios* (communities) tend to reflect the same kind of economic and physical decline as African-American neighborhoods.

In many ways, Mexican Americans epitomize both racial integration and cultural separatism. This duality is clearly seen in a brief review of Mexican history. The Aztecs were intermarried with their Spanish conquerors and with Indian tribes hostile to the Aztecs. The children of these mixed marriages were called *mestizos*. *Creoles*, pure-blooded Spanish people born in Mexico, largely disappeared through intermarriage. Blacks from Africa, brought into Mexico during the colonial period as slaves, married Indians, and their offspring were called *zambos*. Zambos and mestizos later intermarried, causing the so-called Negro blood to disappear.

Although they are a racially mixed people, Mexican Americans have a similar heritage. As noted earlier, some Mexican Americans prefer to be called *Chicanos*. The word *Chicano* stems from the Mexican-Indian Nahuatl word *Mechicano*. The first syllable is dropped and Chicano is left. It is an old term for the American of Mexican descent. The Chicano movement (or Chicanismo) represents a commitment to the improvement of life for all Spanish-speaking Americans and Americans of Mexican descent.

Mexican Americans, like American Indians, Asian Americans, and Puerto Ricans, are truly marginal people. Culturally they are neither black nor white. Their marginality affects individual searches for identity. Few organizations include activities and materials with which Hispanics can positively identify. Black History Week and other African-American oriented celebrations, for example, are not culturally inclusive. Therefore Hispanics and other ethnic group employees feel left out when those programs are presented. As another illustration, programs that honor the cultural contributions of Mexican Americans may not be adequate for other Hispanic employees because of subculture differences.

There are qualitative differences in the language of Hispanics who are monolingual Spanish or bilingual Spanish-English. Furthermore, Spanish has many dialects—those brought to the United States by Hispanic immigrants and several that have developed in this country. A brief discussion of some of the common characteristics of tradition-oriented Mexican Americans follows.

1. *La Raza (The Race)*. Latin Americans are united by cultural and spiritual bonds believed to have emanated from God. Based on the belief that God controls all events, Mexican Americans tend to be more present-oriented than future-oriented. The influence of the Roman Catholic Church on *La Raza* is pervasive. Mexican Americans are born, get married, work, die, and are buried under the auspices of religious ceremonies.

2. *Family loyalty*. The familial role is the most important, and the family is the second most cherished institution in Mexican-American society. Chicanos owe their primary loyalty to the family. The worst sin is to violate one's obligations to the church, but next comes the family.

3. *Respect (Respecto)*. The oldest man in the household is the family leader. Respect is accorded on the basis of age and gender. The old are accorded more respect than the young and men are accorded more respect than women. Latino families are based on family solidarity and male superiority.

4. *Machismo*. Mexican culture prescribes that men are stronger, more reliable, and more intelligent than women. *Machismo* dictates that the man will show a high degree of individuality outside the family. Weakness in male behavior is looked down on.

5. *Compadrazgo*. The Mexican-American family is extended by the institution of *compadrazgo,* a special ceremonial bond between a child's parents and godparents. Often the bond between *compadres* is as strong as between brothers and sisters.

6. *Folk medicine*. Humoral pathology is an important aspect of Latin American and Spanish folk medicine. Their simplified form of Greek humoral pathology was elaborated in the Arab world, brought to Spain as scientific medicine during the period of Muslim domination, and transmitted to America at the time of the Spanish conquest. According to humoral medical beliefs, the basic functions of the body are regulated by four bodily fluids, or "humors," each of which is characterized by a combination of heat or cold with wetness or dryness.

Puerto Ricans

Puerto Rico is an island in the Caribbean approximately 1,000 miles from Miami and 1,600 miles from New York. Puerto Rico's population of over 3.5 million represents a density greater than that of China, India, or Japan. As a result of the Jones Act of 1917, all Puerto Ricans are American citizens. The island population is a mixture of Taino Indians, Africans, and Spaniards; Puerto Rican skin colors range from white to black, with shades and mixtures in between. Puerto Ricans who were reared on mainland America are sometimes called Neo-Ricans. The 2.7 million Neo-Ricans are mainly English speakers; few speak fluent Spanish.

Despite dissimilar backgrounds, Puerto Ricans tend to be labeled African Americans and they are subjected to the same prejudices inflicted on black Americans (Rogler & Cooney, 1984; Masud-Piloto, 1988; Feagin & Feagin, 1993). A cursory review of related literatures shows that Puerto Rican history is not Mexican-American history. It is imperative that managers and supervisors do not consolidate Puerto Ricans or any other peoples into an incorrect category or ethnic group. The following characteristics typify Puerto Rican culture:

1. *Sense of dignity*. Custom requires that proper attention be given to culturally prescribed rituals such as shaking hands and standing up to greet and say good-bye to people. A sense of dignity is present in all important interpersonal relationships.

2. *Personalismo*. Personal contact is established by Puerto Ricans before beginning a business relationship. It is important to exchange personal life data (such as size of family, their names, and their ages) before talking business.

3. *Individualism*. High value is placed on safeguarding against group pressure to violate an individual's integrity. This makes it difficult for some Puerto Rican workers to accept the concept of teamwork in which the individual relinquishes his or her individuality to conform to group norms. This characteristic reduces the importance of the Roman Catholic Church in the lives of Puerto Ricans, most of whom are nominally Catholic.

4. *Cleanliness*. Great emphasis is placed on being clean and well dressed. To some Puerto Ricans, looking good includes wearing "good" clothes and, frequently, avant-garde styles.

5. *Fear of aggression*. Puerto Rican children are discouraged from fighting, even in self-defense. A Puerto Rican idiom describes this conditioning: *Juegos do mano Juego de villano* (pushing and shoving, even in play, makes one a villain). Survival in perceived hostile environments, including the workplace, sometimes forces Puerto Ricans to become villains.

6. *Compadrazgo and machismo*. *Compadrazgo* and *machismo* are operative in Puerto Rican culture in the same manner as in Mexican-American culture.

7. *Folk medicine*. For a discussion of Puerto Rican folk medicine, see the section pertaining to Mexican Americans. Both cultures are quite similar.

American Indians

There are approximately five hundred Indian tribes and 1.8 million Indians in the United States (Snipp, 1989; Vogel, 1968). Some are bilingual and others are not. Nor is there a common tribal language. This is why sign language became the major means of intertribal communication. Currently, American Indians and Alaskan natives are at the bottom of the economic ladder in the United States (Jaimes, 1992). They have the highest rates of unemployment and school dropouts, live in the most dilapidated housing, and in some parts of the country are accorded the lowest social status.

Most government programs have failed to assist Indians in their efforts to maintain individual dignity and cultural identity while achieving success in the larger society. Half the Native American population lives on 40 million acres of reservation in thirty states. Part of their plight is revealed in the following statistics: Indians have 100 million fewer acres of land today than in 1887 (Fixico, 1986). Their average life expectancy is forty-five years. Nearly 60 percent of the adult Indian population has less than an eighth-grade education. Infant mortality is more than 10 percent above the national average. The majority of Native American families have annual incomes below $20,0000; 45 percent of Native American workers on reservations have annual incomes below the official poverty line. Indian unemployment is almost ten times the national average.

Feeling trapped and powerless in a world mainly controlled by non-Indians, most rural and urban Indians have not become militant, but instead have withdrawn. Overgeneralizing from this group, representatives of non-Indian cultures pass on stereotypes about shiftless and drunken Indians. There is a saying in some towns, "If you hire an Indian, never pay him the first day if you want him to come back the second day. He'll take the money and drink it but not come back to work." It is not only what is said about Indians that is detrimental but also what is not said. Until the 1970 United States Census, Native Americans were not even listed as an identifiable ethnic group.

Conflicts between Indian and non-Indian cultures are found on reservations, in small towns, and in big cities (Olson & Wilson, 1984). The strain shows up in many ways, including high job absenteeism and alcoholism rates. Some non-Indians tend to think that because an exceptional Indian has managed to succeed with little help, the others should also. Most people of any culture succeed with a lot of help from significant others. Generally, whether occupational successes or failures, the following characteristics apply to traditional American Indians:

1. *Present-oriented.* They are taught to live in the present and not to be concerned about what tomorrow will bring. Most Euro-Americans tend to be future-oriented; they are constantly destroying the past and building the future.

2. *Time consciousness.* Many earlier Indian tribes had no word for time. Thus, historically the emphasis has been placed on doing as opposed to going to do something or being punctual. Unlike some people who rush to meetings to be punctual, Indians try to finish current activities. (African Americans and Hispanics have similar time consciousness.)

3. *Giving.* The Indian who gives the most to others is respected. In many tribes, saving money or accumulating consumer goods results in ostracism.

4. *Respect for age.* Like the other ethnic groups discussed in this book, respect for the Indian increases with age. Indian leadership is seldom given to the young.

5. *Cooperation.* Indians place great value on working together and sharing resources. Failure to achieve a personal goal is believed to be the result of competition.

6. *Harmony with nature.* Indians believe in living in harmony with nature. They accept the world as it is and do not try to destroy it. Along with this belief goes a belief in taking from the environment only what is needed to live.

7. *Extended family.* The American Indian family network is radically different from other extended family units in the United States. The typical non-Indian extended family includes three generations within a single household. American Indian families include several households representing relatives along both vertical and horizontal lines. Grandparents are official and symbolic family leaders. In addition, namesakes (formalized through a religious ceremony) become the same as parents in the family network.

8. *Folk medicine.* The Indian medicine man is a vivid reminder that long before physicians, nurses, social workers, and counselors intruded into their lives, Native Americans had folk cures for physical and mental illnesses. Upon reflection, it is no more logical to believe in germs that we cannot see than in spirits whom we cannot see. An example of Indian folk medicine is seen in traditional Navajo culture that asserts that illness is a sign that a person is out of harmony with nature. Indian religion and medicine are virtually indistinguishable. Medicine men and women, singing, rituals, and chants are important aspects of treatment for illness.

Asian Americans

As noted earlier, the Asian-American population is not a homogeneous group of people. They represent unique histories, customs, and cultural contributions. However, they share certain characteristics as Asians. The 1990 United States Census lists five distinct Asian-American peoples: Chinese (1.6 million), Filipino (1.4 million), Japanese (848,000), Koreans (815,000), Vietnamese (600,000). A related grouping of peoples, but who are qualitatively different culturally from Asians, are the Pacific Islanders: Hawaiians (200,000), Samoans (63,000), and Guamanians (49,000).

The plight of poverty-stricken Asian Americans is vividly captured in Los Angeles and San Francisco Chinatown statistics: more than one-third of the Chinatown families are poverty-stricken; three-fourths of all housing units are substandard; rents have tripled in the past five years; more than half the adults have only a grade school education; juvenile delinquency is increasing; and the suicide rate is three times the national average (Endo, Sue & Wagner, 1980; Takai, 1989). But most of the 2 million Asian Americans are neither poverty-stricken nor poorly educated (Duleep & Sanders, 1992). Many of the following values that characterize traditional Chinese are applicable to other traditional Asian cultures:

1. *Filial piety.* There is unquestioning respect for and deference to authority. Above all else, there is the expectation that each individual will comply with familial and social authority.

2. *Parent-child relationship.* Children defer to their parents, especially in communication, which is one-way from parents to children.

3. *Self-control.* Strong negative feelings are seldom verbalized. Assertive and individualistic people are considered crude and poorly socialized.

4. *Fatalism.* Resignation and pragmatism characterize the manner in which Chinese Americans deal with change in nature and social settings.

5. *Social milieu.* Chinese Americans are other-directed and therefore greatly concerned with how their significant others view and react to them. Social solidarity is highly valued.

6. *Inconspicuousness.* Taught to avoid calling attention to themselves, Chinese Americans are likely to be silent in public settings.

7. *Shame and guilt.* Since Chinese Americans are taught to respect authority and maintain filial piety toward their parents and their ancestors, a violation of this cultural norm results in feelings of shame and guilt. The Chinese family is a continuum from past to future whose membership includes not only the present generation but also the dead and the unborn.

8. *Folk medicine.* Asian folk medicine and philosophies have a strong Chinese influence. Unlike Western medicine, which emphasizes disease and cure, Asian medicine focuses on prevention. The theoretical and philosophical foundation of Chinese medicine is the Taoist religion, which seeks a balance in all things. Both energy *(chi)* and sexual energy *(jing)* are vital

life energies, with *chi* and *jing* kept in balance by *yin* and *yang*. *Yin* is feminine, negative, dark, and cold; whereas *yang* is masculine, positive, light, and warm. According to Chinese medicine, an imbalance in energy is caused by an improper diet or a strong emotional feeling. Balance or good health may be achieved through the use of appropriate herbs.

Whether or not to integrate into Western society is a question that most ethnic minority peoples ponder. This is an especially sensitive issue for individuals subscribing to traditional cultural values (Levin & Rhodes, 1981; McCready, 1983). The dilemma is somewhat similar to that of the early European immigrants to the United States. When they initially came to this country during the nineteenth century, the Poles, Greeks, Germans, Italians, and other European groups clustered together in their own ethnic enclaves. Gradually, either they or their children moved out of their ethnic neighborhoods into the larger community. This is happening to minority groups too. Along with this change comes a merging of languages, customs, habits, dietary patterns, and housing. Consequently, there are relatively few third- and fourth-generation minority group peoples who adhere strictly to traditional cultural beliefs and practices.

EXECUTIVE ORDER AND LAWS

Executive Order 11246, as Amended (Effective October 14, 1968)

This order prohibits employment discrimination based on sex, as well as on race, color, religion, or national origin, by federal contractors or subcontractors and contractors who perform work exceeding $10,000. To ensure nondiscrimination in employment, contractors must take affirmative action. Further, employers must state in all advertising that they are indeed affirmative action/equal opportunity employers. According to revised orders, employers with over $50,000 in federal contracts and fifty or more workers must file affirmative action plans with goals and timetables with the Office of Federal Contract Compliance.

Title VII of the Civil Rights Act of 1964, as Amended by the Equal Employment Opportunity Act of 1972

This legislation resulted in the creation of the Equal Employment Opportunity Commission (EEOC). Title VII prohibits discrimination in employment based upon sex, as well as on race, color, religion, and national origin, by employers of fifteen or more employees, public and private employment agencies, labor organizations with fifteen or more members, and labor-management apprenticeship programs. Discrimination based on race, color, sex, religion, or national origin is unlawful in hiring and firing;

wages; fringe benefits; classifying, referring, assigning, or promoting employees; extending or assigning use of facilities; training, retraining, or apprenticeships; or any other terms, conditions, or privileges of employment. The Equal Employment Opportunity Commission has issued guidelines that bar hiring based on stereotyped characterization of the sexes, classification or labeling of "men's jobs" and "women's jobs," or advertising under male or female headings. Also, the guidelines prohibit excluding from employment an applicant or employee because of pregnancy.

Civil Rights Act of 1991

Finding that additional remedies under federal law are needed to (1) defer unlawful harassment and intentional discrimination in the workplace, (2) strengthen the scope and effectiveness of federal civil rights protections, and (3) provide additional protections against unlawful discrimination in the workplace, on November 21, 1991, Congress passed Public Law 102-166, known as the Civil Rights Act of 1991.

Title I of the act defines federal civil rights remedies, including limiting compensatory damages to a maximum of $50,000 for future pecuniary losses, emotional pain, suffering, inconvenience, and the like for each complaining party if an employer has up to 200 employees, $100,000 if the employer has 201 to 500 employees, and $300,000 if the employer has more than 500 employees. No limit is set for punitive damages when an employer engages in a discriminatory practice with malice or with reckless indifference to the federally protected rights of an aggrieved individual.

Title II, referred to as the "Glass Ceiling Act of 1991," established a Glass Ceiling Commission to conduct studies and prepare recommendations concerning: (1) eliminating artificial barriers to the advancement of women and minorities in the workplace, (2) increasing the opportunities and developmental experiences of women and minorities to management and decision-making positions in business. (See Tables 2.2 and 2.3.)

Title III, the "Government Employee Rights Act of 1991," provides procedures to protect the right of U.S. Senate and other government employees, with respect for their public employment, to be free of race, color, religion, sex, national origin, age, or disability discrimination.

SELECTED COURT CASES

The U.S. Supreme Court defined discrimination as it applies to Title VII in the landmark case of *Griggs v. Duke Power* (1971). Succinctly, the Court stated that if an employment policy treated one class of individuals differently from another class or had the effect of eliminating employment opportunities of a protected class, this is *disparate impact* and it is unlawful unless a business necessity could be proven. Using the EEOC guide-

Table 2.2

Occupational Employment in U.S. Private Industry by Race/Ethnic Group/Sex and by Industry, 1990*

All Industries (154,894 units)

Race/Ethnic Group/Sex	Total Employment	Officials and Managers	Professionals	Technicians	Sales Workers	Office & Clerical Workers	Craft Workers	Operatives	Laborers	Service Workers
All Employees	100.0	100.0	100.0	100.0	100.0	100.0	100.0	100.0	100.0	100.0
Male	53.9	71.9	52.0	55.2	42.9	16.6	89.4	66.6	65.6	44.5
Female	46.1	28.1	48.0	44.8	57.1	83.4	10.6	33.4	34.4	55.5
White	77.4	89.9	87.0	81.0	81.1	76.9	82.4	71.1	62.6	60.2
Male	42.4	65.5	45.9	45.8	35.5	11.9	74.6	48.8	41.1	25.1
Female	35.0	24.4	41.0	35.2	45.7	64.9	7.9	22.3	21.5	35.1
Minority	22.6	10.1	13.0	19.0	18.9	23.1	17.6	28.9	37.4	39.8
Male	11.5	6.4	6.1	9.4	7.4	4.6	14.8	17.8	24.4	19.4
Female	11.1	3.7	7.0	9.6	11.5	18.5	2.7	11.1	12.9	20.4
Black	12.7	5.0	5.2	10.2	10.7	14.1	9.2	17.2	19.6	24.5
Male	6.0	2.9	1.9	4.1	3.8	2.5	7.7	10.4	12.7	10.9
Female	6.7	2.2	3.3	6.1	6.9	11.6	1.6	6.8	6.9	13.6
Hispanic	6.7	2.9	2.5	4.4	5.9	5.9	6.3	8.7	14.8	11.7
Male	3.9	2.0	1.3	2.7	2.6	1.3	5.5	5.8	10.1	6.8
Female	2.8	0.9	1.2	1.7	3.3	4.6	0.8	2.9	4.7	4.9
Asian/Pacific Islander	2.8	1.9	5.1	4.0	1.9	2.7	1.5	2.4	2.3	3.0
Male	1.4	1.3	2.7	2.3	0.8	0.7	1.2	1.3	1.3	1.5
Female	1.3	0.6	2.3	1.6	1.1	2.0	0.3	1.1	1.0	1.5
AmInd/Alaskan Native	0.5	0.3	0.3	0.4	0.4	0.4	0.6	0.5	0.6	0.6
Male	0.3	0.2	0.1	0.3	0.2	0.1	0.5	0.3	0.4	0.3
Female	0.2	0.1	0.1	0.2	0.2	0.3	0.1	0.2	0.2	0.3

* Excludes Hawaii

Source: U.S. Equal Employment Opportunity Commission.

Table 2.3
State and Local Government Employment: Full-Time, 1991—6,080 Reporting Units

MALE

Annual Salary $M	Total Number	Total Pct.	White Number	White Pct.	Black Number	Black Pct.	Hispanic Number	Hispanic Pct.	Asian Number	Asian Pct.	Indian Number	Indian Pct.
0.1-07.9	19,981	48.6	15,817	38.5	2,954	7.2	924	2.2	188	0.5	98	0.2
8.0-11.9	59,929	39.8	33,959	22.5	19,964	13.2	5,306	3.5	249	0.2	451	0.3
12.0-15.9	202,659	38.9	125,791	24.1	57,278	11.0	16,980	3.3	1,009	0.2	1,601	0.3
16.0-19.9	367,067	44.9	253,311	31.0	81,254	9.9	26,700	3.3	2,954	0.4	2,848	0.3
20.0-24.9	561,856	50.5	413,661	37.2	101,013	9.1	36,909	3.3	6,743	0.6	3,530	0.3
25.0-32.9	809,097	61.1	619,672	46.8	121,918	9.2	49,373	3.7	13,874	1.0	4,260	0.3
33.0-42.9	655,545	70.1	525,218	56.1	70,857	7.6	40,116	4.3	16,430	1.8	2,924	0.3
43.0 Plus	433,671	78.0	358,940	64.6	34,006	6.1	22,258	4.0	16,645	3.0	1,822	0.3
Total	3,109,805	57.0	2,346,369	43.0	489,244	9.0	198,566	3.6	58,092	1.1	17,534	0.3
Median Salary	$28,395		$29,269		$24,117		$27,019		$35,452		$25,449	

FEMALE

Annual Salary $M	Total Number	Total Pct.	White Number	White Pct.	Black Number	Black Pct.	Hispanic Number	Hispanic Pct.	Asian Number	Asian Pct.	Indian Number	Indian Pct.
0.1-07.9	21,105	51.4	15,872	38.6	4,241	10.3	772	1.9	148	0.4	72	0.2
8.0-11.9	90,798	60.2	60,078	39.9	24,626	16.3	5,138	3.4	387	0.3	569	0.4
12.0-15.9	318,441	61.1	215,489	41.4	78,578	15.1	20,433	3.9	1,808	0.3	2,133	0.4
16.0-19.9	450,079	55.1	305,314	37.4	108,529	13.3	29,087	3.6	4,388	0.5	2,761	0.3
20.0-24.9	550,692	49.5	368,087	33.1	134,065	12.1	35,087	3.2	10,545	0.9	2,908	0.3
25.0-32.9	515,279	38.9	365,221	27.6	102,734	7.8	29,857	2.3	14,827	1.1	2,640	0.2
33.0-42.9	280,048	29.9	198,859	21.3	50,407	5.4	15,338	1.6	14,237	1.5	1,207	0.1
43.0 Plus	122,323	22.0	89,344	16.1	18,408	3.3	5,739	1.0	8,353	1.5	479	0.1
Total	2,348,765	43.0	1,618,264	29.6	521,588	9.6	141,451	2.6	54,693	1.0	12,769	0.2
Median Salary	$22,669		$22,885		$21,672		$22,180		$30,434		$21,461	

** TOTAL **

Annual Salary $M	Total Number	Total Pct.	White Number	White Pct.	Black Number	Black Pct.	Hispanic Number	Hispanic Pct.	Asian Number	Asian Pct.	Indian Number	Indian Pct.
0.1-07.9	41,086	100.0	31,689	77.1	7,195	17.5	1,696	4.1	336	0.8	170	0.4
8.0-11.9	150,727	100.0	94,037	62.4	44,590	29.6	10,444	6.9	636	0.4	1,020	0.7
12.0-15.9	521,100	100.0	341,280	65.5	135,856	26.1	37,413	7.2	2,817	0.5	3,734	0.7
16.0-19.9	817,146	100.0	558,625	68.4	189,783	23.2	55,787	6.8	7,342	0.9	5,609	0.7
20.0-24.9	1,112,548	100.0	781,748	70.3	235,078	21.1	71,996	6.5	17,288	1.6	6,438	0.6
25.0-32.9	1,324,376	100.0	984,893	74.4	224,652	17.0	79,230	6.0	28,701	2.2	6,900	0.5
33.0-42.9	935,593	100.0	724,077	77.4	121,264	13.0	55,454	5.9	30,667	3.3	4,131	0.4
43.0 Plus	555,994	100.0	448,284	80.6	52,414	9.4	27,997	5.0	24,998	4.5	2,301	0.4
Total	5,458,570	100.0	3,964,633	72.6	1,010,832	18.5	340,017	6.2	112,785	2.1	30,303	0.6
Median Salary	$25,523		$26,421		$22,723		$24,491		$32,798		$23,587	

Source: U.S. Equal Employment Opportunity Commission.

lines, the Court illustrated a manner in which disparate impact can be determined: the selection rate for minorities is less than 80 percent of the selection rate for the other applicants. Judicial approval was given to the formula in *Albermarle Paper Co. v. Moody* (1975).

The term *disparate treatment* is not the same as *disparate impact*. In the case of disparate treatment, an employee is treated less favorably than other people because of his or her race, sex, and so forth through policy or action of an employer. These are individual cases, and the plaintiff must show that the employer had an unlawful motive or intention to discriminate against him or her (*Furnco Construction Co. v. Waters*, 1978; *Texas Department of Community Affairs v. Burdine*, 1981). In summary, disparate impact relates to discriminatory treatment toward a group of employees, while disparate treatment complaints are individual cases. An employer can treat an individual member of a protected class differently as long as there is no intent to discriminate and a nondiscriminatory reason can be shown.

It is important for employers to know the difference between equal employment and equal opportunity (Turner, Fix & Struyk, 1991). There is a common belief among managers and supervisors that they are not engaging in discrimination when a minority applicant is rejected or denied a promotion if they already have on their workforce members of protected classes. In *Connecticut v. Teal* (1982) the court ruled that Title VII is designed not only to protect groups but to protect individuals as well. The law provides members of the protected classes legal redress if they are denied the opportunity to compete equally for *all* jobs they are qualified to fill. The fact that other protected class workers were not discriminated against is not an acceptable defense. Equal opportunity means an *equal opportunity to be employed;* equal employment means *equal treatment once an individual is employed.*

SPECIAL PROGRAMS

Equality of treatment and opportunity has been the official policy of some organizations for many years. In their standards of recruitment, training, and promotion, government agencies and human services organizations have been more effective as equal opportunity employers than the private business sector (Woods, 1989). But even in government and human services agencies there is room for improvement. Many equal opportunity employers are merely paper compilers; their behavior is anything but exemplary of equality in action (Leigh, 1978; Work, 1984).

If the policy of equal employment opportunity (EEO) is to apply without regard to sex, race, creed, color, or national origin, an important first step is to ascertain whether influential members of an organization harbor prejudices. The next step is make sure they put these prejudices aside when they are on the job (Blanchard & Crosby, 1989). Unless administrators carefully monitor on-the-job activities, prejudice will be manifested in official and semiofficial actions. Therefore CEOs must not assume that it is adequate merely to issue memoranda and directives setting forth their policy of equal opportunity. They must find out for themselves whether their subordinates are accorded equal treatment. The following are several effective methods by which managers and supervisors can make certain that their subordinates understand the policy of equal opportunity:

1. Discuss the policy in staff conferences.
2. Discuss the policy in informal talks with subordinates.
3. Issue periodic statements of the policy in newsletters or memoranda.
4. Explain the policy during the orientation of new employees.

Resolving cases involving discrimination always involve value judgments (Bowie, 1988). Administrators should, however, try to abate discriminatory practices in such a way as to cause those doing the discriminating to alter their behavior. Transferring the individual being discriminated against or transferring the discriminator does not solve the problem; it merely leaves the discriminator free to repeat the act. *Good human relations cannot be delegated—they begin and end with each manager and supervisor.*

An organization culture embodies common core values held by its members regarding the acceptability of certain behaviors (Robbins, 1988). When an organization's culture is set up in such a way that it provides advantages to some ethnic groups at the expense of others, it is practicing institutional racism (Krantz, 1992; Mizell, 1992). Institutional racism exists because of the acts of individuals who either make and carry out discriminatory practices or, through their passive acceptance, allow them to continue. Intention is not a necessary ingredient in racism. Intended or not, it is the effect of the law, practice, or behavior that determines whether it is racist (Mizell, 1992).

Techniques and Tips

Many diversity-related problems proceed from employees' lack of information, job misinformation, inadequate human relations skills of managers, and decisions that do not resolve the problem. In summary, most equal opportunity/affirmative action problems can be resolved by:

1. Following equal opportunity regulations and exercising proper jurisdiction
2. Getting all the facts
3. Correctly analyzing the facts

4. Involving all persons in the deliberations
5. Assigning responsibility for corrective action
6. Following up to see that corrective action is carried out

The process of getting the facts involves both verbal and nonverbal communication. *How* something is said is just as important as *what* is said. *What is not said* is also important. Good human relations involves learning to listen. Organizational problems are usually solved by supervisors who listen to subordinates before rendering a decision. (Specific change strategies are presented in Part 2 of this book.)

Most minority workers need time to talk, to listen, and to learn about job opportunities and equal opportunity practices. Relatedly, supervisors who tell minority workers not to be embarrassed or feel guilty because they do not fully understand job procedures may inadvertently suggest that they *should* experience those feelings. When minority workers' jobs needs are expressed and received, the psychosocial distance between minority-group employees and the supervisors is spanned. As the minority-majority relationship unfolds, the facilitative skills of the manager or supervisor come to the center of the interaction. Both verbally and nonverbally, an effective administrator will communicate and demonstrate the depth and breadth of his or her human relations skills. For minority-group workers, this means their supervisor will help them define and achieve their employment goals.

It is important for managers and supervisors to explain the technical aspects of job opportunities or complaint procedures in terms that will make sense to all their subordinates. If employees are to willingly and correctly pursue available job opportunities, they must be given and accept helpful guidance. This is a basic human relations principle: *Individuals affected by a diversity action plan must understand their options if optimum job success is to occur.*

When a worker is nourished and sustained by contact with his or her supervisor, the relationship is not only good but it is also helpful. Administrators would do well to remember that most employees are like the Philosopher in Stephen's (1945) *The Crock of Gold*, who said, "I have learned that the head does not hear anything until the heart has listened, and that what the heart knows today the head will understand tomorrow" (p. 128). The following tips for managers are a compilation of common-sense suggestions which, upon reflection, are almost too obvious to require repeating—but they frequently are ignored:

1. If subordinates' points of view differ from yours, thank them for giving you other ways to conceptualize things. This does not commit either party to altering their views.

2. Do not extrapolate from past experiences and expect minorities to be like those whom you knew in the past. They may be—or they may not.

3. Do not ascribe to the "super minority" theory, which defines successful minorities as being better than their "slow" or "dumb" brothers and sisters. Like majority-group workers, minority workers' abilities reflect the full range of human performances—not just the two extremes.

4. Avoid remarks that suggest to minority employees that they should consider themselves lucky to be in the organization. And comparing their employment opportunities and conditions to people in Rhodesia, Mexico, China, or some other Third World country is humiliating and insulting.

5. If it is not a practice to call majority-group employees by their first name, do not do so to minorities. For example, Native American employees should not be called by their first names if you refer to their Anglo peers as "Mr." or "Miss."

6. Avoid clichés and platitudes such as "Some of my best friends are Mexicans" or "I went to school with blacks."

7. Do not expect a minority-group employee to know all the other employees of his or her ethnic group or to speak for them. They share ethnicity, not necessarily the same experiences, friendships, or beliefs.

8. Avoid phraseology that may be considered offensive by some minority employees. Examples would be referring to Mexican-American workers as "boy," "girl," "son," "gal," "you people," "your people."

In all instances, racial stereotyping must be avoided. And pejorative comments or joking in a racial nature is, at a minimum, offensive. When carried to extreme, it is emotionally destructive. "Jap" jokes, for example, are just as offensive as "dumb Irish" or "redneck" jokes. Equally offensive is ignoring minority employees—treating them as nonpersons. The challenge to managers and supervisors is to minimize unfair, nonprofessional treatment and to maximize fair, professional treatment of *all* workers.

Problems centering on intergroup communication are more complex than many authors suggest. Seldom are managers and supervisors taught to elicit cross-cultural information (i.e., how to talk, listen, and provide feedback). But this is not to suggest that there are no managers and supervisors who can effectively communicate with ethnic minority workers. There are many who possess this skill, though most of them are self-taught. Something as important as cross-cultural communication should not be left to intuition or chance. Nor should minority employees' understanding of their organization culture be left to chance.

Numerous studies conclude that a large number of minority workers receive insufficient information about their present job conditions and future opportunities. Specifically, many minority workers quit or retire from organizations without ever having understood what their supervisors diagnosed as their needs, why certain procedures were followed and, if failure resulted, what their failures consisted of and the reasons for them. The minority workers' rights include the right to courteous, prompt, and the best supervision. They have the right to know what is wrong, why, and what can be done about skill deficiencies.

We could build a case of minority workers' ignorance as being a by-product of the managerial mystique. That is, administrators and supervisors are commonly perceived as being people whose training and predilections place them in a special ability category. To put it even more bluntly, there is a tendency for ethnic minority employees to be in awe of administrators. Minority workers who are the most confused about their employment situation and what their supervisors are or are not doing to help them succeed are less actively involved in discussions about their careers than minorities who are better informed.

Too many supervisors are unable to accurately judge the level of their subordinates' job skills knowledge. Paraphrasing an old adage: When in doubt, they should ask their subordinates. There are several ways the more effective supervisors communicate with ethnic minority workers. Most of them verbally communicate relevant information; some use printed materials, including diagrams and leaflets. Still others refer subordinates to commercial audiovisual materials. And a few use all of these methods. In the end, the quality of the information a supervisor is able to give a worker is directly related to the quality of information he or she gets from the worker. Additional tips are:

1. Call people by their right names. In Spanish, for example, individuals are given two last names. The first last name is from the father's family and the second last name is from the mother's family. In written communications, managers should use both last names so as not to insult the Spanish worker. Also, it is appropriate to ask individuals for the correct pronunciation of their names.
2. Try to understand local minority-group customs.
3. Study local minority histories.
4. Analyze your feelings about various ethnic minority groups.
5. Avoid patronizing or condescending approaches to minority clients and employees.
6. When giving information, don't merely ask individuals if they understand what you have said; ask them to repeat it.

Establishing Rapport

The challenge to managers and supervisors is to demonstrate that competence and empathy are not unique to members of a particular group. For example, a competent white administrator can be as "black" as any of the black employees in his or her organization. Blackness is more than a condition of the skin; it is thinking black, behaving black, and accepting black. Just as some black people admit that there are white people who have "soul," there are many white people who acknowledge that some black people have "culture." Skin color may be a help or a hindrance in establishing rapport. The major determining factor is the quality of interaction among people.

The first step in establishing rapport with minority workers is to help them relax. To do so, the administrator must be relaxed. If a supervisor is worried about being verbally or physically attacked or sued, it will show. Besides, minority employees may also be anxious about the encounter. They may wonder about the supervisor's hidden agenda. For some employees, regardless of their race or ethnicity, conferences with supervisors produce feelings of great discomfort. It is typical for people to bring their community-related anxieties with them to the workplace. As an example, fear of police brutality is not easily left in the community outside the workplace. The spread effect can cause some employees to fear all authority figures. During the initial encounter, organization problems or conversations about community problems exacerbate feelings. A few minutes of "small talk" can often reduce the stress. Effective administrators know when to slow the pace and talk about nonthreatening subjects. However, not even the most tactful administrators always succeed in establishing trust.

A small number of minority (and majority workers) approach managers and supervisors in ways that are outright defensive—they use profanity and behave indiscreetly. Such defense mechanisms do not usually reflect faulty personalities. Rather, protection of the ego is normal; but a disproportionate use of defenses indicates a lack of security. Culturally different workers, particularly ethnic minorities, seek to maintain their psychological balance during times of stress in several ways, such as by rationalizations, reaction formation, overcompensation, or projection. People who believe they are members of an underclass or out-group often develop rigid, persistent, and chronic ego-protection devices. Before overreacting to these situations, the administrator should ask himself or herself: "If I were in the same situation, would I behave in similar ways?"

Managers and supervisors who are most different from minority-group workers in terms of culture generally have more difficulty communicating empathy, congruence, respect, and acceptance than individuals who share or understand the workers' cultural perspectives. To be more specific, managers and supervisors who understand the psychological and sociological backgrounds of minority-group employees are better able to counsel them than their colleagues who lack this knowledge. A meaningful relationship with a supervisor can do much to reduce employees' negative feelings. In the end, the most successful managers and supervisors are linguistically compatible with their subordinates, empathic, and well trained.

As employees move into the highest echelons of an organization, it is evident that promotion is based more on competence and "chemistry" than merely competence. Minorities and women have greater difficulty than white men getting into the "club." But it is a mistake to assume that all—or most—white male workers have an opportunity to get into the club. They do not. It is an exclusive group into which even few white employees are accepted.

Implicit knowledge of how an organization works and how policies and systems evolved is to a lesser degree shared with minorities and women. Fortunately, there are success stories. Abby Livingston (1991) examined Fortune 500 companies and concluded that the following companies had made significant progress in recruiting and promoting minorities: Apple Computer, Avon, Corning, Digital, DuPont, Hewlett Packard, Honeywell, Pacific Bell, Procter & Gamble, Security Pacific Bank, U.S. West, and Xerox. They succeeded by using most or all of the following strategies:

1. Improved the skills of the workers they had
2. Shared secrets of success with underrepresented employees
3. Found out what motivated different employees
4. Hired to match their market
5. Restructured the work week

In summary, they used the synergy of diverse groups to achieve organization goals (Gordon, 1992). Cultural diversity is desirable for everyone in an organization, not just members of underrepresented groups.

HELP!

You have just been appointed diversity officer for your organization. You are new to the company—on the job for two weeks. Your CEO has given you the following instructions: "I want you to help me get this place on the right diversity track. Your predecessor made too many slow, bad decisions. I want action now! Don't let me down."

Respond to the following situations. Record your answers in written, audio, or video form. After you have read this book, see if you would have handled the situations differently.

1. Paul, an American Indian, comes to you for help. He believes that his Anglo co-workers are trying to get him fired. "They are," he states, "spreading lies about my job qualifications. They say I'm a token Indian employee." What will you tell Paul and why?

2. Belinda, a white accountant, is having an affair with Charles, an African-American colleague. She is very much concerned that if her supervisor finds out it will

cost her a promotion. She comes to you for advice. What will you tell her and why?

3. Alberto has lost his desire to be an integral part of your company's informal structure. He is a Chicano militant who believes that too much socialization within racially mixed groups is socially undesirable. He calls the minority workers "Uncle Toms" and "Aunt Thomasenas." The minority workers come to you for advice. What will you tell them and why?

4. Marsha, a black supervisor, has an all-male work team. The white males have accepted her leadership. The black males are uncooperative and sometimes sexually offensive. Marsha is angry and confused by the behavior of her "black brothers." She comes to you for insight and advice. What will you tell her about the behavior of the black workers? What would you advise her to do?

5. Richard, an employee with a physical disability, drinks alcoholic beverages on the job and admits to you, his supervisor, that he is a "drunken cripple." He is one of the most productive workers you supervise. He has come to work intoxicated several times. What will you do and why?

6. The white males in your organization constantly talk to each other about "reverse discrimination." You overhear one of the conversations. What will you tell the individuals who are obviously upset?

CHAPTER 3

Women

From a historical perspective it is evident that capitalism, through its wage-labor system, introduced an important distinction between the sexes: men began to work for wages outside their homes, while women continued to work within their homes without wages. Despite mechanical aids altering the way women work, this did almost nothing to change the type of work assigned to women (e.g., domestic, family maintenance, reproduction, socialization of children). The so-called women's work continues to be seen by some people as natural functions, instinctive, and of little importance when compared with men's work. The downgrading of women's work has been a foremost cause of current status problems of women. Even when pre-1970 women supplemented their families' income through work at home by taking in boarders, laundry, or children, for example, their efforts continued to go unheralded; it was viewed as a part of their routine household chores.

Until World War II, most married women living with their husbands worked outside their homes only if they were extremely poor or if a hardship was experienced, such as the husband being unable to work or pay the bills. Middle-class and upper-class mothers were expected to remain at home with their children. If they did not their employment meant that their husbands were inadequate in some respect, and this was a blow to the men's self-esteem and that of their families.

Numerous rationalizations were used by employers for paying women less, but the major reason was quite simple: it was profitable. Not only were women forced to accept underemployment, seasonal employment, and tedious tasks, but they were also viewed as being expendable during periods of economic recession. Excluded from most skilled jobs and the opportunity to learn trades, women had few choices but to accept low wages and poor working conditions. As a result of these conditions, countless women opted for housework, especially since they had to do it anyway, even those who worked outside their homes. Things have changed since 1970 but women still lag behind their male peers in terms of those employed as executives. This issue is not women but, instead, sexism.

DEFINITIONS

Sexism is the process of assigning life roles according to gender. This system fosters sex-related roles that usually relegate men to positions of authority in government, industry, education, science, and business. Although sometimes used only in reference to prejudice against females, sexism means any stereotyping resulting in arbitrary discrimination against females or males. *Sex discrimination* is differential employment decisions based on an employee's gender. *Sexual harassment* is unwelcome behavior of a sexual nature.

Sexism is an integral part of most societies. It is an insidious infestation hidden in the very core of social relationships, and it has a cumulative effect upon all societal functions as reflected in lifestyles, economic institutions, religious doctrines, and personal relations. It is perpetuated and supported by the manner in which males and females are socialized. The basic institutions of socialization are education and the family. Sexism begins in the family. The behaviors associated with sexism are so deeply ingrained into our minds that sexist behaviors are generally unconscious. Both men and women practice sexism in their daily behaviors by means of speech, dress, attitudes, and goals.

Sexism respects neither race nor color nor culture. It can be compared with racism in that it identifies a portion of the population and designates them "different" and, therefore, inferior. Sexism, like racism, involves the combination of power and prejudice. The power originally assumed by men was generally ascribed to them because of their greater physical strength and speed needed as hunters and warriors in early civilizations. Male dominance and female passiveness have remained in cultural, institutional, and individual practices even though technological advancements have negated strength and speed as required factors of dominance.

Both sexism and racism have been documented throughout history, but racism has received more attention in the news media; consequently, minority males have gained more in the area of social justice. For example, although companies that have contracts with the federal government are bound by law to hire and promote regardless of race and sex, most companies have until recently done a better job locating, hiring, and integrating minority males into their workforce. This is not to suggest that the racial struggle has been won, but only to note priorities. In addition, it should be noted that sexism exists within racism, thus becoming a double problem for minority women.

STEREOTYPES

John Stuart Mill (1970) regarded women as a subject class. But he recognized that the state of female bondage in at least one respect was a refinement over that of the black slave; each man wants his woman to be "not a forced slave, but a willing one; not a slave, merely, but a favorite" (p. 50). In *The Subjection of Women* he emphasized the subtle and pervasive social conditioning by which women are prepared to accede to roles as the servants of men. Sigmund Freud (1967) was critical of Mill's study of women, believing that it gave insufficient consideration to what Freud construed to be inborn temperamental differences between the sexes. Freud said, "Despite my thirty years in research into the feminine soul, I have not yet been able to answer . . . the great question that has never been answered: What does a woman want?" (p. 18).

One of the answers that those active in the contemporary women's liberation movement would give is cessation of the stereotypes of female status—the casual acceptance that women are less than human. Simone de Beauvoir (1952), one of the intellectual stalwarts of the women's equality movement, wrote in *The Second Sex* that society, being codified by men, decrees that the female is inferior. Betty Friedan (1963) documented the problems of middle-class homemakers and observed that the American society seemed bent upon persuading women that all that is requisite for the fulfillment of their gender can be found in the cleaning, cooking, and child-rearing climate of the home. Mill observed:

When we consider the positive evil caused to the disqualified half of the human race by their disqualification—first in the loss of the most inspiring and elevating kind of personal enjoyment, and next in the weariness, disappointment, and profound dissatisfaction with life, which are so often the substitute for it—one feels that among all the lessons which men require for carrying the struggle against the inevitable imperfections of their lot on earth, there is no lesson that they more need, than not to add to the evils which nature inflicts, by their jealous and prejudiced restrictions on one another. (p. 162)

Socialization

Many of the roots of the contemporary women's rights movement stem from the prejudices and frustrations women encounter regularly when they attempt to leave their "designated" role and enter the world of work, research, or study. Psychologically and professionally, many women find that established legal principles are not operative for them in daily practice in the world of trade and service. Perhaps the most damaging of all the handicaps a woman faces when she enters that world is the general assumption that a man by his very nature is capable of more than she is and in every respect. The subtle psychological implications of this are reflected in early toys and unwittingly absorbed in childhood. On the one hand, toys are constructed to imply that boys are activistic and will grow up to create and produce. Girls' toys, on the other hand, cater to a more passive nature and point toward a feminine role meant to nourish and consume.

Further psychological reinforcement for submissiveness is added when females are admonished that having an intellect may, in fact, be a hazard that will discourage proposals of marriage—the only worthy, ultimate goal for women. The effectiveness of this conditioning would tend to be supported by the fact that girls outperform boys in academic work *until* their late teens, when culturally established goals of marriage assume paramount importance, and a degree of reversal occurs.

Despite fairly pervasive efforts over a long period of time to determine the role and direction women should take, the results achieved, both past and present, have been far from uniform. Some women are very interested in female equality, some are apathetic, and some stand firmly against it. Kathleen Snow (1973) concluded, "Some women confess that their pro-liberation thinking is at odds with their anti-liberation feelings; they have been intellectually persuaded, but their hearts belong to the old order" (p. 87).

Pat Crigler (1973), a psychologist at Northwestern University in Chicago, became interested in why the active feminist role attracts some women and repels others. Finding no satisfactory answers at hand, she set about querying 750 women in Atlanta and Chicago. Two organizations were selected for this study: the liberal National Organization for Women (NOW) and a more conservative organization, the League of Women Voters. She reported: "If I were going to say what has the most bearing on why a woman becomes a feminist, my answer would have to be that when there is a girl in the house who is for women's rights, it is the influence of her father" (p. 10). This study further concluded that the more education the father has, the more likelihood there is that the daughter will be a feminist. Still another significant factor determined by this study is that the higher the educational level in the home, the more likely girls are to believe in equal rights. An only child, it was determined, has a natural impetus toward a role beyond that of the traditional woman.

Nonfeminists, the study showed, were likely to be women busy with large families. The more children a woman has, particularly if she does not work outside the home, the more likely it is that she is not going to be in favor of equal rights. Based on this study, there is considerable difference in perspective between women who passively advocate equal rights and those active in women's liberation. There is a broader philosophical base for current trends than some of the most vocal spokespersons in both the pro and the con fringe areas of women's equality movements would have us believe. The term *feminism* is a misnomer for what we are seeing. It is not women's liberation; it is not the battle of the sexes. These are very inadequate synonyms for an interest in equal rights for all people—females and males.

Commenting on the prevailing stereotype of a wife's role, Judy Syfers (1973) noted that most men say, " 'I want a wife who will take care of my physical needs . . . keep my house clean . . . keep my clothes clean, ironed, and replaced when need be . . . take care of the details of my social life . . . remain sexually faithful . . . understand that my sexual needs may entail more than strict adherence to monogamy.' My God, who wouldn't want a wife?" (pp. 23–25). In an empathetic vein, David Riesman (1973) mused: "I think what I would ideally like to see in our society is that sex become an ascribed rather than an achieved status. That one is simply born a girl or a boy and that's it. And no worry about an activity's de-feminizing or emasculating one" (p. xiii). Riesman will not get his wish if the prediction that the family of the future will remain deeply ingrained in institutions influencing employment, income maintenance, marriage, sex relations, divorce, and mental health comes true.

Off the Pedestal

Just as some white males used paternalism to keep blacks in "their place" during slavery, chivalry is being used to keep women in their place today. The old masculinist places women on a pedestal so that he knows where they are at all times. Women in the world of work frequently step down from their pedestals. When Garda Bowman (1968) interviewed business executives, she uncovered a great deal of hostility toward female executives. Countless men and women accept the stereotypes that (1) women work only to earn extra spending money, (2) women who work take jobs away from men, (3) women are absent from their jobs because of illnesses more than men, and (4) women are too emotional to supervise subordinates. These stereotypes cause many employers to question female workers' commitment to work. And men are more likely than women to be perceived as "serious" about their careers. This places the extra burden on women to convince employers that they are not job risks.

MYTHS

Earlier researchers postulated that most workers believed women to be less competent than men in the workplace (Brenner, 1972; Broverman et al., 1972; Burgen, 1977; Fabian, 1972; Goldberg, 1967; Malcolm, Hall & Brown, 1976). Both male and female respondents favored male supervisors, who were believed to possess the characteristics of good managers— emotional stability, ability to make correct decisions, analytic ability, and the like. The erroneous belief that males are more competent than female workers has resulted in a hierarchy of preferred leaders in the following descending order: (1) white males, (2) nonwhite males, (3) white females, and (4) nonwhite females.

Schellenbarger (1993) reported the following illuminated conclusion made in the *National Study of the Changing Workforce* conducted by the Families and Work Institute: "Despite myths to the contrary, there is no difference, as judged by workers, between men and women supervisors" (p. 88). Most of the 2,958 wage and salaried workers in the most comprehensive survey so far of American workers did not see much difference in the way men and women manage—though women managers were viewed as being a bit more empathic to family and personal problems. Men and women managers were rated the same in terms of keeping subordinates informed, offering recognition and support, and being fair. Yet the myths pertaining to gender differences persist.

Women in leadership positions are often in a Catch-22 situation: They are devalued if they display "feminine" behaviors (nurturing, cooperative, passive) and chided when they exhibit "masculine" behaviors (assert-

Table 3.1
How to Tell a Businessman from a Businesswoman

Businessman	Businesswoman
A businessman is aggressive.	A businesswoman is pushy.
He is careful about details.	She's picky.
He loses his temper because he's so involved in his job.	She's bitchy.
He's depressed (or hung over), so everyone tiptoes past his office.	She's moody, so it must be her time of the month.
He follows through.	She doesn't know when to quit.
He's firm.	She's stubborn.
He makes wise judgments.	She reveals her prejudices.
He is a man of the world.	She's been around.
He isn't afraid to say what he thinks.	She's opinionated.
He exercises authority.	She's tyrannical.
He's discreet.	She's secretive.
He's a stern taskmaster.	She's difficult to work for.

Source: Robert M. Fulmer, *Practical Human Relations*, 2d ed. Copyright © 1983 by Richard D. Irwin. Reprinted by permission.

iveness, independence, aggressiveness). Thus, for example, a female supervisor who handles a situation differently than a male supervisor is frequently judged ineffective by her male boss. Conversely, he labels her "pushy" and "abrasive" when she is assertive—an important characteristic for career success among males. (See Table 3.1.) This is even more of a problem for black American women than white women because of the perceived role reversal. As a whole, the disparity between the expected behaviors of women and the appropriate professional behaviors makes it extremely difficult for most women to prove to their male peers and supervisors they have "what it takes" to be leaders. In many organizations, perceptions have changed little since George Biles and Holly Pryatel (1978) wrote "Myths, Management, and Women."

Myth 1: Women are poor economic risks because they are frequently sick and quit work when they have children. *Reality:* There is no statistically significant difference in the absenteeism of men and of women employees. Women who leave the workforce to have children reenter the workforce once the children reach school age; many mothers take a brief leave and return within a few weeks.

Myth 2: Women do not make good managers because they are too emotional. *Reality:* Many female managers are calmer than their male peers.

Myth 3: Women have a low commitment to the world of work. *Reality:* Men job-hop more than women. The perceived lack of commitment may be due to the fact that disproportionately more women than men are employed in dead-end, mundane jobs.

Myth 4: Women lack education and experience. *Reality:* As a whole, female employees possess more education than males. Their major problem is getting promotions.

Myth 5: Women are not interested in certain phases of business. *Reality:* This may be partly true, as a result of socialization.

Myth 6: Women should be banned from certain organizational groups because of their disruptive influence. *Reality:* Disruptions occur in all-male organizations, too.

Myth 7: Man is the protypical worker. *Reality:* There are almost as many working women as men.

Myth 8: Women lack the motivation to compete and achieve. *Reality:* When they are given the opportunity, many women compete with men and achieve top-level goals.

It would be erroneous and grossly simplistic to assume that the problems women have in the workplace would be solved when all organizations recruit female executives and promote them to the highest echelons. Karen Peterson (1993) cited the following findings in a recent nationwide Gallup poll conducted for *USA Today* and Cable News Network (CNN): (1) More women (44%) than men (33%) preferred a male supervisor. (2) Almost half (49%) of the men surveyed said a supervisor's gender did not matter; one-fourth (25%) of the women respondents said that a supervisor's gender did not matter. (3) More than half (61%) of women respondents aged eighteen to twenty-nine preferred a female supervisor. But most (60%) of women over fifty years of age preferred a male supervisor. (4) About half of the men (51%) and women (52%) said men have reacted positively and satisfactorily to national efforts to improve the status of women.

With a margin of error of plus or minus 3 percent, the Gallup poll chronicles progress and challenges. Younger men and women tend to be more progressive than older ones in terms of the "women's movement." A critical mass of people believe that the women's movement is a misnomer for the changes occurring in the workplace. It is not women's liberation; nor is it the battle of the sexes. These are inadequate descriptions of an interest in equal rights for all workers—males and females trying to be accepted on their merits and not to be stereotyped. Therefore the major issue is not men versus women. Instead, it is fairness for all workers regardless of their gender. However, the low numbers of women in managerial and supervisory positions indicate that workplace practices lag behind employee readiness to accept women in management. And the disparaties in job opportunities available to men and women have augmented numerous debates about gender differences in job readiness.

One could argue that women have less access to education than men and, therefore, are confined to lower-paying jobs. This, however, is not supported by evidence. According to 1992 U.S. Department of Labor statistics, the average female worker is as well educated as the average male worker—both having completed high school. The truth of the matter is that, on the whole, women with college degrees earn a mean annual income less than their male counterparts or males with only a high school education. In 1990, for instance, females with four years of college education earned an annual mean income of $28,911, while males with four years of college earned $44,554. Males with four years of high school education earned $28,043. Females with five or more years of college education earned $35,827, whereas males with similar education earned $55,831. A 1992 survey of 439 women who were vice presidents or higher in Fortune 500 companies revealed an average salary of $289,000 for men and $187,000 for women (Swingle, 1993).

The fact that statistics confirm women are earning much less than men and are still, for the most part, entering a narrow range of occupations seems to support the view that our social attitudes and values about what is and is not appropriate behavior for men and women are hard to alter. Even in the helping professions women are underrepresented in administrative positions. As long as girls are encouraged to pursue "feminine" interests and boys are encouraged to pursue "masculine" interests, the status quo will be reinforced—some jobs will be seen as suitable for males and others for females.

THOSE WHO ARE AFFECTED

Statistics reveal that between 1980 and 1990, the number of female workers increased from 45.5 million to 56.6 million—a 24.4 percent increase during this period. The number of male workers grew from 61.5 million in 1980 to 68.2 million in 1990—only a 10.9 percent increase. This reflects an increase of about twice as many female workers than the male workers. As a result, there were about eight female workers for every ten male workers in 1990 compared to seven female workers for every ten male workers in 1980. Increases occurred among women twenty-five years old and over, but they were especially pronounced for women thirty-five to forty-four who had a total increase of 6 million in ten years. The second highest female worker increase, 3.7 million, occurred in the twenty-five to thirty-four age category. With a total increase of 2.3 million, the forty-five to fifty-four age group was third. There was a four hundred thousand increase in each of the fifty-five to sixty-four, and sixty-five and over age groups. Equal Employment Opportunity Commission (EEOC) reports (1991) vividly capture the following American employment trends:

- While the percentage of the male population in the civilian labor force has remained steady over the past decade, the percentage of women has increased substantially.
- Women have substantially increased their share of employment in both the private sector and state and local government, whereas the participation rate of men has declined.
- Women also increased in their participation in managerial, administrative, and professional jobs in the private sector and in state and local government.

Declines in labor force participation rates have occurred in most age groups for men, whereas women have experienced increasing labor force rates in all age groups under fifty-five years. The decline of men reflects, in part, the spread and liberalization of pension, disability, and retirement plans as well as changing social attitudes toward work and leisure. The fact that employment rates for women have risen in the presence of some of these same forces attests to the strength and durability of the movement of women into the labor force. (See Figures 3.1 and 3.2.) With this general statistical background, let us now examine some other facts that seem to

Figure 3.1
Private Sector Employment Participation Rates of Minority Men and Women:
U.S. Summary, 1966–1990

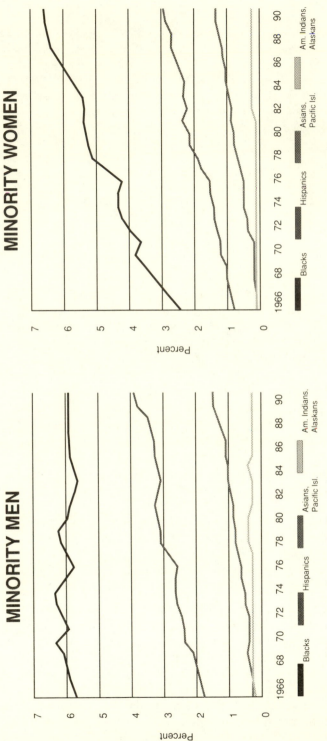

Source: U.S. Equal Employment Opportunity Commission.

· Each minority group, except black men, increased its employment participation in the private sector.

· The employment participation rate for black women increased more than two and one-half times, so that their 1990 participation rate (6.6%) slightly exceeded that of black men (5.9%).

· Hispanic women had employment participation rates that significantly lagged behind their male counterparts.

Figure 3.2
State and Local Government Full-Time Employment Participation Rates of
Minority Men and Women: U.S. Summary, 1974–1990

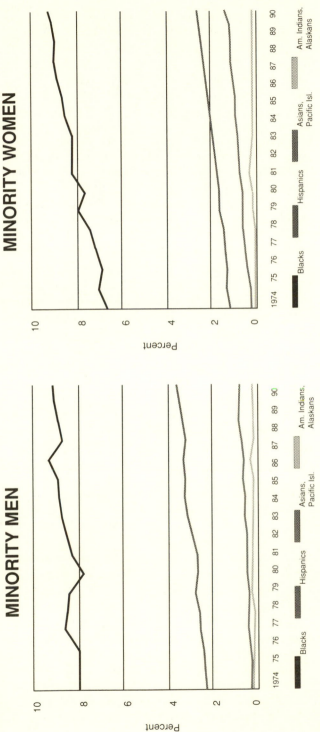

Source: U.S. Equal Employment Opportunity Commission.

- Within each minority group, both men and women increased their full-time employment participation.

- The participation rates for all minority groups, except Hispanics, were fairly equal for men and women. For Hispanics, however, men had participation rates that were higher than those of Hispanic women.

suggest reasons why participation rates for women are on the rise. Data provided by the United States Department of Labor indicate that:

- Of the 56.9 million women workers in the labor force in 1991, the majority worked because of economic need. More than four-fifths of all women in the labor force in 1991 were single, widowed, divorced, separated, or had husbands whose earnings were less than $20,000.
- Forty-three percent (6.8 million) of all black women were in the labor force in 1991; they accounted for nearly half of all African-American workers. Thirty-four percent (3.8 million) of Spanish-origin women were in the labor force in 1990; they accounted for 39.6 percent of all Hispanic workers.
- The more education a woman has, the greater the likelihood she will seek paid employment. Four out of five women with a bachelors degree or more education are in the labor force.

During the past decade, various women's organizations worked to dispel the notion that women did not want better jobs, or that most of them preferred to stay at home. They worked toward asserting women's rights within the workforce, gradually moved women into leadership positions, highlighted women's concerns during collective bargaining sessions, and supported women who ran for public office. Women's caucuses insisted that public policies that reinforced domestic roles created self-images and behavior patterns that fostered inferior positions for women in the workforce. In higher education institutions all over the country, women's studies courses have been developed to satisfy demands for more and better information about women.

Some experts predict improvement for women as a result of shifts in the structure of work itself. Technological improvements have decreased the amount of physical strength needed to do most jobs, thus rendering groundless many physical reasons for discrimination against women. Even with these changes, it is painfully clear that much is left to be done in the war against sex discrimination. For example, Social Security benefits, still structured on the premise that each family has one breadwinner, have the net result of being more advantageous to women as dependents rather than as income earners. Furthermore, when women workers are unemployed, they face a dual discrimination (Stolz, 1985). If they are pregnant, they may be denied unemployment benefits because they are not able to take another job. Also, women who give up jobs to follow their husbands who are relocated may not collect unemployment benefits in some states because they were not laid off.

Pay and promotional opportunities are usually based on the official job description rather than actual performance. Despite many gains, women are still grossly underrepresented in professional and managerial jobs (Stolz, 1985; Wall, 1992). Further, female executives are much more likely than male executives to be assistants to high paid professionals, and they are disproportionately overrepresented in special staff jobs that have no line responsibilities (affirmative action officers, diversity officers, community relations specialists). Assistants do much of their supervisors' work. In addition, women and minorities are concentrated in a few job categories, whereas white males span the range of jobs. In other instances, female workers are performing the same duties as men for significantly less pay.

Usually, female assistants are responsible for training the new male executives; however, because assistants belong to a certain sex, age, or racial group, they may find themselves discreetly blocked from joining the management staff, as well as locked into a dead-end job. Thus, job opportunities produce employees Kanter (1977) called "stuck" and "movers." People become stuck either because they are hired into dead-end positions or because they have been passed over too many times for promotion. Still others are stuck because they are in jobs that have promotion opportunities but they lack the background and experience for promotion. That is, they are misplaced and poorly trained after placement. "Movers" are upwardly mobile people—the "water walkers." Relatedly, "stuck" individuals have low job aspirations because their chances of moving up in the organization are minimal; "movers," on the other hand, aspire upwardly.

More females and minorities than white males hold low job expectations. In a recent national survey, minority men and white women rated their chances for job advancement lower than white men did themselves (Schellenbarger, 1993). But when opportunities are factored in, the differences are greatly reduced. Racism and sexism cause minorities and women to correctly be negative about their job opportunities. There is an irritating downside for "stuck" females: As a whole, minority men exhibit the same sexism as white men. In fact, minority men have their own "old boy network" that propels them to the higher echelons. With relatively few female mentors in most organizations, female executives also find few male mentors. And some male mentors are hesitant to sponsor women because the relationship may be misinterpreted as sexual. Mentoring typically involves informal social contact such as lunches, athletic activities, and cocktails. Consequently, women in management positions more so than males are social isolates.

As a result of discriminatory behaviors, many women have the skills needed for upward mobility but their skills are not reflected on personnel records or in job descriptions. Thus, a sex barrier is created, especially if there is a lack of initiative on the part of male administrators to give female workers recognition when it is due. This leaves female workers locked into a few job categories. But males are not the only culprits. Some women who achieve supervisory positions also discriminate against women. Ultimately, countless women discriminated against discourage other women from thinking of themselves as having potential for higher-level jobs. These employees become so convinced of their limited abilities that they lose the initiative to apply for training and promotion. They become a prophecy that fulfills itself. The effects of this not-too-subtle type of discrimination are evident in the higher ranks of many administrative staffs.

Sexual Harassment

It is common for female employees to be subjected to unwelcome sexual advances, requests for sexual favors, and other verbal or physical conduct of a sexual nature. Although not illegal per se, such behavior is illegal when it is used by managers and supervisors to decide whether to hire or fire someone; when it is used to determine pay, promotion, or job assignment; and when it creates an intimidating, hostile, or offensive work environment. If an employee submits to a sexual request and receives job benefits from it, then the employer may be sued by the other employees who were equally qualified but denied similar benefits. "Examples of verbal harassment could include sexual comments, suggestions, jokes, or innuendos; nonverbal harassment could include suggestive looks, leering, or ogling; and physical harassment could include accidentally brushing against someone's body, 'friendly' pats, squeezes or pinches, and forced sexual relations" (Webb, 1981, p. 5). According to the Equal Employment Opportunity Commission, sexual harassment can occur in a variety of circumstances, including but not limited to the following:

- The victim as well as the harasser may be a woman or a man. The victim does not have to be of the opposite sex.
- The harasser can be the victim's supervisor, an agent of the employer, a supervisor in another area, a co-worker, or a nonemployee.
- The victim does not have to be the person harassed but could be anyone affected by the offensive conduct.
- Unlawful sexual harassment may occur without economic injury to or discharge of the victim.
- The harasser's conduct must be unwelcome.

Ellen Wagner (1992) provided evidence that sexual harassment not only causes lower productivity but also higher turnover and poor morale. Further, the costs are astronomical. Norma Fritz (1989) reported that, excluding costs of litigation, Fortune 500 companies surveyed for *Working Woman* estimated their sexual harassment costs at almost $7 million per company per year.

The U.S. Merit Systems Protection Board (1988) conservatively estimated the cost to the federal government from May 1985 to May 1987 to be $267 million. That cost included replacing harassed employees, sick-leave payments, and reduced productivity. Diversity training and other preventive activities would cost only a fraction of what it takes to remedy the abuse.

Sexual harassment is an outgrowth of individual and institutional sexist behaviors. Often it takes a considerable amount of courage for women to report harassment. Sexually harassed workers are embarrassed, intimidated, and demeaned. They become victims of external stress and frequently suffer from headaches, stomach pains, and inability to concentrate on job-related activities. Extreme stress leads to increased absenteeism, loss of efficiency, and reduced productivity. Employment turnover also increases because many harassed workers quit their jobs and rehiring and retraining costs go up.

LAWS

The Equal Pay Act of 1963 (Effective 1968)

As an amendment to the Fair Labor Standards Act (FLSA), this act requires the same pay for men and women doing equal work, requiring equal skill, effort, and responsibility under similar working conditions in the same establishment. Where discrimination exists, pay rates of the lower-paid sex must be raised to equal those of the higher-paid sex. In a landmark decision, a federal court rejected a claim that the jobs of men and women have to be identical for them to receive equal pay and asserted that they need only be "substantially equal." The act, which is enforced by the Labor Department's Wage and Hour Division, permits wage differentials based on a bona fide seniority or merit system, or a system that measures earnings by quantity or quality of production, or any other factor other than sex.

The laws discussed in Chapter 2 also apply to women.

SELECTED COURT CASES

The legal parameters of sexual harassment are extracted from several court decisions. Initially the courts only decided whether women in the workforce were treated differently from men, and whether there was a bona fide occupational qualification (BFOQ) that justified the treatment. In *Phillips v. Martin Marietta Case* (1971) the U.S. Supreme Court ruled that a company policy that precluded the employment of women with preschool children, but hired men with preschool children, was unlawful.

Dress and grooming codes can also violate Title VII. In *Cornell v. Sparrow Hospital Assn.* (1985) the court awarded back pay to nurses discharged when they refused to wear full white uniforms but men were allowed to wear street clothes under their white laboratory coats. The court found unpersuasive the employer's argument that patients are accustomed to seeing women dressed like nurses and men like doctors. In a leading case on dress, *Meritor Savings Bank, FSB v. Vinson* (1986), the court found discriminatory the employer's requirement that the receptionist wear provocative clothes but did not require men to do so.

Meritor was the first case on sexual harassment to come before the Supreme Court. Ms. Vinson alleged that Taylor, a vice president in the bank, had sexual relations with her about forty to fifty times in the previous four years, during and after business hours. But she never lodged a complaint of harassment against Taylor to any of his supervisors. Further, she alleged that on other occasions, Taylor fondled her in front of other employees. In other instances, he followed her into the women's restroom when she went there alone, exposed himself, and on occasion forcibly raped her. Taylor's behavior stopped when she got a steady boyfriend. About a year later she went on sick leave for an indefinite period. Three months after Ms. Vinson was on leave the employer fired her for excessive sick leave. Thereupon she brought suit alleging sexual harassment during the four years of employment.

The district court dismissed the suit as the manifestation of a broken love affair. The appellate court reversed the decision on the grounds that the action was a violation of Title VII. The court concluded the employer knew or should have known about Taylor's behavior since he was its representative. In a unanimous decision, the U.S. Supreme Court held that a violation of Title VII is based on two types of harassment: (1) those involving economic benefits, and (2) those where a hostile environment is created. In order for sexual harassment to exist there must be three elements:

1. There is unwelcomed sexual behavior.
2. The employer must have actual or imputed knowledge of the behavior.
3. Either job opportunities must be involved or a hostile environment must be created.

Succinctly, there are two types of sexual harassment: quid pro quo and hostile environment. *Quid pro quo* (a Latin phrase meaning something for something) harassment occurs when a manager or supervisor makes unwelcome sexual advances. For example, a supervisor tells a subordinate, "Go to bed with me if you want to keep your job." Submission to the ultimatum is an expressed condition for receiving job benefits, while refusal to submit will result in the loss of the job. Quid pro quo harassment can be implicit, too. For example, a supervisor tells a subordinate, "We can resolve your salary request more quickly at dinner. Would you like to have dinner with me tonight?"

A *hostile environment* is relentless and continuing unwelcome sexual conduct in the workplace that interferes with an employee's job performance, or conduct that creates an intimidating, hostile, abusive, or offensive job environment. On the one hand, sexual flirtation, sexually explicit vulgar language, or sexual innuendos fall within the category of unwelcome sexual advances. On the other hand, extreme rudeness directed exclusively at one sex, such as women, is an example of a hostile environment. Harassment in the workplace violates Title VII when a member of a protected group is treated differently from other people. There is no specific provision in Title VII prohibiting harassment as such, but the courts have made such an interpretation (*Williams v. Saxbe,* 1976). Racial harassment would be found in a situation where black employees were subjected to racial slurs, pranks, or other bigoted acts by their co-workers or supervisors (*Hamilton v. Rogers,* 1986).

Costly Misunderstandings

Jan Bohren (1993) listed the following six myths about sexual harassment that are spread by either misinformed or culpable persons: (1) "It's not a problem here"; (2) "It's human nature. They'll work it out"; (3) "If there's no intent to harass, you're not liable"; (4) "It's hard to determine guilt—it's one person's word against another's"; (5) "Women harass men as much as men harass women"; (6) "There's not much [law enforcement] they can do to us." CEOs, managers, supervisors, and other high-level organization personnel must be vigilant to prevent and abate the harassing behaviors of others—and themselves. Victims and perpetrators almost never voluntarily work things out to the satisfaction of either party.

The law does not deal with the issue of *intent;* rather, it is enough to prove the sexually oriented activity occurred. Even when there are no witnesses, most harassers admit the act, claim there was no intent to harass the other person, and/or claim ignorance of the law. Seldom do these cases end up "judgment calls" after a thorough investigation. It is true that women can and do harass men. However, the vast majority of perpetrators are men. Fortune 500 legal costs for harassment are vivid examples of what "they can do" to harassers and the organizations they work for.

The nonlegal expenses caused by lower productivity, higher turnover, and poor morale can be even more considerable. The *Working Woman* survey estimated sexual harassment costs at $6,719,593 per company per year. That figure included such expenses as turnover costs, falloffs in production, and leave of absence. It did not include the costs of litigation. Even more striking is the estimate, considered as conservative, of the U.S. Merit Protection Board, of the costs of sexual harassment to the federal government from May 1985 to May 1987: $267 million. Government estimates include the cost of replacing employees who leave because of sexual harassment, sick-leave payments to employees who are absent from work because of sexual harassment concerns, as well as the cost of reduced productivity, both individually and in groups. In one nationwide survey women who reported experiencing sexual harassment at work, 42 percent felt compelled by continued harassment or post complaint retaliation to quit their jobs. (Wagner, 1992, p. 13)

SPECIAL PROGRAMS

While it has been stated that the women's liberation movement is not the major reason for women's increasing participation in the workforce, it is clear that the renewed interest in women's rights in the late 1960s had a significant impact on public policy. Antidiscrimination legislation can be credited in large measure to pressure from feminists, many of whom worked in Fortune 500 corporations. The problems of women may have originated at home, but public and private organizations have perpetuated sexism. These organizations now have the clear obligation to obey the laws enacted to end discrimination against women.

The Fourteenth Amendment to the United States Constitution provides that "no state shall deny to any person within its jurisdiction the equal protection of the laws." It would appear that this affords women constitutional protection of their rights. However, contrary to the Fourteenth Amendment, women have been treated so differently from men that the equal protection clause has not been meaningful to them. As early as 1977, Margaret Henning and Anne Jardin wrote:

In order to take advantage of equal opportunity women must believe they are, in fact must be, as competent as their male counterparts. In-depth competence in their chosen field has traditionally been one of women's outstanding strengths, almost an employment characteristic, but competence as a manager requires understanding and skill at working in and with the informal system of relationships in which management jobs are embedded. Such competence represents a stage most women in organizations have not yet reached, and the guarantee of equal opportunity is empty unless opportunities are created for women to acquire the knowledge and skill which will make it possible for them to understand, to enter and to compete within the informal system of middle management. (p. xiv)

Equal employment opportunity programs that are the most effective do the following:

- Have a publicly shared affirmative action plan.
- Identify and abolish barriers to recruiting women.
- Encourage women to apply for all positions they are qualified to fill.
- Encourage and support women to take advantage of job-relevant skill-training workshops, classes, and programs.

- Have a policy of promoting qualified women to supervisory positions.
- Publicly recognize supervisors who successfully recruit, train, and promote women.
- Have a procedure for dealing with personnel engaging in sexual harassment (e.g., verbal warning, written warning, probation, and termination).
- Continually monitor affirmative action progress.

Specific acts of discrimination may be difficult to pinpoint. However, statistics are essential tools that can be used to identify problem areas. Managers and supervisors have a significant impact on hiring, firing, training, promoting, delegating disciplinary action, and appraising and assigning agency employees. They control, directly or indirectly, the employment and advancement of women.

TECHNIQUES AND TIPS

Since the vast majority of senior executive positions are held by white males, and since they are responsible for most of the hiring and promotions, it is reasonable to focus on them as the alpha and omega factors of American workforce decisions. The values white male executives tend to internalize—individuality, unwavering toughness, control, and dominance—are not generally the qualities Third World peoples and women value. Even in interpersonal situations, white males tend to dominate—or at least they try to. Equally telling is their reluctance to admit errors or to apologize for them. Females fare even worse than minority-group males when competing with white males for the dominant (white, male, middle-class) society success goals. The unconscious disdain males often have for females is ingrained in literature. In 1975 Peter Swerdloff analyzed 2,760 stories in 134 children's books. In most cases the male characters—almost exclusively white—were adventuresome, brave, and socially active; while the female characters—almost exclusively white—were sedentary, timid, and socially passive. Today's managers are mainly products of this kind of fantasy. And so, too, are today's employees.

One of the more significant conclusions gleaned from the many studies reviewed for this chapter is the need for procedures to aid and assist female workers in adjusting to their work environment. All employees have feelings, emotions, and attitudes that directly influence the quality of their work. The potpourri of behaviors, hopes, fears, and emotions that people bring with them to their jobs exerts tremendous influence on their professional growth. Therefore, to be effective, women must adjust to some situations and challenge others, especially sexist language and acts of discrimination and harassment.

The toll on gender relationships in the workplace can be quite high. Bob

Filipczak (1994) opined that poorly conducted sexual harassment training programs can cause men and women not to trust each other. Such training escalates the battle of the sexes into a cold war in which both sides are caught in a crossfire of hostility and fear. A 1993 *Men's Health* survey of 500 men ages eighteen to sixty-four documented that two-thirds of the respondents were unsure about what to say or do around female co-workers (Peterson, 1994).

Typically, males take offense at females who are offended by sexist words. "When I say men," a male diversity workshop trainee said, "I mean women, too." "We have always had the job titles 'salesman' and 'foreman' in our company," another participant chimed in. "Yeah," another male smiled, "the ladies in here are too sensitive." Finally, when she had listened to enough of the rationalizations, the lone female participant looked at the black supervisor who started the conversation and said, "You black boys have come a long way." She then pointed to a white participant, "Not too many years ago poor white trash couldn't get a job in this company." The males protested her caustic comments. She smiled and asked, "Now who's being too sensitive?" Their words were certainly not neutral. Each of the participants behaved like Humpty Dumpty in Lewis Carroll's (1982) *Through the Looking-Glass:*

"When I use a word," Humpty Dumpty said, in rather scornful tone, "it means just what I choose it to mean—neither more nor less."
"The question is," said Alice, "whether you *can* make words mean so many different things."
"The question is," said Humpty Dumpty, "which is to be master—that's all." (p. 190)

A message, "Let's Get Rid of 'The Girl,' " published in the *Wall Street Journal* by United Technologies Corporation (1985) is even more direct:

Wouldn't it
be great
to take one giant
step forward
for womankind
and get rid of
"the girl"?
Your attorney says,
"If I'm not here
just leave it with
the girl."
The purchasing agent
says, "Drop off your
bid with the girl."

A manager says,
"My girl will get
back to your girl."
What girl?
Do they mean
Miss Rose?
Do they mean
Ms. Torres?
Do they mean
Mrs. McCullough?
Do they mean
Joy Jackson?
"The girl"
is certainly
a woman when she's
out of her teens.
Like you,
she has a name.
Use it.
©United Technologies Corporation 1985

Great care must be taken by managers and supervisors to avoid using language that demeans or treats female employees as a low-status, homogeneous group. Referring to people by name is an important way to empower them.

Another way supervisors can help female employees adjust to their work environment is through counseling. Many supervisors believe that theories of counseling are fine but not very practical because of the lack of time. However, if done effectively career counseling can be an extremely valuable managerial tool for establishing an open, honest climate with all subordinates, female or male. Even if they do not consider it counseling, supervisors must learn to listen to subordinates and help them talk out their problems. The purpose of this is to promote a greater degree of understanding and possibly prevent acts of discrimination.

Managers and supervisors who dismiss the importance of counseling are extremely foolish. Like it or not, wherever a superior-subordinate relationship exists, counseling situations will inevitably arise. Therefore, to be an effective manager one must be an effective counselor. By its nature, employee counseling is broad. However, in some circumstances counseling may be for specific, predetermined reasons: (1) employment interviews, (2) job evaluations, (3) disciplinary cases, (4) morale surveys, and (5) exit interviews.

Training is another important aspect of job enculturation and success. Thomas Wells (1973) listed five ways organizations enculturate and promote employees: (1) on-the-job training; (2) formal training programs, that is, a series of planned job-related experiences; (3) employer-supported outside study programs; (4) informal sponsors; and (5) participation in conferences. Women and minorities typically are excluded from on-the-job training, formal training, and employer-supported outside study because they disproportionately are hired into low-skill, dead-end jobs that do not require additional training. Thus they are stuck. Further, women and minorities seldom have mentors to shepherd them through the system. They also are less likely than their white peers to participate in conferences.

Another disadvantage to women and minorities are company training programs specifically designed for them. These programs tend to stigmatize the participants and also give them superficial exposure to various departments but few, if any, challenging job responsibilities. This kind of training perpetuates "token" and "reverse discrimination" beliefs of white workers. Ergo, some companies unintentionally reinforce stereotypes about incompetent women and minority workers. Such programs seldom provide trainees exposure to available role models farther up in the hierarchy. It is important for organizations to link women and minorities not only to female and minority mentors but also to white male mentors. However, all training for new employees should be available to every employee. Ideally a job-rotation system would be implemented for as many leadership positions as feasible.

As stated earlier, people bring their emotions with them to work. As a group, females are stressed by pressures of outside forces to a greater degree than their male counterparts. Not only must a disproportionate number of women adapt to the work environment; they must also adapt to changing family and gender roles. While these changes impact both men and women, the values and attitudes of society put extraordinary pressure on women. Both male and female supervisors should consider the following do's and don'ts. First, supervisors in general and male supervisors in particular should:

1. *Have and be able to convey a genuine sensitivity for the concerns of female workers.* These concerns include (a) role conflict and personal fragmentation that many female workers face as a result of being torn between the job and home, (b) lack of equity in pay, (c) inadequate promotion opportunities, (d) too few training opportunities, (e) occupational segregation, (f) sex discrimination, (g) sexual harassment, and (h) unfounded beliefs about what is appropriate behavior for men and women.

2. *Have an understanding of how interpersonal problems can affect an organization.* Supervisors must be aware of female workers as persons who frequently bring to work problems, values, and attitudes that affect their performance. It is important to remember that a woman's work performance may not reflect lack of commitment to the job.

3. *Get to know individual female workers and convey sensitivity to each worker in a noncondescending manner.* The supervisor must establish

rapport with female workers and convey his or her desire to assist in problem solving and job enhancement.

4. *Be fair and insure that all employees know and understand the standards, policies, and procedures.*

5. *Listen carefully for negative and positive feelings.* Feed back this information; seek clarity and understanding.

6. *Recognize the limits of their authority and expertise.* Know when it is appropriate to refer female workers to someone else or some agency with more specialization in abating problems (e.g., marital, affirmative action, and chemical abuse specialists).

On the other hand, do not: (1) *Make unsubstantiated assumptions about women and what they can and cannot do.* (2) *Argue with or admonish women who need counseling.* This will cause them to become defensive and they will not share their feelings. (3) *Flaunt authority (organizational or intellectual).* Talk with workers, not *at* them or *to* them. (4) *Give advice.* Help women by encouraging them to consider the advantages and disadvantages of various options to relieve job stress. Offer understanding of problems and answer questions about organizational policies and procedures. Ask questions, but allow workers to make the choice as to which option, if any, they will take.

Supervisors must learn, if they do not know already, how to deal effectively with female workers. They are extremely important human resources. They are absolutely essential to the functioning of business and industry and the economic survival of our society. To unleash the full potential of these resources is an enormously complex task. On a small level, supervisors and co-workers can realize amazing gains by being sensitive to women's concerns and creating a climate where affirmative action is more than words.

HOW TO DEAL WITH SEXUAL HARASSMENT

If an employee complains about sexual harassment, managers and supervisors should:

- find out what action she (he) wants to take.
- offer to help by talking to the offending person privately or by meeting with both of them together.
- advise the harassed worker to say "no" to the offender.
- follow the organization's disciplinary procedures if the offender repeats the harassment.

Under no circumstances should managers and supervisors:

- tell the harassed employee to ignore the harassment.
- assume that the complaining worker "asked for it."

- joke about it.
- tell the complainant to embarrass the harasser or to get physical.
- let the harassment continue.

If managers and supervisors see possible incidents of sexual harassment, but are not sure, they should:

- ask the potential victim if she (he) finds the behavior offensive or intimidating.
- tell the potential victim that she (he) does not have to accept harassment.

Questions to ask the complainant:

- "Where and when did the alleged behavior occur?"
- "Who was involved?"
- "Were there witnesses?"
- "Has this behavior or other offensive behavior happened before? If so, what happened and when did it happen?"
- "What did you tell the person(s)?"
- "What was his/her/their reaction?"
- "Have you told anyone else about this?" "Who?"

When talking with the alleged harasser:

- Begin by stating the purpose of the meeting. For example, "I want to talk to you about an allegation of sexual harassment involving you." Maintain a calm, unbiased demeanor.
- Do not initially reveal the name of the complainant. Describe the complaint and ask him (her) if it occurred.
- If there is more than one allegation, discuss each of them separately. Ask for a response to each allegation.
- If the individual acknowledges the behavior in question, tell him (her) that it must stop immediately.
- If he (she) denied the allegation(s), advise him (her) that you will try to determine the truth of the allegation(s) through further investigation to gather relevant facts.
- Document the dates and pertinent points of the meeting with the complainant and the alleged harasser(s).
- After a thorough investigation, take appropriate action based on your organization's policies. Notify all parties involved of your findings and action.

Et Cetera

Generally, women who elect to leave their protective pedestals still encounter problems in being accepted by men as equals. The altering and meshing of sex roles do not occur easily. But in the end the conservation and proper use of our human resources, female and male, is the key to success in the workplace. If companies want to react correctly to the changing workforce, they will recruit, retain, and promote more women (Hughey & Gelman, 1986; Pennar, 1988). This may include instituting or expanding benefits such as family care, wellness programs, and flexible work schedules.

SEXUAL HARASSMENT QUIZ

Sexual harassment means many things. Of course, the facts of the situation determine whether or not harassment has occurred. Check all of the behaviors listed below that you believe may constitute sexual harassment.

_____. Actual or attempted rape or sexual assault.

_____. Unwanted requests for sexual favors.

_____. Unwanted deliberate touching, leaning over, cornering, or pinching.

_____. Unwanted sexually suggestive looks or gestures.

_____. Unwanted letters, telephone calls, or materials of a sexual nature.

_____. Unwanted requests for dates.

_____. Unwanted sexually related stories, teasing, jokes, remarks, or questions.

_____. Referring to an adult as a "girl," "hunk," "doll," "babe," or "honey."

_____. Whistling at an individual.

_____. Cat calls.

_____. Shifting from job-related discussions to sexual topics.

_____. Asking about an individual's sexual fantasies, preferences, or history.

_____. Personal questions about an individual's social or sexual life.

_____. Sexual comments about an individual's clothing, anatomy, or looks.

_____. Directing kissing sounds, howling, and smacking lips at an individual.

_____. Telling lies or spreading rumors about an individual's personal sex life.

_____. Giving an individual an unsolicited neck massage.

_____. Touching an individual's clothing, hair, or body.

_____. Giving personal gifts.

_____. Hugging, kissing, patting, or stroking an individual.

_____. Touching or rubbing oneself sexually around another person.

_____. Standing close to or brushing up against an individual.

_____. Looking an individual up and down (elevator eyes).

_____. Staring at an individual.

_____. Displaying or circulating sexually suggestive visual materials.

_____. Winking, throwing kisses, or licking one's lips at another person.

The answers are in the Appendix.

CHAPTER 4

Older Workers

American business, government, social agency, and labor leaders have become concerned with the obvious but momentous fact that our nation is growing older. In 1980 the median age of our population passed thirty for the first time since World War II. That disclosure by the United States Census Bureau shattered the myth that the United States is still a youthful country (Anderson, 1981). The recent history of older Americans is not a story of humane relations. Older people in America have by and large been separated from the mainstream of society, either by design or through neglect. Many social agency and industrial leaders seem convinced that older citizens cannot serve a useful purpose. Some of those leaders do not want them to try to be useful. Whatever the reason, neglect and disdain of older workers appear to be increasing. This does not alter the fact that older people are the fastest growing segment of the population.

DEFINITIONS

Social gerontology is one of the youngest of the behavioral sciences. Most of the literature pertaining to the aged and the aging in the United States written before 1940 was devoted primarily to analyses of the biological processes of aging. Moreover, those studies seem to have been conducted with a noticeable degree of nonchalance. The apparent casualness of the interest in aging may be explained largely by the fact that the average life expectancy for persons of either sex never exceeded 63.7 years until 1940. Today, the situation is quite different; it is common knowledge that recent scientific advances have substantially increased the average life expectancy. After 1940, "the United States, like a woman who [had] just taken a good look in the mirror, [realized] that it [was] no longer as young as it used to be. The result [was] a feeling of shock followed by an earnest search for remedies to the creeping problems of age" (*The Economist*, 1960, p. 54).

The "search for remedies" had to be extended into new areas, since the very fact that the aged population had increased in size presented problems beyond the scope of biology. Most gerontologists came to the realization that our society was not oriented toward solving these problems, which included such realities as the older person's need for employment, housing, and recreation. As Clark Tibbitts (1950) observed, "Our population has been oriented toward youth. Most of our attitudes and institutions have been developed with reference to an essentially young population. This has been particularly true of our employment practices, of our educational and recreational facilities, of the medical specialties, of social welfare services, and even of our religious institutions" (p. 1).

Some researchers have hypothesized that the majority of older Americans want to continue to be useful, participating, recognized, and wanted members of the community—in essence, to remain an integral part of society. They conclude that the fulfillment of this desire would be reflected in suitable living arrangements, physical comforts, financial security, emotional outlets, and companionship. From a business perspective, the question is being asked: Are the more than 30 million older persons not potentially valuable human resources? Many of them have acquired and honed job-related skills through decades of tough, practical experiences. From a practical point of view, older workers represent a reserve of proven talent.

The Graying of America

The United States no longer has an under-thirty-years-of-age majority population and it is becoming increasingly older. Life expectancy in the United States has increased approximately ten years in the past three decades. Four-fifths (87.3%) of the population now reach age sixty-five. But sixty-five is just the beginning. On the average, those who reach sixty-five live an additional fifteen years. The increase in the number of older Americans is quite remarkable. Each day about 4,200 Americans over sixty-five die, while four thousand enter that age group. This aging population profile is not unique to the United States. Western Europe, Japan, and the Eastern European countries are experiencing the same phenomenon. All industrial nations must deal with increasing numbers of older people who do not seem to fit very well into today's swift-paced, highly technological, youth-oriented culture.

The United States Department of Labor (1981) conducted a statistical study that examined the characteristics of "older workers" (those forty-five years old and over) and trends in their participation in the labor force.

The report stated that the employment patterns of older workers are expected to change significantly in the coming years. Tomorrow's older workers will be better educated and more skilled than those of today.

The issue that few people discuss is *ageism*. The aged are stereotypically described as more slow, tired, ill, forgetful, defensive, withdrawn, self-pitying, and unhappy than younger people (Kalish, 1982; Levin & Levin, 1980; McTavish, 1971). The negative stereotypes are most often perpetrated by people who fear their own loss of control, loss of sexuality, and loss of intelligence (Palmore, 1990; Perdue & Gurtman, 1990). In terms of perceived differences, the words *old* and *young* are frequently used as the equivalent cultural antonyms. Robert Butler (1969) coined the term *ageism*:

Ageism can be seen as systematized stereotyping of and discrimination against people because they are old, just as racism and sexism accomplish this with skin color and gender. Old people are categorized as senile, rigid in thought, old-fashioned in morality and skills. . . . Ageism allows the younger generation to see older people different from themselves; thus they subtly cease to identify with their elders as human beings. (pp. 1, 9)

Derogatory expressions of the old abound: *old bag, old fogey, old maid, dirty old man, old fart, old goat, old hag, old lecher* (Saporta, 1988). These terms are augmented by insulting metaphors for people "past their prime": *over the hill, dead wood.* Consequently, through speech the stereotypes are created, nourished, and perpetuated. Indeed, through myths and stereotypes, the prophecy of inferior beings fulfills itself. "Society and the North American media don't treat older people well: too much patronizing, too much stereotyping, too many stories dwelling on the problems and foibles of old age, and too few about its joys and rewards" (IABC, 1982, p. 47).

MYTHS AND STEREOTYPES

Younger employees who stereotype older people as inferior beings and discriminate against them set in motion their own negative conditions in later life. Paraphrasing an old saying: The sins of the sons and the daughters accrue to the grandmothers and grandfathers. Contrary to the previously mentioned stereotypes, most older workers are not only able to continue working but they are also extremely productive (Kelly, 1990). The national trend is toward a longer, healthier life; toward more years with more energy, more ability, and more need to remain active. While it is true that most people want to enjoy at least partial retirement, few want to be forcibly, totally retired. In summary, a substantial number of older citizens are willing and eager to work.

There does not appear to be any way to grow old gracefully in the United States. Equally important, it is difficult for most workers to grow old and remain useful. The old are not out of sight and, consequently, they are not out of the minds of younger workers. The encounter is daily. Less than 6 percent of our aged are in institutions. Within organizations they frequently are perceived as standing in the way of the young, upwardly mobile employees. Away from the job, they remind people of the final life cycle. In *As You Like It*, Shakespeare painted this literary portrait of growing old:

> The sixth age shifts
> Into the lean and striped pantelone
> With spectacles on nose and pouch on side;
> His youthful hose, well-sewed, a work too wide
> For is shrunk shank, and his manly voice
> Turning again to childish treble, pipes
> And whistles in his sound. Last seen of all,
> That ends this stage eventual history,
> Is second childishness, and mere oblivion,
> Sans teeth, sans eyes, sans taste, sans everything.

Movies and television specials perpetuate the image of older citizens wasted to bones and waiting to be buried. This is not to say that the elderly are without problems. They have many problems—some of them similar to younger workers. Personnel officers tend to be less empathetic toward older workers, preferring to see them retire rather than retrain them or reduce their hours. Some of the myths and stereotypes pertaining to the aged are the beliefs that most old people are senile, mentally ill, or in poor health; are set in their ways and unable or unwilling to change; are poor workers; are isolated and lonely; have incomes below the official poverty level; are happy to retire from jobs and abandon the hassles of work; are hypochondriacs; and are basically alike.

Based on data pertaining to ethnic minorities, to be an old ethnic minority person is to be in double jeopardy. Along with the stereotypes about ethnic groups (e.g., shiftless, lazy, docile) are also added the stereotypes about growing old. People of color do not live as well as Caucasian citizens; nor do they live as long.

Although numerous studies conclude that while differences in hourly output among age groups are insignificant, older workers suffer from the stereotypic notion that they are doddering, unproductive, inflexible, uninformed, and inactive. Most majority-group Americans typically face job discrimination around age forty-five (it is much earlier for ethnic minorities). Many of them are forced out of the workplace in their middle sixties or earlier and are left to the questionable pleasures of a retirement that is too often devoid of personal challenges and frequently full of financial struggles. This kind of retirement definitely is not the "golden years" in the storybook dreams of most people.

THOSE WHO ARE AFFECTED

A generation ago, seven out of ten American workers were men and fathers of families. As a rule, their wives did not work outside the home, and they had one or more children living at home. This was the classic *nuclear family*. The major pool of the labor force was determined to be white males, and jobs were designed to meet the needs of those workers (Anderson, 1981; Palmore, 1990). They were the "traditional" workers. In 1990 they were about 75 percent of the labor force. They shared jobs with working wives, single parents, husband and wife teams, minorities, and others. Business, government, and public agencies were slow to accommodate this demographic change.

Almost 70 percent of American men aged sixty-five and over were gainfully employed or seeking employment in 1900. By 1990, both men and women over sixty-five represented 2.8 percent of the labor force. Unless the trend is reversed, the percentage will be even lower in the year 2000. The sheer numbers of people without jobs will be financially and socially staggering. America must, as R. O. Anderson (1981) stated, "take them off the shelf" (p. 207). The elderly population is growing, as well as getting older. The population aged eighty-five and over is one of the fastest growing groups in the country and it is expected to more than double from the year 1990 to 2030, from 3 million to over 8 million people.

According to the U.S. Administration on Aging, more older people are retiring long before age sixty-five. Consequently, the labor force participation declines with age. There has been a rapid drop in workers past forty years of age. In 1950, almost half (46%) of all men aged sixty-five and older were in the labor force. This figure had dropped to 27 percent by 1970. In 1989 only 17 percent of older men were in the labor force. Historically, labor force participation for black women aged sixty-five and older has been somewhat higher than for their white peers. In recent years, however, the rates have converged and less than two percentage points separated the two groups in 1989: 8.2 percent for elderly white women and 9.8 percent for elderly black women. The labor force participation rate for older black men (14.3%) was lower in 1989 than the rate for older white men (16.8%).

The decline in the poverty rates for the elderly since 1959 has been dramatic, from 35.2 percent to 12.4 percent in 1991. Despite the decline in poverty, however, there are still disproportionately high levels of poverty among certain groups of elderly, especially members of ethnic minority groups, the very old, and older women. The "discard shelf" simply is not big enough to hold all of the discarded workers. Those who support our nation's social insurance programs—the employed workers—are buckling under the load of future generations. Numerous economists have pointed out that never in the history of the Social Security Act have so many people depended on so few for their income. The program is not going to survive much longer unless something is done to ease the load.

In 1935, when the Social Security Act was passed, there were eleven adults in the labor force for each Social Security recipient. Today only six active workers support each retiree, and the situation is getting worse because of an increasing longevity and a decreasing birth rate. This trend toward what is sometimes referred to as "intergenerational interdependence" affects the federal budget and, relatedly, each wage earner. The long-term viability of Social Security must be put on a fiscally sound footing. Many private and public sector employer pension plans are also close to being insolvent. Soon the unfunded liabilities of public and private pension programs may exceed the national debt. Retirement, specifically early retirement, appears to be unrealistic.

A 1981 Harris poll concluded that 46 percent of retired people would prefer to work part-time or full-time. This same poll indicated that 51 percent of younger workers—tomorrow's retirees—expressed the desire to work in some meaningful activity after they retire. It is widely accepted that work is therapeutic for older people who choose it. This is also good for business and the nation. The rewards older people get from working are both economic and psychic. Part-time work is needed to supplement pensions as savings are increasingly eroded by inflation. Work also fosters a sense of usefulness, of being involved, active, and needed. When businesses and agencies offer work opportunities to older persons, they supplement their own talents with a vast reservoir of skills, experience, knowledge, and past productivity. As the pool of younger workers grows smaller in the future, it clearly is in the self-interest of organizations to look to older workers for more than token help (Lawrie, 1990; Rhine, 1978).

In regards to America in general, the benefits of using older people will be multidimensional. Studies prepared for the 1981 White House Conference on Aging suggest that expanded employment of older workers would boost the entire U.S. economy. Some economists believe this would add to U.S. gross national product by almost 4 percent by the year 2005. In terms of money, this economic growth could add approximately $40 billion in 1980 dollars to federal, state, and local tax revenues in the year 2005 (Beach, 1981).

Common Characteristics

Many elderly workers exhibit a high level of *anxiety*. Fear, shame, and physical deterioration add to the stress inherent in most work situations.

Hearing loss is a common phenomenon: almost one-third of the older workers experience this sensory loss. Fewer older workers (15%–20%) experience extreme visual problems. Older workers tend to be more cautious than younger ones. Most of their errors are of omission rather than commission. Afraid that mistakes may cost them pensions, promotion, or just plain praise, they are likely to do only what is required. Part of this is because many elderly workers develop an unrealistic perception of their supervisors. In psychiatric terms, this is *transference:* They view supervisors as parents or children. In either case, elderly workers in this category have an obsessive need not to disappoint their supervisors.

Loss is a persistent theme of the elderly. They lose bodily functions, friends and loved ones, employment, and often self-esteem. Some even lose their memory of previous events. Perhaps their greatest fear is that they will lose their minds and go crazy. Most older workers do not seem obsessed with losing their lives, but almost all of them fear being alone at death. It is not merely older workers who are affected by aging and impending death; all employees who work with them are also affected. The older worker is the conduit of many problems—racism, burnout, sexism, alcoholism, mental illness, and terminal illness. In many ways, how organizations care for their older workers is a valuable clue of how they care for younger ones with problems.

Both young and old employees frequently are torn between the desire on the one hand to stay with familiar and on the other hand to venture forth into new activities. *New experience* occurs when individuals encounter something that, in part or in whole, they have never faced before. A new experience may be a job situation to which a new variable has been introduced—for example, minority groups who suddenly must adjust to newly achieved equal employment opportunities. The need for new experience is the antithesis of the wish for maintaining the status quo. New experience describes actions that disturb the status quo, such as the behavior of an individual who takes a vacation or quits his or her job. Experiences that are too radical are usually disturbing rather than stimulating. To be interpersonally pleasing, for example, a new job assignment must be the familiar done in a slightly different manner.

The need for *security* can be seen in all actions that contribute to keeping things as they are. Efforts to keep a job or retain one's youth are examples of wishes or motives for security. Most people tend to resist revolutionary changes. Most of the social history of the later Middle Ages is a chronicle of the efforts of majority groups to prevent minority groups from introducing novel inventions and methods. The history of early science is characterized by the struggle against conservatism. Even today, most people cling tenaciously to old cultural norms, however willing they profess to be for change. To illustrate, most industries still have double promotion standards for older and younger workers, with older workers generally receiving fewer opportunities for supervisory positions. Much of human conservatism is traceable to the fact that once a reasonably effective pattern of behavior is learned, any change that makes that pattern less effective is psychologically or socially distressing.

Older workers, like younger ones, also have a need for *recognition*—the need to be acknowledged for an accomplishment. To fail to be recognized by people important to us is one of the most dreaded forms of punishment. For instance, a company may decide to recognize a retiring worker. It schedules a banquet in her honor and invites many people, including representatives of the press. No matter how elaborate the preparation of food and decorations and certificates of honor, if the invited guests do not attend the banquet, the retiree has not received recognition. In highly competitive organizations, a great amount of human action has no other objective than that of individuals trying to diminish the importance of their associates. Members of competitive work groups are, by conditioning, egoists, each trying to rise above the others. Generally, old age brings less recognition.

Closely related to recognition is the need for *response* from members of one's organization. Because employees derive their definition of success from others, they need feedback from significant others to help them shape their behaviors. An individual's corporate identity arises in interaction with other employees. In some organizations, older workers are left out of significant informal social interactions. When this happens, they become the equivalent of nonpersons.

All individuals have the need to receive *respect,* which provides confirmation of their positive self-worth. This kind of reinforcement is the basis of healthy personalities. It is a simple but significant fact that all individuals need respect from their co-workers in order to develop and maintain healthy personalities. Some organizations do not foster such interactions. For example, little respect accrues to individuals whose productivity decreases or who are perceived as being superfluous to long-range organization goals. Older workers frequently fit that characterization.

LAWS

The Age Discrimination in Employment Act (ADEA)

Passed in 1967 and effective June 1968, the purposes of the ADEA are to promote employment of older people between the ages of forty and sixty-five based on their ability rather than age; to prohibit arbitrary age discrimination in employment; and to help employers and workers find ways to solve problems arising from the impact of age on employment. Specifically, the act prohibits age discrimination in hiring, referral, classification, compensation, and other terms and conditions of employment (and related advertising) on the part of employers with twenty-five or more employees, employment agencies, and labor organizations.

In order to save money, businesses are prone to cut their biggest expense: the workforce. Employees with the most seniority and the largest salaries, most expensive retirement plans, and most costly health care packages are replaced by employees at entry-level positions (Thompson, 1992). Many older employees were forced into an early retirement. According to the law, early retirement must be voluntary (Lacey, 1992).

The 1974 Employee Retirement Income Security Act (ERISA)

Although complicated and full of flaws, the ERISA gives employees greater protection for their pension programs. Prior to ERISA, employees enrolled in private pension plans frequently lost their pensions, sometimes after decades of participation. Among the causes for such losses were job transfers, companies going out of business, and employers' mismanagement of pension funds.

The 1978 Amendments to ADEA (Public Law 95-256)

This act rendered legally unenforceable most mandatory retirement policies for people up to age seventy. The act also prohibits employers from discriminating against persons aged forty through seventy in hiring, firing, promotions, compensation, and other conditions or privileges of employment. Interestingly, the previous mandatory retirement age of sixty-five as outlined in the original 1967 ADEA was arbitrarily selected by New Deal planners because this age was used in Otto von Bismark's social welfare system in Germany in the nineteenth century. In fact, Congress accepted the age of sixty-five for retirement without even considering any other age or related factors. Public Law 95-256 reflected an awareness by Congress of changing economic and social conditions in the United States. (Mandatory retirement after age seventy was abolished in a 1986 amendment to ADEA.)

The 1990 Older Workers Benefits Protection Act (OWBPA)

Effective in 1991, this act provides additional safeguards against employers pressuring workers to accept early retirement. The OWBPA prohibits capricious and discriminatory acts to get employees to waive their employment and retirement rights. Employees are empowered to negotiate retirement terms. And they have twenty-one days to decide whether or not to sign a job waiver. If the waiver is presented to a group of workers, each individual has an additional seven days to change his or her mind if the waiver was signed. Other key requirements placed on employee agreements not to sue include the following:

- The agreement must be understandable to the average worker.
- The employers must offer employees something of value in addition to what is already owed them.
- The employer must advise the employee in writing to consult an attorney before signing the waiver.

SELECTED COURT CASES

Belatedly, many older workers learn that the new legal protections have limited value in practice as evidenced by the large number of lawsuits and complaints filed with the EEOC that are dismissed in court. Proving age discrimination is difficult. Judicial interpretations of the laws are constantly changing. A December 1991 *Newsweek* article described a controversial ruling in the federal appeals court in New York in 1990. The court held that "employers may replace highly paid executives with lesser paid ones for financial reasons, so long as age is not a factor" (Beck et al., 1991, p. 66). The court stated that former employees must prove discriminatory intent on the part of the employer. With the current backlog of complaints facing the EEOC many older workers who have left their jobs because of discrimination may not get the chance to prove their dismissals were not in accordance with the law. Private lawyers are expensive and many of them are reluctant to take age discrimination suits because proving bias of any kind is difficult. The evidence suggests that age discrimination is the most virulent in the employment area.

Proving why someone was not hired is even more difficult than proving why someone was fired. In 1991 there were between 1.1 million and 1.9 million men and women aged fifty through sixty-four out of work. Most of those people were willing, able, and well qualified for work but were unable to find jobs. As a whole, older Americans are very aggressive about asserting their rights. During economic downturn, older workers are at an even greater disadvantage when competing with younger workers for jobs.

The ADEA does not apply to employees over forty years of age who do not perform their jobs satisfactorily. In *Cova v. Coca-Cola Bottling Co. of St. Louis* (1978) the employer was upheld because the plaintiff was warned several times about his unsatisfactory performance prior to being terminated. The record actually showed that Cova's sales record was unsatisfactory when judged by company standards. The court ruled that the employers had the right to determine job standards and could make a decision to terminate Cova. A similar conclusion was reached in *Bohrer v. Hanes Corp.* (1985), where a salesman with twenty years' employment with a company was fired and replaced with a twenty-eight-year-old person. Here, too, the plaintiff had received several consultations focusing on his unsatisfactory sales record. In *Huhn v. Koehrnig Co.* (1983) an employee of thirty years alleged that he lost his job as a sales representative because of his age even though he had been a good employee.

When employers discharge older workers because of their age, they may be assessed very high punitive damages. In *Rawson v. Sears, Roebuck and Co.* (1985) a sixty-year-old store manager with thirty-three years' service was discharged in a manner the jury described as "callous and demeaning" without regard to the plaintiff's feelings. The evidence showed Rawson to be a loyal, dedicated, and productive employee who was discharged as a result of a company-wide plan to phase out older employees in order to promote younger ones. The jury awarded Rawson $580,000 for lost wages, $264,000 for future lost wages and reduction in pension funds and other benefits, and $5 million for pain and suffering. And because there was malice and wanton disregard of the plaintiff's rights and feelings, the jury awarded $10 million for exemplary (punitive) damages even though his attorney only asked for $1 million.

The Supreme Court of Montana upheld a $100,000 award for emotional distress and $1.3 million for exemplary damages in *Flanigan v. Prudential Federal Savings & Loan Assn.* (1986). The court stated the punitive damages may seem excessive, but it also acknowledged such damages were within the jury's discretion. Flanigan worked for Prudential Savings and Loan for twenty-eight years and had progressed from teller to assistant loan counselor. Prior to filing the lawsuit, Ms. Flanigan was told her position was being eliminated and she was offered a teller position. One week after she worked as a teller, she was fired without notice. During the trial, the president of the company referred to older employees as "deadwood," "old deadwood," and "ballast." The court concluded that he had "blatant disregard for older workers."

The Problem Grows

Age discrimination is a growing problem among America's older workers. According to the American Association for Retired Persons (AARP), requests for information on fighting age discrimination have increased 55 percent since 1990 (Beck et al., 1991). Charges of age discrimination nearly doubled during the 1980s and by 1990 there were 22,537 new cases filed (O'Conner, 1991). In 1990 the Equal Employment Opportunity Commission (EEOC) had a backlog of age discrimination cases exceeding 45,000, and it received 17,000 more complaints in 1991. By September 1992, a record 60,000 discharge because of age cases were filed with the EEOC (Thompson, 1992). Along with the cases filed through the EEOC, private lawsuits alleging age discrimination increased 2,200 percent from

1969 to 1989. Thus, although there are state and federal laws prohibiting age discrimination, complaints continue to grow.

SPECIAL PROGRAMS

The federal government and several state governments have almost completely abolished compulsory retirement before age seventy for their own employees. Also, Social Security laws have been liberalized so that retired workers can earn a limited amount of money without losing benefits. Although all of those changes help, much more needs to be done. The fact still remains that few people over sixty-five who want to work actually do work.

Workforce Analysis

A workforce analysis could identify occupations with high concentrations of older workers and predict the consequences for an organization if large numbers of these workers retire in masses. In addition, the analysis could ascertain older workers' interest in delaying their retirement and determine preferred alternative work options. Organizations anticipating a high turnover of experienced workers or a shortage of employees with particular skills could develop formal retention and rehiring policies for older workers and retirees. All organizations should carefully weigh the costs of implementing such policies against the cost of hiring and training replacements for their older workers (Anderson & Weagant, 1972).

Part-time Work

When considering the alternative of part-time work for older employees, most organization budgets are restricted to a fixed number of positions. Program managers usually are prohibited from hiring two part-time workers to fill one full-time position without building a case of unique circumstances. One solution is to count the number of part-time workers on a prorated basis. Another fact that can be taken into consideration by employers interested in converting full-time jobs into equivalent part-time jobs is the difficulty in finding employees with similar skills. For this reason, employers must develop policies to encourage part-time workers to be recruited from within as well as outside the organization. Indeed, a few organizations are experimenting with procedures allowing two persons to jointly apply for the same position (e.g., job sharing by married couples).

Job Transfers

Frequently, productive older employees who find their jobs too demanding retire early and look for work with different employers. Sometimes this is done because lateral job changes in the same organization are viewed as demotions by co-workers. It is important that employers recognize this problem and, as some are doing, develop opportunities for lateral transfers into newly created or restructured jobs with recognized status. This removes the stigma of demotions for older workers who change jobs. An example of this would be a company creating "emeritus" positions for older, highly valued workers who could continue working but in the role of mentors and consultants. Although such positions might be at a lower salary, they would connote elevated or special status, which may alleviate the psychosocial problems accompanying reduced or different work loads. Modifying work schedules and redesigning jobs are relatively new ideas. The mechanics of implementing alternative work options take time to develop and will not be worked out unless employers perceive an advantage in doing so.

Retirement Planning

The more progressive organizations are assisting older workers to become aware of opportunities, if any, for alternative work options and their impact on retirement benefits. In organizations where work options are available, the information provided to employees usually includes an explanation of the financial impact of the alternatives on retirement benefits. This is especially important because many older workers who are interested in alternative work options wish to extend their work lives but not at a financial loss. Several organizations use preretirement seminars to stimulate workers' interest in alternatives to full retirement. If employees wait until just before their retirement dates to participate in such seminars, it may be too late to seriously consider alternative work options. Therefore, some employers organize and encourage worker participation in preretirement seminars at least several years prior to retirement in order to allow sufficient time to evaluate several work arrangements as alternatives to full retirement.

Economic Incentive Programs

Most pension regulations penalize older workers who utilize alternative work options with the same employer. For example, pension regulations often prohibit employees from drawing their pensions while still working for the same employer and, in some cases, even disallow working a postretirement job in the same industry. In other instances, the rules governing pension benefits penalize workers interested in most alternative work options. For example, in some organizations if individuals were to work half time, it would take them two years to accumulate one additional year of service based on existing organization pension regulations. Additionally, there is a disincentive to work part-time when calculations for retirement benefits are based on an employee's average salary for the years immediately preceding retirement.

A method now being tried by some private organizations is a separate in-house entity that serves as a job shop or employment service. In essence, retirees are rehired as temporary employees, and able to draw their pensions to supplement their wages, but they are ineligible for pension accrual or other fringe benefits. The public sector is adjusting pension regulations through legislative change. For example, modifications in the Kansas Public Employees Retirement System permit employees to retire at age sixty or later, draw their pensions, and be rehired into their former jobs or other jobs for which they are qualified. Also, the Wichita Public School System has taken advantage of similar legislative change provisions to encourage job sharing.

A growing number of organizations are exploring the feasibility of permitting older workers who want reduced work schedules to continue having their pension contributions calculated as though they were working full-time and earning full salaries. Several organizations have adopted such a plan, which has met with considerable success. In this case, part-time employees do not collect their pensions.

The slowness of American organizations to recognize problems unique to older workers is part of the reason there are few carefully planned programs for older workers (Abbasi & Hollman, 1991). It is anticlimactic to wait until people retire before designing retirement programs. The majority of older workers need preretirement programs.

TECHNIQUES AND TIPS

Subtle discrimination of older workers can lead to what is sometimes called the "Detroit syndrome": devalue them, demote them, discount them, and dump them. Perhaps one of the most obvious forms of ageism is seen in organizations that assign older middle- and lower-level employees slower, less important responsibilities. Because these employees are believed to be less productive than younger workers, they are given less productive assignments, and in the end they *are* less productive. Lawrie (1990) recommended eleven organization policies and practices to combat ageism: (1) Acknowledge that ageism probably exists. (2) Provide training programs for older workers that have longer lead and learning times. (3) Implement incremental changes in work activities. (4) Use praise instead of punishment to bring about changes. (5) Do not allow a young versus older worker caste system to develop. (6) Provide ample guidance and role models for older workers. (7) Set goals in terms of brackets and ranges instead of absolute marks. (8) Do not expect productivity to occur at a constant rate. (9) Provide clear, helpful feedback and encourage trainees to tell supervisors what they understand their assignments to be. (10) Where possible, let the employees rehearse their new assignments. (11) Managers must communicate to the employees that change is a way of life.

For administrators who want to prevent or abate problems growing out of old age, it is necessary to focus on the past, the present, and the future. The major emphasis, however, should be on immediate reality, that is, what is occurring today, not what happened yesterday. Employees who dwell exclusively on historical grievances such as ethnic, age, or sex discrimination are likely to become hardened, bitter people who see little hope in the present or the future. Those who spend most of their time dreaming of the future are likely to lose touch with reality. Ultimately, leaders of organizations must be able to design older-worker activities that are relevant for today and tomorrow.

The foremost goal of any older-worker program should be to aid each individual in realizing his or her optimum individual and organization growth. This goal necessarily includes freedom for individuals to express themselves as long as they do not infringe on the constitutional rights of others. Specifically, an older-worker program should point out to all employees that age differences are not valid reasons for rejecting others. Everyone must become willing to live with and accept age differences.

EFFECTIVE COMMUNICATION

A slow and relaxed pace can do much to relieve an older worker's anxiety. However, this does not necessarily require the younger person to talk slower. "Just because I move slowly doesn't mean I think slowly," an elderly worker said to his supervisor. It is important that older workers be treated with respect. To some older workers, words such as "old man" or "old lady" are as offensive as "boy" and "girl" are to many African Americans. The key to most human relations problems is effective communication. Administrators and co-workers who refuse to listen to what others are saying miss opportunities for positive interaction. In this instance, they *hear* the words but they do not *listen* to the social and psychological implications.

At all times managers must be alert for obstacles to good listening that may be caused by prejudice against the elderly employee, whether it is caused by his or her age, dress, or basic beliefs. Effective communication systems do not just happen; they are created. Nor should quantity of communication automatically be equated with quality. Informal gatherings, staff meetings, and individual conferences are occasions when organization communications can be checked for accuracy. Whenever possible, managers should send messages to older workers that convey the thought "I'm okay, you're okay." When there are so many positive things that can be said about people, it is an act of gross insensitivity to send only negative messages. In summary, communicating with older workers is the same as communicating with other workers: It is hard work that requires constant monitoring and refining.

Many organizations such as the American Association of Retired Persons (AARP) are working "to better the lives of older Americans through service, advocacy, education, and volunteer efforts" (Maxwell, 1992, p. 2). The AARP has increased its efforts to focus national attention on age discrimination. Its goal is to change negative societal attitudes toward middle-age and older workers, to improve workplace conditions, and to increase opportunities for all workers. Age discrimination is harmful not only to individual victims but also to the nation's economy. Older workers are valuable resources and an asset to the nation. Therefore, how effectively the United States uses this valuable resource will determine our productivity and global competitiveness in the 1990s and in the twenty-first century as well.

ATTITUDES ABOUT AGING

This survey will help you assess your own attitudes and opinions about the aged and about your own aging. This is best done in an extended discussion or exploratory interview or through rigorous self-examination. Inventories, such as this one, however, can help in this process. The statements listed below are opinions. Identify your opinions about each statement by circling a number between 1 and 10. Circling a 1 means that you very much agree, circling a 10 means that you very much disagree with the statement. Circling a 5 means that you have no opinion one way or another.

1. Some people stay young in their beliefs no matter how long they live.

   Agree   Disagree
   1   2   3   4   5   6   7   8   9   10

2. No one who is retired and over sixty-five years of age should be allowed to drive a car.

   Agree   Disagree
   1   2   3   4   5   6   7   8   9   10

3. Retired people are happiest when they are in the company of people their own age.

   Agree   Disagree
   1   2   3   4   5   6   7   8   9   10

4. Anyone can keep young if he or she only tries.

   Agree   Disagree
   1   2   3   4   5   6   7   8   9   10

5. I usually feel depressed at the thought of getting old.

Agree   Disagree
1   2   3   4   5   6   7   8   9   10

6. We should not expect old people to be physically active.

Agree   Disagree
1   2   3   4   5   6   7   8   9   10

7. When people retire they should realize that the best years of life are yet to come.

Agree   Disagree
1   2   3   4   5   6   7   8   9   10

8. We will never get old if we remain active.

Agree   Disagree
1   2   3   4   5   6   7   8   9   10

9. It would be sad to still be alive after all my friends are gone.

Agree   Disagree
1   2   3   4   5   6   7   8   9   10

10. The future is so uncertain that there is little point in thinking about it or planning ahead.

Agree   Disagree
1   2   3   4   5   6   7   8   9   10

11. All community organizations should have older persons on their boards of directors.

Agree   Disagree
1   2   3   4   5   6   7   8   9   10

12. It was a shock to look in the mirror and find that I am showing signs of aging.

Agree   Disagree
1   2   3   4   5   6   7   8   9   1

Scoring Instructions: There are three attitudes that are measured in this inventory. Place the number that you have circled measuring your agreement or disagreement with the item in the column below beside the item number. Multiply the number you entered by the weight number and place this result in the Score Column. Add the scores and enter the total on the last line.

Attitude 1: Denial of Aging

Item #	Raw Score	Weight	Score
4		1	
7		1	
8		1	

Total

Attitude 2: Anxiety about One's Own Aging

Item #	Raw Score	Weight	Score
5		4	
9		3	
10		2	
8		1	

Total

Attitude 3: Favorable or Unfavorable Response to Older Persons

Item #	Raw Score	Weight	Score
1		2	
2		4	
3		2	
6		2	
11		1	

Total

Scoring

In Attitude 1, Denial of Aging, the range of possible scores is from 3 to 30. The lower the score, the greater the degree of denial. If, for example, your score total is 15, you are in the midrange of denial. If you score 10 or under, you are engaging in considerable denial of the aging process.

In Attitude 2, Anxiety about One's Own Aging, the range of scores is from 10, the highest possible degree of anxiety, to 100, the lowest. A total score of 21, for example, indicates considerable anxiety about one's own aging. Likewise a very high score would indicate a low degree of anxiety.

In Attitude 3, Favorable or Unfavorable Response to Older Persons, the range of scores is from 8, the most unfavorable response to elders, to a high of 83, most favorable response. A total score of 54 is midrange. It is likely that a score of around 30 and below indicates strong aversion to older persons.

CHAPTER 5

Workers with Disabilities

Work takes on increased meaning for people who have physical disabilities (Vash, 1981). Such individuals are generally viewed as not being capable employees when emphasis is put on physical abilities. Indeed, some employers believe that individuals with disabilities are less than normal. These employers are likely to recall a negative stereotype of physically disabled people and consequently expect less of their own workers with disabilities. They also often believe that individuals with disabilities should expect less of themselves. Thus, they are not surprised when an individual with a disability is unable to get a job.

From a societal perspective, work: (1) is a source of self-respect, a way of achieving recognition or respect from others; (2) defines a person's identity, his or her role in society; (3) provides the opportunity for association with other people for building friendships; (4) allows for self-expression and provides the opportunity for creativity and new experiences; and (5) permits people to be of service to others. Work is a basic ingredient in modern culture; most people organize their lives around their occupations. Grave psychologic disturbances can result when individuals with disabilities who are able to work are barred from participating in this most important societal activity (Eisenberg, Griggins & Duval, 1982). When individuals are unable to find or keep a job because of prejudices about their disabilities, physical disability becomes a handicap. The work capabilities of most people with physical disabilities have been demonstrated many times. Indeed, there are several factors more important than physical prowess for the performance of most jobs.

DEFINITIONS

The words *disability* and *handicap* are most often used interchangeably. Definitions of words and the way in which they are used often create problems, such as the projection of undesirable images of people. Beatrice Wright (1960) warned against using shortcuts to describe individuals with disabilities: "It is precisely the perception of a person with a physical disability as a physically disabled person that has reduced all his life to the disability aspects of his physique. The shortcut distorts and undermines" (p. 8). She concluded her remarks by pointing out that the use of shortcuts is a major factor in the derogatory connotations of *disabled* and *handicapped*.

Even so, unless they are professionals in a medical field or in some other human services profession, most people do not make a distinction between *disability* and *handicap*. In fact, professional helpers in the field of rehabilitation contributed to the confusion during the many years they used the words *handicapped persons* to identify people they now call *disabled*. Wright argued that using these terms is a shortcut and *individuals with disabilities* and *individuals with handicaps* should be used instead. Is this much ado about nothing?

Disability

Wright (1960) defined a disability as "a condition of impairment, physical or mental, having an objective aspect that can usually be described by a physician" (p. 9). James Bitter (1979) added to the definition by pointing out that the physical or mental condition limits a person's activities or functioning. Jeffrey Koshel and Carl Granger (1978) cautioned against the use of unidimensional definitions of disability:

Use of the term disabled should assume interaction between the individual and the environment. However, in common usage the word disability is frequently equated with separate and specific physical or mental impairments, or both, thus omitting the contributory effects of the environment. When impairments are viewed as sufficient cause for disability, then the unfortunate use of diagnostic labels as shortcut proxies for disability can lead to a pessimistic outlook regarding the rehabilitative potential of individuals. (p. 102)

Handicap

The dictionary defines a handicap as a deficiency, especially an anatomical, physiological, or mental deficiency that prevents or restricts normal achievement. Wright added to this definition by stating that a handicap is "the cumulative result of the obstacles which disability interposes between the individual and his maximum function level" (p. 9). The term *handi-capped* should be used only when specific life processes or social activities are adversely affected. That is, an individual can be handicapped in certain aspects of functioning and, at the same time, be fully functional in many others. In most textbooks, Franklin Delano Roosevelt and Helen Keller are used to illustrate this point. There are countless less well known persons whose lives also attest to the relativity of handicaps.

Impairment

The definition of impairment depends on the functions that are being emphasized. For example, the definitions most commonly used in vocational rehabilitation state that an individual with an impairment is someone who has a physical or mental condition that constitutes a handicap or results in hindering employment. Other social institutions define impairment in relation to functions that are important to their organization focus. Succinctly, an impairment is any condition that prevents individuals from adequately performing particular functions that are important to them. If people have impairments or disorders that are severe enough to constitute a disability or a dysfunctional condition, then it can be said they are handicapped to the degree their social role performance is adversely affected. Even when impairment is constant rather than intermittent, it is possible that an individual may be socially dysfunctional only in a limited way. In short, one cannot know the effects of an impairment without knowing the person with the impairment.

A disability is an undesirable thing. To think otherwise can cause unnecessary pain and embarrassment. A disability does limit an individual's capabilities. Thus, the term *disabled person* (for which I prefer to use *individual with a disability*) refers to *an individual with impaired functioning, mental or physical, that is sufficient enough to interfere with one or more major aspects of his or her living*. A disability can be due to vision, speech, hearing, or motor impairment; birth defects; disease; or accident. An impairment limits mobility or mental functioning, but it is societal attitudes that make people handicapped.

MYTHS AND STEREOTYPES

Although all people with physical disabilities are not handicapped, there is the tendency for others to think of them as being handicapped and for them to think of themselves as being handicapped. Generally, people do not consider children to be handicapped because their physical or mental abilities are less than those of their parents. However, they frequently consider them handicapped if their physical or mental abilities are less than those of their peers. Somewhere in this conceptualization is a nebulous but important concept of the "normal person," who is able-bodied and visually attractive. To be different is to be set apart, to be abnormal.

"Being different" can include confinement to a wheelchair, slurred speech, impaired vision or hearing, a limp, or a missing part of the body. Interestingly, these differences are comparable to those of ethnic minorities, who may be different because of skin color, language, hair texture, physical features, and religious beliefs. Individuals who accept definitions of themselves as abnormal usually try to minimize contact with "normal" people or hide their deviance to avoid intruding unnecessarily into social relationships (McDaniel, 1970). Indeed, it is expected by most people that individuals with disabilities will know and stay in their place away from their rejectors. As a friend counseled a person with a disability: "You're a blind man, now, you'll be expected to act like one. People will be firmly convinced that you consider yourself a tragedy. They'll be disconcerted and even shocked to discover that you don't" (Wright, 1960, p. 15).

Disabilities are deficiencies, and some people look down on individuals who have them. Physical disabilities seem to be inextricably linked with shame and inferiority. And physical limitations produce suffering and despair much greater than the physiology of the impairment, and these feelings often affect the individual's psychological well-being. Beliefs that cause employers to be reluctant to hire workers with disabilities stem primarily from false assumptions that are deeply entrenched. (See Nathanson, 1979, for refutation of these assumptions.) Common myths relate to safety, insurance, liability, productivity, attendance, accommodations, and acceptance in the workforce.

Safety Myth

Myth: Because workers with disabilities deviate from what employers generally consider normal, that is, they walk differently, walk with the aid of something, or have a hearing or visual impairment, they are likely to injure themselves or cause other employees to be injured.

Reality: In 1981 a survey conducted by the DuPont Company showed that, with respect to safety, 96 percent of their employees with disabilities rated average or above average, compared with 92 percent for employees who did not have disabilities. Other studies have also indicated that individuals with disabilities are safe employees. A 1978 International Telephone and Telegraph Company (ITT) study of their Corinth, Mississippi plant, where 125 persons with disabilities were part of a 2,000 member workforce, showed an all-time safety record of 3,700,000 job-hours worked without lost time that was injury related. At the time of the survey, no worker with a disability had suffered more than a minor on-the-job injury since starting with the company (President's Committee on Employment of the Handicapped, 1982).

Other large companies such as IBM, Sears, Roebuck and Co., and ConEd have been leaders in hiring people with disabilities. If these companies had not found them to be safe workers, they would not continue to recruit and hire them. Employers' past experience with workers who have disabilities correlates positively with their readiness to hire them (Florian, 1978).

Insurance Myth

Myth: Insurance companies will not let employers hire workers with disabilities. "My insurance company will penalize me if I hire a disabled person. My insurance rates will go up. My workers' compensation rates will go up."

Reality: Insurance companies do not tell employers whom to hire, nor are employers required to get approval for workers' compensation insurance before hiring workers with disabilities (Brantman, 1978). Insurance premiums are based on a company's safety record, not its workers' physiques. Employees with disabilities are proportionately as safe as, if not safer than, workers who do not have them. Aware of this, the insurance industry does not oppose but actually encourages the employment of individuals with disabilities. Workers' compensation insurance rates are determined by three factors: (1) nature of the business, (2) size of payroll, and, for larger employers, (3) accident experience. In determining workers' compensation insurance rates, occupations are classified so that the cost of accidents can be assessed proportionately to the accident risks involved (i.e., hazardous occupations have higher rates than sedentary occupations).

The DuPont Company did not experience an increase in workers' compensation or health, accident, or other medical insurance costs. A survey of 279 companies made by the United States Chamber of Commerce and the National Association of Manufacturers revealed that 90 percent of the respondents reported no change in insurance costs as a result of hiring persons with disabilities (President's Committee on Employment of the Handicapped, 1982).

Liability Myth

Myth: An on-the-job accident that, when added to a worker's prior disability, results in permanent total disability will make the company liable for permanent total disability.

Reality: All fifty states and the District of Columbia now have a Second Injury Fund built into their workers' compensation law. The Second Injury Fund assumes the responsibility of compensation to people with physical disabilities who become totally disabled through industrial accidents allocating to the employer's expense only the single injury sustained at work.

Because each state develops its own Second Injury Fund, specific provisions and the way they are applied vary from state to state.

Productivity Myth

Myth: Workers with disabilities are not capable of performing their jobs; therefore, the other employees have to "take up the slack."

Reality: An employer should know what skills are required to accomplish a job. If applicants with disabilities possess the skills, there is no reason they should not be hired. For example, if a job's primary skill requirement is eye-hand coordination and the applicant is in a wheelchair, assuming he or she has good eye-hand coordination, there is no reason he or she should not be hired. Relatedly, if applicants with disabilities do not possess the required skills but are capable of learning them with reasonable training, there is no reason they should not be hired. Conversely, if applicants with disabilities do not possess the needed skills and training is not feasible, they should not be hired.

Job applicants with physical disabilities should fill out the same employment forms, take the same tests, and be given the same interview as other applicants. In short, they should be given an equal opportunity, but if they do not have the aptitude for the job, they should not be hired. They deserve the same, not unequal breaks. The DuPont study showed that 92 percent of their workers with disabilities were rated average or above average, compared with 91 percent for their workers who did not have disabilities. ITT found that individuals with disabilities were more productive than their co-workers. These results are similar to findings in other studies (Weissman, 1965; Yuker, Cambell & Brock, 1960).

Attendance Myth

Myth: Workers with disabilities are absent from their jobs a great amount of time because of their physical problems.

Reality: If they are job-ready via physical or vocational rehabilitation, individuals with disabilities should have no more absences than other employees. There may be a few exceptions such as persons with arthritic conditions or allergies who are affected by climatic changes. ITT discovered that the workers with disabilities in their Corinth plant had fewer absences than their nondisabled co-workers: Eighty-five percent of the workers with disabilities were average or above average in attendance. Employees with disabilities are keenly aware of the difficulty of securing employment; therefore, once they obtain jobs, most of them will not risk losing them by faking illnesses.

Accommodations Myth

Myth: Most job sites would have to be specially redesigned to suit people with disabilities. "Our company will have to spend a fortune to accommodate disabled workers. They need a lot of special equipment," a CEO mused.

Reality: The expenditures that most companies must make to accommodate workers with disabilities are not exorbitant. Once experts evaluate their needs, most organizations are pleasantly surprised at the results. For example, engineers at Kaiser Aluminum estimated it would cost $160,000 to bring their California corporate headquarters into compliance, but a consulting firm reviewed the facilities and concluded that it could be done for less than $8,000 (Koestler, 1980). ITT spent $22,750 at its Corinth plant to make it accessible to individuals with disabilities, and most of that amount ($22,000) was for an elevator. When modifying a corporate headquarters building to aid employees with disabilities, the Rehabilitation Institute of Chicago reduced an outside contractor's estimate for necessary alterations from $96,000 to $5,000. The saving was accomplished by making selective modifications rather than wholesale changes and by doing the work in-house.

Sears, Roebuck and Co. made structural changes at its executive headquarters to accommodate persons with disabilities for very modest costs— $300 for cassette tape recorders for six blind telephone salespeople; $800 to lower desks, widen doors, and install restroom grab-bars for catalog order-takers who use wheelchairs; between $300 and $600 for similar accommodations for service technicians in wheelchairs; and $3,800 for a reading machine for the blind and instruction in its use (President's Committee on Employment of the Handicapped, 1982).

Acceptance Myth

Myth: Employees who do not have disabilities will not accept individuals with disabilities. The special accommodations (e.g., parking spaces, wheelchair ramps, elevators) will be resented.

Reality: The DuPont survey did not find that special accommodations resulted in much resentment of workers with disabilities. When "able-bodied" employees work with individuals with disabilities and discover that they are capable of doing their jobs, acceptance or rejection occurs for reasons other than physical disabilities.

The importance of myths and stereotypes should not be minimized, however. People with physical disabilities gain much of their feelings of inferiority from initially false myths and stereotypes. When employers unequivocally state that individuals with disabilities are poor employees and then either deny them jobs or relegate them to low-paying, dead-end jobs, many of these individuals in fact begin to exhibit inferiority complexes. Caroline Vash (1981) concluded:

Most of us have three types of goals. We want to get specific materialistic rewards, such as homes, cars, adult play toys, and so forth. We also want to *do* identified activities, either for the pleasure of the process, the outcomes or both. And we want to be a certain way, viewed by ourselves or others as good or honest or tough or whatever characteristics are deemed desirable. Disabled workers have little chance of reaching these goals through their work, or at all, if they are relegated to traditional or conveniently available jobs. (p. 106)

If people with disabilities become a contrast to those without disabilities, then poverty-stricken people with disabilities become an enigma to all people. In recent years, people with physical disabilities have become a topic for public conferences, frequent subjects for research, and prime recipients of architectural innovations. Each year, they seem to become more infamous and less financially secure (Burdette & Frohlich, 1977). It is not the American dream that is repulsive to unemployed and underemployed people with disabilities but instead their inability to achieve it.

THOSE WHO ARE AFFECTED

A cursory review of statistics pertaining to people with disabilities in the United States is overwhelming. There are approximately 25 million adults with disabilities between the ages of sixteen and sixty-four; between the ages of three and twenty-one there are approximately 10 million people with disabilities who are impaired enough to require special education in the public schools. One-fourth of all American citizens sixty-five years of age and over have disabilities. Frank Bowe (1980) put the various statistics into chilling perspective:

Of the 15 million disabled Americans between the ages of 16 and 64 who are not institutionalized more than 7.7 million are either out of the labor force or unemployed. Most have given up, and they have because they cannot obtain the education they need for employment, cannot get a job training in many fields, cannot secure transportation to and from work, and cannot find suitable places to live. Our failure to invest in these people and their potential has forced them into dependency programs. (pp. 8–9)

These overlapping statistics give estimates of 36 million to 50 million Americans with disabilities, and the number is growing as the population ages. People with disabilities comprise the nation's largest open minority group—anyone may join at any time. Disability is not restricted to any race, ethnic group, gender, age, social class, religion, or geographic boundary. Whatever the cause or nature of his or her disability, each person is an individual who must overcome barriers to his or her functioning as an integral member of the community. In 1991 the numbers of people with chronic conditions resulting in some type of severe disability were as follows:

- 31.1 million had arthritis and rheumatism.
- 27.8 million had hypertension.
- 22.7 million had hearing impairments.
- 20.5 million had heart ailments.

If the people who have mild disabilities are included in these statistics, the numbers are even larger:

- 20 million Americans have hearing problems.
- 200,000 Americans are deaf.

In 1991, 43 million Americans had one or more physical or mental disabilities. Disability is more prevalent among women than among men. In 1989, for instance, there were about 78 women and 74 men with heart conditions in every 1,000 persons; there was about 128 women and 98 men with hypertension problems in every 1,000. There were also 157 arthritis female cases as compared with 96 men in every 1,000 people the same year. African Americans and other ethnic minorities comprise 18 percent of the total working population, but African Americans alone make up 21 percent of the U.S. population with disabilities.

According to a 1985 survey conducted by the International Center for the Disabled, 24 percent of "working age" adults with disabilities held full-time jobs; 10 percent held part-time jobs; and 11 percent, while in the labor force, were unemployed. Of those unemployed, two-thirds indicated that they would like to work (Weaver, 1991, p. 35). Countless individuals with disabilities are discouraged from seeking gainful employment for a variety of reasons. A survey conducted by the Developmental Evaluation Clinic (Kiernan & Brinkman, 1985) identified the following barriers individuals with disabilities face when seeking employment: economic disincentives; employers' negative attitudes toward people with disabilities; and co-workers' negative attitudes toward people with disabilities.

Women

Numerous writers (Fine & Asch, 1981; Greenblum, 1977; Thurer, 1982; Vash, 1982) have statistically documented the occupational plight of women with disabilities: Approximately 70 percent of women with disabilities and 30 percent of men with disabilities are unemployed. This means that males with disabilities are more likely than females with disabilities to be referred to vocational schools and on-the-job training. Women with disabilities are more likely to be underemployed than men with disabilities and they are less likely to be college educated. Women earn substantially less than their male peers and have lower levels of disability coverage and insurance benefits.

Women with disabilities are largely employed in traditional "female" jobs that have low salaries. In 1988 the mean weekly wage for women in rehabilitation programs was $100 compared with $150 for their male peers. Only 2 percent of the women earned $200 or more per week at the end of their rehabilitation program, compared with 10 percent of the men (Thurer, 1982). However, as women with disabilities become more socially and politically active, many of the leadership roles once held by men with disabilities are being shared with women with disabilities, to the point that in isolated instances, males with disabilities are crying "reverse discrimination," as employers fill their EEO quotas with females instead of males.

Paula Franklin (1977) pointed out that women with disabilities are socially disadvantaged because they are less likely than other women to marry, are more likely to divorce, and have more absent spouses (separated, divorced, or widowed) than men with disabilities. There is a larger percentage of female heads of households with disabilities than male heads of households with disabilities. Ruth Mauer (1979) suggested that the disadvantages begin early in life; females with disabilities have lower self-images during childhood than their male peers. The females in her study were more likely than males to identify with a story character with a disability; most males identified with the characters without the disability. Social forces push a disproportionate number of women to behave like their negative stereotypes. Although there are relatively few socially successful models for people with disabilities in general, there are even fewer for females with disabilities.

The Elderly

Since the 1880s, the increase in the number of births, advances in medical technology, development of more disease-fighting drugs, and better understanding of the functions of the body and diseases have led to increases in life expectancy. According to the National Center for Health Statistics, the life expectancy for women is approximately seventy-nine years; for men, it is seventy-two years. The elderly population in the United States is estimated at 25 million and growing. The United States Bureau of the Census projects that by the year 2000, there will be more than 30 million elderly persons in the United States. (A person in America is defined as being elderly at age sixty-five.)

As crude as it may sound, it is true that the body is a machine and that, as with all machines, it becomes less functional with age. Brittle bones, less stamina, and decreased range of motion are but a few of the factors that can cause the elderly to become less active. However, as discussed in Chapter 4, there are many older individuals who are physically active, and their mental abilities are sharp enough to allow them to manage their own affairs. Conversely, some individuals who are younger than sixty-five show some of the classic signs attributed to the elderly: physical frailty and slow mental processes. Workers differ greatly in their mental and physical characteristics at all ages, although as a group, older workers tend to be more heterogeneous than other workers (Butler, 1975).

Elderly persons with disabilities have a double disability. They must struggle to survive two types of stigma—one associated with normal physical limitations and one with being placed in a category that presupposes great intellectual limitations. (This latter principle especially relates to ethnic minorities with disabilities.) Robert Atchley (1980) explained the overall stigma attached to old age:

By far, the most important aspect of the stigma of old age is its negative disqualifying character on the basis of their age; older people are often relegated to a position in society in which they are no longer judged to be of any use or importance. Unless they have special talents or skills, or can afford to support themselves well in retirement, older people often find that the stigma of old age limits their opportunities. Like most "expendable" elements in society, many older people are subjected to poverty, illness, and social isolation. (p. 16)

Elderly people with disabilities may be the most discriminated against people in America. In terms of productivity, very little is expected of the elderly in general, and almost nothing is expected of those with disabilities (Butler, 1975; Rosen & Jerdee, 1976). And very few attempts are made to provide them with ways of maintaining their self-esteem. Some views of the elderly are quite morbid: their lives are perceived as being over, and all that remains for them to do is to lie down and close their eyes.

Men, Too

Generally, the most important factor for men who have disabilities is whether they are still able to perform physical tasks. In many instances, cosmetic devices do little more than hide the disability, while the functional limitations remain. Jerome Siller (1963) and Irving Zola (1982) documented that artifical limbs and other prostheses create an illusion of no disability but that these devices often do little to curb negative attitudes and behavior toward physical disability. For men who perceive themselves as heads of households and the general leaders and protectors of their families, adjustment to disability is particularly difficult. As a growing number of females are receiving treatment equal to that of men, they, too, are becoming concerned with tasks rather than physical appearance (Thurer, 1982).

Because the population with disabilities has a disproportionate number of women and ethnic minorities, two groups that have historically been paid less than white males, it is not surprising that a large proportion of this population is classified as low income. Disability is more prevalent among women than among men; almost 20 percent of American women have some degree of disability, compared to slightly more than 15 percent of the men. African Americans and other ethnic minorities comprise 12 percent of the total working population, but they make up 15 percent of the population with disabilities and over 18 percent of persons with severe disabilities.

LAWS

In 1917 Congress passed the Smith-Hughes Act, a landmark education act that set the precedent for subsequent federal funding of educational programs, not only for people with disabilities but also for other people (Cull & Hardy, 1973). In addition, it called for a Board of Vocational Education to spearhead the drive for vocational education. This board was to become the foundation for vocational rehabilitation in the United States. The first Board of Vocational Education was funded in 1918 under the Soldier Rehabilitation Act to operate a program of vocational rehabilitation for World War I veterans. Better known as the Smith-Sears Veterans' Rehabilitation Act of 1918, it provided the following general purview for federal vocational rehabilitation services: "An act to provide for the vocational rehabilitation and return to employment of disabled persons discharged from the military or naval forces of the United States and for other purposes." After this seed had been planted, state and federal vocational rehabilitation programs developed. However, before these programs evolved to their present status, they progressed through several stages.

Smith-Fess Act (1920)

President Woodrow Wilson's signature on PL-236 (the Smith-Fess Act) in 1920 made public rehabilitation programs a long-awaited reality. This act established federal and state rehabilitation programs and provided for an equal sharing of expenditures for them. The act was not without limitations, however. Funds were provided only for vocational guidance, training, occupational adjustment, prostheses, and placement services. In short, rehabilitation services for persons with physical disabilities were to be vocational in nature; physical restoration and sociopsychologic services were excluded.

Actually, the Smith-Fess Act was an extension of earlier vocational education legislation. It added the provision making rehabilitation services available to people with physical disabilities. Also, this was temporary legislation and remained operative only by additional legislation. In 1924 federal legislation was passed that extended the life of state and federal vocational rehabilitation programs for an additional six years. It was not until the 1935 Federal Social Security Act that state and federal vocational rehabilitation programs became permanent. The long and tedious battle to institutionalize vocational rehabilitation for the disabled was finally won.

Barden-LaFollette Act (1943)

More commonly known as the Vocational Rehabilitation Act of 1943, the Barden-LaFollette Act strengthened vocational rehabilitation programs by providing physical restoration services to people with disabilities. In addition, it extended vocational rehabilitation services to the mentally handicapped and the mentally ill. In 1954 this act was again amended, and the following significant changes made:

1. More funds and additional program options were provided to state agencies.
2. Federally funded research programs were established.
3. Training funds were added for physicians, nurses, rehabilitation counselors, physical therapists, occupational therapists, social workers, psychologists, and other specialists in the field of rehabilitation.

Vocational Rehabilitation Act Amendments (1965)

These amendments further strengthened vocational rehabilitation programs by (1) providing monies to states for innovative projects that developed new methods of providing services and otherwise serving individuals with severe disabilities; (2) creating a broader base of services to individuals with disabilities, including individuals with socially handicapping conditions; and (3) eliminating economic need as a requisite for rehabilitation services. Slowly, the related pieces to comprehensive care were coming together to form a meaningful whole.

Rehabilitation Act of 1973

PL-112 of the 93rd Congress replaced the Vocational Rehabilitation Act as amended in 1968 with this new act, which maintained the major provisions of the 1968 amended act and added the provision that before receiving funds a state must conduct a thorough study to determine the needs of its handicapped citizens. Other significant provisions of the act were the inclusion in Title V of Sections 501, 502, 503, and 504.

Section 501. This section established the Interagency Committee on Handicapped Employees. The committee consists of federal agency heads, who have the responsibility to review annually the adequacy of federal hiring, placement, and job advancement of persons with disabilities. Based on each review, the committee can recommend further legislation and administrative changes.

Section 502. This section established the Architectural and Transportation Barriers Compliance Board, which has the responsibility of monitoring the construction of new federal buildings and the remodeling of old ones to ensure that they are accessible to individuals with physical disabilities. Existing federal buildings that are not being remodeled do not have to be made accessible.

Section 503. The words *affirmative action* were introduced into the vocabulary of rehabilitation in Section 503, which requires that every employer doing business with the federal government under a contract for more than $2,500 take affirmative action in hiring individuals with disabilities. Throughout the various states of employment (recruiting, hiring, upgrading, transferring, advertising for recruitment, establishing rates of pay, and selecting persons for apprenticeships), affirmative action must be taken.

Section 504. If the law contained within Section 504 were followed to the letter, at least 80 percent of the employment problems of individuals with physical disabilities would vanish. This section calls for nondiscrimination in employment. Every U.S. institution that receives federal financial assistance must take steps to ensure that individuals with disabilities are not discriminated against in employment.

It is important to note that the enactment of Sections 503 and 504 began a major change in America's national commitment to citizens with disabilities. Until the 1990s, these laws were more symbolic than concrete. They codified the concept that all people have the right to reach their full potential.

The Rehabilitation Act of 1973 was amended in 1974 and 1978. The 1974 amendments significantly strengthened programs for the blind that were first authorized in 1936 by the Randolph-Shepard Act. (This act had authorized states to license qualified blind persons to operate vending stands in federal buildings.) In addition to providing increased funding to states, some provisions of the amendments to the Rehabilitation Act of 1973 focused on employment opportunities and independent living for individuals with disabilities. Specifically, the provisions provided for (1) community service employment pilot programs; (2) projects with industry and business to accelerate the training and employment of persons with disabilities; (3) grants and contracts with individuals with disabilities to start or operate business enterprises; (4) loans from the Small Business Administration to persons with disabilities when other financial assistance is not available; (5) funds for comprehensive services for independent living for individuals with severe disabilities; and (6) grants to states for the establishment and operation of independent living centers.

Americans with Disabilities Act of 1990

Passed on July 26, 1990, by the 101st Congress, this act was created to (1) provide a clear and comprehensive national mandate for the elimination of discrimination against individuals with disabilities; (2) provide clear, strong, consistent, enforceable standards addressing discrimination against individuals with disabilities; (3) ensure that the federal government plays a central role in enforcing the standards established in the act on behalf of individuals with disabilities; and (4) invoke congressional authority, including the power to invoke the Fourteenth Amendment to regulate commerce, in order to address major areas of discrimination faced day-to-day by people with disabilities.

It is important to note that the act substitutes the term *individuals with disability* for the term *handicapped workers* that was used in previous acts. Title I includes *employment.* Any person, including his or her agents, engaged in industry affecting commerce who has fifteen or more employees for each working day in each of twenty or more calendar weeks in the current or preceding calendar year are covered by the act. No covered entity can discriminate against a qualified individual with a disability because of the disability in regard to job application procedures, the hiring process, job advancement or discharge, employee compensation, job training, and other aspects of employment.

Title II of the act includes *public services* for any qualified individual with a disability—an individual with a disability who, with or without reasonable modifications to rules, policies, or practices, the removal of architectural, communication, or transportation barriers, or the provision of auxiliary aids and services, meets the essential eligibility requirements for the receipt of services or the participation in programs or activities provided by a public entity. Title III includes public accommodations and services operated by private entities. Title IV includes telecommunications.

SELECTED COURT CASES

To avoid liability for discrimination against individuals with disabilities, employers must make a good faith effort to accommodate them. *Southeastern Community College v. Davis* (1979) is a landmark case defining some of the rights of individuals with disabilities. Ms. Davis, a deaf person, was an applicant to the nursing program at Southeastern Community College. She was denied admission on the ground that her hearing disability made her unfit to be a nurse. That is, it would be an unsafe career for her because she would not be able to hear job-related conversations. She could not understand speech without lip reading. This fact, the court reasoned, meant that she could not meet all the requirements of the program unless the program's standards were substantially lowered. And the college was required to do so. Other courts have not required substantial modifications in programs (*Strathie v. Department of Transportation*, 1983; *Carter v. Bennett*, 1988).

The courts have decreed that employers do not have to employ a person who cannot safely perform the essential functions of the job he or she is seeking. This is referred to as a *bona fide occupational qualification*. This standard was established in *Weeks v. Southern Bell Telephone and Telegraph Co.* (1959). The employer "must show that all or substantially all members of the class would not be able to perform safely and efficiently the duties of the job." *Lewis v. Metropolitan Transit Comm.* (1982) concluded that unless there are objective facts to substantiate such claims, they will not be accepted in court (*Maine Human Rights Comm. v. Canadian Pacific Ltd.*, 1983).

SPECIAL PROGRAMS

In the early 1960s the staff of the Vocational Rehabilitation Division of the Federal Board for Vocational Education studied 6,097 persons with physical disabilities who were employed after being rehabilitated. The investigation confirmed that: (1) rehabilitated persons could perform adequately in a wide range of occupations; (2) persons with disabilities, even those with similar diagnoses, differed greatly from each other in many occupational factors; and (3) it is not possible to equate disability and occupational capability (Obermann, 1965). Relatedly, Anne Roe (1956) said the following about persons with disabilities and their ability to work:

Unlike special abilities which may qualify their holder for desirable, unusual jobs, special disabilities are more likely to function as only limited factors. Blindness, deafness, orthopedic disabilities, chronic illness all have very real effects upon occupational selection. Some of these effects, it is true, are the result of inadequate knowledge on the part of everyone, the disabled, the employers and society generally, as to just what performance limitations are the necessary results of certain disabilities, but some of the effects are genuinely inevitable. A man with one arm cannot perform activities which really require two fully functional ones, but he can do many more things with one arm and one prosthetic device than might be imagined. Furthermore, there are a large number of occupations for which a second arm is really unnecessary. (pp. 64–65)

Job Training Programs

Employers' apprehensions, due to a lack of experience or an unpleasant employment experience with individuals with disabilities, greatly limit employment opportunities (Hasazi et al., 1985; Maxwell-Hanley et al., 1986). This is less true for employers involved with federally supported employment programs for people with disabilities (Will, 1984). The more effective programs integrate workers with disabilities into a competitive work setting, while providing continuous support services for them. Prior to placement, each worker's abilities are evaluated in an effort to ensure a successful, compatible match with employer's needs. In addition, proper job attendance and punctuality are stressed. The nation benefits as supported employment helps decrease government subsidies and increases tax revenues and productivity. And, of course, these programs provide employers with a labor force of trained individuals (Kiernan & Schalock, 1989).

Prior to integrating individuals with disabilities into the workplace, some employers assess co-workers' attitudes and perceptions. They want to know if co-workers will readily accept a particular worker with a disability. Unfortunately, our society places great emphasis on physical appearance. "Attractive" people tend to be perceived as being competent, likeable, and possessing good communication skills, acceptable social skills, and athletic ability (Yuker, 1988). Individuals with disabilities may be social isolates, may be ostracized, and may be less competent than their co-workers. The degree of disability influences acceptability. Individuals with visible disabilities tend to be less accepted than those with nonvisible disabilities (e.g., hearing impaired). Physically attractive individuals with disabilities are more readily accepted than those perceived to be physically unattractive.

Barrier Removal

Physical barriers also limit employment opportunities. Most buildings and other work environments have been constructed for nondisabled workers, and most employers are concerned that necessary adaptations will be costly (Wehman & Moon, 1988, p. 247). However, as discussed earlier, the benefits outweigh the costs. Job accommodation results in higher productivity, a safer and more efficient job site, and increased employee independence. Employers also receive tax incentives, up to $35,000, if modifications make the job site more accessible for individuals with disabilities and the elderly.

To help employers make the necessary accommodations, the Job Accommodation Network (JAN) has been established. JAN, which was initially funded by the National Institute of Handicapped Research, and now by the Rehabilitation Services Administration and several other organizations, collects and distributes information to anyone interested in accommodating people with disabilities. Various solutions, as well as the names of manufacturers and suppliers, are provided free of charge. However, the network does request that users furnish information on the accommodations they have made in order that other users of the service may benefit by learning about them.

The Architectural and Transportation Barriers Compliance Board succinctly described the following barriers that confront people with disabilities: (1) architectural barriers (e.g., steps and entrances); (2) attitudinal barriers (e.g., pity and sympathy); (3) educational barriers (e.g., texts not in Braille and lectures not in sign language); and (4) informational barriers (e.g., uncaptioned films and unraised letters in elevators). In addition, barriers may include unemployment and underemployment; transportation (e.g., buses too high from the ground to be boarded safety); housing (e.g., only public, institutional housing for persons with disabilities); and recreation (e.g., turnstiles in theaters and overly gravelled paths in parks).

TECHNIQUES AND TIPS

Most people with disabilities want to know where they fit in the larger organization scheme of things. That is, they want to know if they are part of their organization's in-groups or out-groups. By placing physical and economic barriers in the paths of individuals with disabilities, organizations send messages to them that, when decoded, mean: "You are not wanted. You are not respected. You are not as good as those who are not restricted. You are, in summary, inferior." Few managers and supervisors openly admit to feeling superior to people with disabilities. However the statement "There but for the grace of God go I" succinctly captures a thought that runs through the mind of many of them.

The manner in which most persons with physical disabilities are treated would cause casual observers to believe that they are either unable to speak or retarded or both. For example, even if they have only an orthopedic handicap for which they must use a wheelchair, many persons with paraplegia are treated like imbeciles. People who treat a paraplegic this way believe that a physical disability goes beyond the physical realm and contaminates all areas of the person's being, both physical and psychological. Taking the gargantuan leap from one perceived characteristic (physical disability) to other characteristics (emotional or mental problems) is referred to as the *spread phenomenon*. Of course, there are instances when an accident or a disease does indeed impair a person's intellect or emotions; however, this generally is the exception rather than the rule. People with physical disabilities are too often perceived as being totally impaired. This misperception is symbolized by a supervisor shouting at a nondeaf employee with total loss of vision in order to communicate.

Just as few individuals will admit to feeling superior to people with disabilities, few will admit to thinking that people with physical disabilities are less intelligent than those without them. However, their actions frequently expose their hidden perceptions. Generally, the severity of the disability has a bearing on the general perception of an individual's intelligence. An employee whose body is twisted and distorted by cerebral palsy is more likely to be considered retarded than a blind employee or someone with one limb amputated or missing. Individuals with a speech impairment are likely to be perceived as being learning disabled. Again, the reason for these perceptions is their deviation from the amorphous norm. The more an individual's disability deviates from what organization standards consider as physical normality, the greater the chances he or she will be perceived as being less intelligent.

The following behaviors extrapolated from E. Paul Torrance (1970) will help managers and supervisors interact constructively with employees with disabilities:

1. *"Wanting to know."* This is evident in the curiosity of administrators who ask questions, become absorbed in the search for the truth about disabilities, try to make sense out of this knowledge, make guesses and test them, and try to develop the skills needed to help workers with disabilities.

2. *"Digging deeper."* The genuinely caring person is not satisfied with quick, easy, superficial answers about disabilities.

3. *"Looking twice and listening for smells."* The effective administrator is never satisfied with learning about disabilities from an intellectual distance or reading reports about them. He or she will want to get to know it from different angles, perspectives, and senses. That is, to know it personally.

4. *"Listening to a cat."* Too many administrators can neither talk to nor listen with understanding to a cat. Most human communication is nonverbal. In the helping process, words usually are insufficient for communicating the deepest and most genuine concerns of one person for another. Administrators must learn to communicate nonverbally with employees with disabilities and to understand their nonverbal communications, too.

5. *"Crossing out mistakes."* Administrators who help workers with disabilities achieve their potentialities inevitably make mistakes. But they must not avoid doing difficult and worthwhile things because of the fear of failure.

6. *"Getting into and out of deep water."* Testing the limits of one's skills and abilities and personal resources means taking calculated risks. It means asking questions for which no ready answers exist.

7. *"Having a ball."* To be truly human is to be able to laugh, play, fantasize, and loaf. Effective administrators encourage their subordinates to take time out to relax.

8. *"Cutting a hole to see through."* This is a tolerance for complexity. By opening up the windows of their subordinates' lives, administrators and supervisors see more of themselves. An effective administrator is a window through which his or her subordinates can gain a better understanding of the world beyond themselves.

9. *"Building sand castles."* In order to build a sand castle, one must be able to see sand not only as it is but also as it might be. To believe that workers with disabilities can move from dependency to independence requires managers and supervisors to see their existence as it might be. Employees with disabilities must plan and strive for their dreams but do so in terms of the materials and resources they can realistically draw upon.

10. *"Singing in your own key."* Thoreau stated this idea very poetically: "If a man does not keep pace with his companions, perhaps it is because he hears a different drummer. Let him step to the music he hears, however measured or far away. It is not important that he matures as an apple tree or an oak. Shall he turn his spring into summer . . . ?" Administrators should let their subordinates know that it is all right to do things differently, to be slightly out of step with employees who do not have a disability.

11. *"Plugging in the sun."* A major source of energy for most employees with disabilities comes from organizations that focus on their needs. An effective administrator learns the names and unique conditions of his or her subordinates with disabilities.

One only has to say the word *welfare* in a public or private gathering to elicit a variety of not-too-complimentary terms: lazy, shirkers, gold-bricks, good-for-nothings. It is true that most employees with disabilities depend on some type of assistance, whether for special devices, economic assistance, or interpersonal acceptance. However, few, if any, of them are malingerers or good-for-nothings.

DIFFERENTLY ABLED

Everyone has a disability. In the space below, list four or five of your disabilities and briefly describe the jobs these disabilities preclude you from performing satisfactorily.

CHAPTER 6

Foreign Workers

One strong and persistent pull of foreign workers to the United States is the availability of jobs. The labor market has always demanded huge pools of both skilled and unskilled workers. Labor and government have often acted together to procure additional human resources through the use of immigration legislation. Nativistic government and business frequently seek immigrants to help build the country, but they do not want them to stay and become permanent citizens (Ross & Weintraub, 1982). Nevertheless, immigrants have had major impacts on the U.S. labor market. In many instances they have reduced overall production costs in factories because they usually work excessively long hours for very low wages. And because foreign workers are not citizens, they are unable to join labor unions. Without recourse to union protection, foreign workers are essentially at the mercy of their employers (Asher & Stephenson, 1990).

The admittance of large numbers of foreign workers into the United States has always been viewed with ambivalence by Americans. This attitude was summed up concisely in a 1992 U.S. General Accounting Office report entitled *Immigration and the Labor Market:* "There is widespread interest in the entry of alien workers into the American work force. Some see foreign workers as a solution to problems with the size or capability of our work force, while others are concerned over threats to jobs of U.S. workers" (p. 1). But in spite of the concerns that have frequently been voiced by American workers over the importation of foreign labor, business leaders tend to have a different view of the situation. Foreign workers usually enter the U.S. workforce in the most menial positions, often in service industries or as agricultural workers, even if they held higher positions in their native land.

Companies can save great sums of money by hiring people who work for less than union negotiated wages. Often, these workers are employed in the underground job market, where their credentials are less likely to attract undue scrutiny, and where employers do not have to pay their share of workmen's compensation insurance and withholding taxes. In effect, these foreign workers are modern-day scab workers whose employment allows their employers to cut labor costs and make higher profits. Robert Asher and Charles Stephenson (1990) contend that whenever American businesses needed a fresh supply of low-wage labor, state and federal authorities allowed millions of poor Mexicans, for example, to move across the Southwestern border and disperse throughout the nation.

DEFINITIONS

Most twentieth-century immigrants and foreign workers are from countries often referred to as *Third World* countries: Africa, Asia, and Latin America. The new immigrants are opposed by diverse groups of American citizens, including nativists, political conservatives, union members, and a few political liberals (Gold, 1992; Haines, 1989). On the one hand, there is fear that immigrants will destroy the cultural values and moral fiber that have made America great. On the other hand, political liberals believe the new immigrants will adhere too closely to right-wing political philosophies and thus will tilt local American voting patterns in that direction.

In the context of international business and cultures, cross-national interaction involves complex human relations dynamics. From this perspective, the interchange of ideas, thoughts, and motives must be communicated at appropriate levels of cultural awareness. Thus, for our purpose, the term *cross-national interaction* is used to mean the interchange and interrelation of culturally different ideas, thoughts, and motives in business dealings. Being in a foreign country brings most people face-to-face with their foremost fear: fear of the unknown (U.S. Commission on Civil Rights, 1980, 1986). Consequently, foreigners (or strangers as they are frequently called) are cultural outsiders.

Words cannot adequately describe the fear that comes from being a stranger in a strange land. The stranger, no matter how cultured in his or her native country, is often unable to read signs, menus, newspapers, or legal documents. Further, he or she must learn to survive in a place filled with unintelligible sounds, unfamiliar smells, and "foreign" people. Reasons such as this cause countless foreign workers who are glib and socially facile in their homeland to resort to grunting, gesticulating, and otherwise acting like impatient children.

The distinction between foreign workers and immigrants is a hazy one. Many writers believe that immigration is a one-step process wherein an individual leaves his or her home country with no plans of returning. In practice, however, most foreign workers who never intended to move to the United States permanently have stayed either as legal or illegal aliens, or as citizens (Bailey, 1987). Nevertheless, it is prudent to consider immigrants as being foreign workers, at least until they become American citizens.

A large number of immigrants come to America as *sojourners*—people who do not plan to settle here permanently. Their motives differ greatly from other ethnic peoples who are forced to sever ties with their home country. Most African and Asian immigrants are temporary residents in the United States, who set out to get a college education or earn a sizable amount of money and then return to their homeland. To accomplish this mission, the sojourners tend to select occupations that do not tie them to a territory for long assignments. Instead, they seek jobs that allow them to be mobile. Relatedly, they are willing to endure short-term deprivations to achieve their long-term goals. They often work excessively long hours and spend little money on conspicuous consumption. They come to save money or to send some of it home, not to spend it.

Because they plan to return home, many sojourners have little motivation to develop intimate, lasting relationships with host country people. Ethnic and regional associations are maintained within ethnic enclaves that resist marriage to nonethnic group people. These enclaves also perpetuate residential self-segregation and the sojourners' native language. Further, the enclaves encourage traditional religions and family institutions. And, of course, enclave residents are insulated against local politics—except those that directly affect their group members. These are the most difficult individuals to integrate into the workforce.

MYTHS AND STEREOTYPES

Culturally debilitating behaviors on the part of Americans when interacting with peoples from different countries are most dramatically seen when Americans travel abroad. This behavior is magnified when foreigners come to the United States. We will focus first on Americans who work and live in foreign countries. Specifically, it is their negative attitudes, stereotypes, prejudices, and ethnocentrism that become barriers to including foreigners in diversity plans. Americans often become defensive and feel threatened by foreign workers. Even when they are in other countries as foreigners and must adjust to a dominant culture, they resist.

Typically, Americans assign positive or negative attributes to citizens of other countries on the basis of the category or group to which they belong. For example, negative stereotypes might lead to the belief that peoples of "developing" countries are uncivilized or of lower intelligence. Conversely, positive stereotypes foster the belief that the peoples of Western industrialized countries are highly civilized and quite intelligent. Indeed, Americans are predisposed to behave in certain ways toward people solely because of their national group membership. For example, countless Americans who visit Mexico avoid eating in Mexican restaurants because they attribute an inferior or unacceptable quality to the foods of the host country. The same individuals may believe French foods are desirable.

The belief that one's own culture is superior to all others, *ethnocentrism,* is the major source of cross-national problems. Ethnocentrism makes it difficult for employees to communicate with colleagues and subordinates from other cultures, who are believed to be inferior. Failure to acknowledge an individual's equality leads to antagonisms that curtail or abort the interaction. A classic example is found in a confrontation between an American executive and his African colleague. The American not only ridiculed his co-worker's belief in evil spirits but also assumed that the individual, despite his M.B.A. degree from a prestigious American university, was "backward" in his comprehension of business issues and managerial techniques. In the end, however, it was the African's *behavior,* generated by negative attitudes and beliefs, which caused the relationship to fail.

The reluctance of some Americans to learn the language and customs of other people is partially perpetuated by a commonplace myth: Anything worth reading is written in English. In the world of business this can be a costly myth. Consider the following faux pas committed by U.S. businesses. An American airline in Brazil advertised *rendez-vous lounges* in its airplanes, until they learned that in Brazilian Portuguese this means a place to make love. Without proper translation, companies may inadvertently urge people who use their products to set fire to their clothes, weld false eyelashes to their eyes, or become pregnant. Several years ago the Ford Motor Company tried to sell Pinto automobiles in Brazil (*pinto* is slang in Brazil for "a small male appendage"). The name of the car was changed to Corcel (which means "horse" in Portuguese). General Motors could not sell many Nova cars because in Spanish *nova* means "it does not go." Sales improved when the car was renamed "Caribe." The phrase "Body by Fisher" is translated in some foreign languages to "Corpse by Fisher." A North American company tried to sell tooth whitening paste to nut chewing Latin American Indians who consider stained teeth a status symbol.

In the past two decades U.S. advertisers seem to have had an almost unique penchant for insulting their hosts by featuring such things as green hats (symbolic of dunce caps in China), storks (signifying maternal death in Indonesia), and animals (considered dirty in some Middle East countries). Then there is Coca-Cola®'s error of not providing a name translation for its soft drink when it was introduced in China. Local shopkeepers made their own signs announcing the drink. Unfortunately, their translation of Coca-Cola® was *ke kou ke la,* which means "bite the wax tadpole." Pepsi Cola's initial effort to capture the Chinese market was equally unsuccessful: "Come Alive with Pepsi" was translated to read "Pepsi brings your ancestors back from the dead."

Although U.S. private enterprises and business schools are slowly adopting a combined technical and communication skills approach to training and education, there is a growing national awareness of the need for even more cultural diversity in business education. Joseph DiStefano (1979) made this observation:

Neither educators in North American business schools nor managers in its enterprises are sufficiently aware of the culture-bound nature of much of what is taught and practiced. Thus it should hardly be surprising . . . that training programs fall woefully short in preparing or helping managers to deal sensitively and effectively with people in other countries. Too often the businessman who experiences difficulties while working abroad explains away the problems by a pejorative litany of natives' shortcomings. Furthermore, both he and his business professors falsely assume (or at least behave as if they did) that U.S. business practices are the only means to accomplish tasks efficiently. (p. 431)

Cultures Are Different, Not Better

American culture is depicted in the literature as being quantitatively and qualitatively different from most other cultures in certain important ways that impact behaviors within organizations. As an example, Sondra Thiederman (1991) provided a comprehensive list of U.S. culture characteristics and contrast culture perspectives, adapted in the next few pages to describe Eurocentric American culture and traditional Third World cultures beliefs and behavior.

Control versus fatalism. Americans believe they have the power to control the future. Third World peoples believe their future is influenced or controlled by a higher power or fate.

Control of nature versus harmony with nature. Americans believe nature can, and should, be controlled to benefit human needs. Third World peoples believe humans are an integral part of nature and therefore must live in harmony with it. This requires disturbing nature as little as possible.

Change versus tradition. Americans believe change is not only necessary but it is usually good. Third World peoples believe in maintaining the old ways; change should be accepted only when it is an obvious improvement of the status quo.

The future versus the past and the present. Americans believe in anticipating and planning for the future. Third World peoples believe it is important to remember the past and enjoy the present.

Reality as order versus reality as disorder. Americans believe in the scientific approach to reality; it can be categorized and ordered. Third World peoples do not believe that ultimate reality can be categorized nor can it be objectively organized.

Rational versus intuitive thinking. Americans believe that the most productive thinking is linear, cause and effect, and rational in nature. Third World peoples rely more on intuitive, often circular, thinking.

Differentiated time versus undifferentiated time. Americans value efficiency, punctuality, and speed within predetermined time frames. Third World peoples do not measure the quality of interaction by efficiency, punctuality, and speed. The quality of interaction is based on undifferentiated units of time.

Transient versus lifelong friendships. Americans establish quick, transient business friendships. Third World business friendships are formed slowly but tend to last a lifetime.

Individual versus group identity. Americans gain their identities from individual achievements, particularly those accomplished in competition. Third World peoples gain identity from family and other communal achievements gained from cooperative activities.

Questioning versus respecting authority. Americans believe it is their right to question people in authority positions. Third World peoples believe it is disrespectful to question people in authority positions. Relatedly, Americans complain to their superiors more readily than Third World workers, who consider such behavior defiant.

From these differences have come myths and stereotypes about backward, ignorant foreign workers. It is foolish to dwell on the "great race" theory; that is, the belief that different races differ significantly in terms of intellectual ability. There are ample reasons to assume that all races and ethnic groups are approximately equal in native endowments of the mind. For one thing, there are no pure races—all nations are mixed races. Furthermore, the so-called advanced or developed cultures were recently backward, while the so-called underdeveloped or developing Third World cultures were sometimes the advanced nations. This does not mean that the peoples of African, Asian, and Latin American stocks have degenerated during the last two hundred years. Instead it shows that unless nations continuously maintain and, where necessary, improve technological aspects of their cultures, they will undergo technological stagnation. As an illustration: The Spaniards used gunpowder (invented by the Chinese) to destroy the Aztec civilization. The Japanese have only recently borrowed technological aspects of Western civilization, and they have regained the world prominence they lost during World War II. These illustrations highlight cultural conditions, not biological inferiority or superiority. The decline of Greek, Roman, and African cultures, or the German shift to intellectualism in the early nineteenth century and to militarism in the early twentieth century are additional illustrations. Managers must not succumb to ethnocentrism. Of course, there are cultural differences in ways peoples of various cultures interact. However, these are learned differences; they are not innate.

Researchers have identified Latin Americans, Arabs, and Southern Europeans as "contact" cultures and Asians, Pakistanis, Indians, and Northern Europeans as "noncontact" cultures. In contact cultures, people face each other more directly, touch more, stand closer, talk more, and have more eye contact. However, there is a progressive decline in the frequency of contact from Central America to South America. The most extreme differences exist between Colombians and Costa Ricans.

We can also compare national cultures to the "Type A" and "Type B" personalities of individual people. Type A cultures are aggressive, goal-oriented, competitive, and under constant time pressure. Type B cultures are relaxed, easygoing, and less task-oriented. Anglo, Germanic, and Nordic cultures tend to be Type A, and people in other countries tend to be Type B. Stress is more evident in Type A employees. Symptoms of stress include high blood pressure, stomach ulcers, migraine headaches, nervousness, and heart disease. But these generalizations mask individual similarities. Failure to understand cultural variances has caused managers to react inappropriately to peoples from other countries by lumping them together as being all Type A or all Type B.

THOSE WHO ARE AFFECTED

The number of immigrants living in the United States is uncertain. Rough estimates range from a low of 1.3 million to a high of 4.2 million (U.S. Department of Labor, 1991). Immigrants, or foreign workers, initially are either pulled or pushed to the United States, depending on their reasons for leaving their home country (Abowd & Freeman, 1991). Factors that constitute a pull are such things as a desire for freedom, economic betterment, or to be reunited with relatives who are already in the United States. The largest number of immigrants—legal and illegal—are Mexicans and Central Americans who come to the United States in search of better jobs. Conditions that tend to push people from their homeland to the United States include political unrest, growing imbalances between population and food supplies, and high income taxes. When they arrive in the United States, most immigrants find few well paying jobs initially available to them. (See Table 6.1.)

Arab immigrants comprise more than one million American immigrants. More than half of them are assimilated third- and fourth-generation descendants of Arabs who migrated to the United States between 1875 and 1948. Almost all of the original Arab immigrants were Christians from the Ottoman Empire. Most of them called themselves Syrians, since the Republic of Lebanon was not established until 1946. The Arabs who experienced the most problems were Muslims, however. Muslims who live and

Table 6.1
Occupations of Applicants for Legalization

	Total
Number Reporting Occupation	1,268.317
Percent	100.0
Executive, Managerial and Administrative	4.2
Technicians	0.6
Other Professional Specialists	2.5
Sales Workers	3.6
Administrative Support	5.7
Service	29.7
Farming, Forestry and Fishing	5.5
Precision Prodeuction, Craft and Repairs	15.1
Operators, Fabricators and Laborers	33.7

OCCUPATION	Job Held Just Prior to Entering U.S.	Job Held First in U.S.	Job Held at Time of Application	Percent Changing Job 11 to 22 Months After Application
Total	100.0	100.0	100.0	37.2
Managerial, Professional	8.3	1.8	3.9	23.4
Executive, Administrative and Managerial	3.5	0.6	2.4	24.0
Professional Specialty	4.8	1.2	1.5	22.3
Technical, Sales, Administrative	18.8	6.9	10.5	36.0
Technicians, Related	1.0	0.2	0.7	28.8
Sales Workers	10.1	4.1	5.2	39.5
Administrative Support	7.7	2.6	4.6	33.1
Service Occupations	10.9	35.7	29.8	37.4
Private Household	4.1	13.0	7.4	38.4
Food Preparation	3.5	14.7	13.7	37.3
Other Services	3.3	8.0	8.7	33.6
Precision Production, Crafts and Repairs	13.4	7.6	14.3	34.2
Mechanics, Repairers	3.3	1.8	3.1	34.8
Construction Trades	5.3	3.0	6.7	38.3
Other Precision Production	4.8	2.8	5.0	27.7
Operators, Fabricators and Laborers	23.3	31.6	33.5	39.4
Machine Operators, Assemblers, Laborers	10.7	18.1	20.0	38.5
Transportation and Material Moving	4.5	1.4	3.7	33.6
Handlers, Cleaners, Helpers and Laborers	8.1	12.1	9.8	43.6
Farming, Forestry, Fishing	24.7	15.7	7.1	42.0

Source: U.S. Department of Labor, 1992.

work in non-Muslim communities have great difficulty exercising their religious rituals. For many of them, it was not possible to observe the Sabbath on Friday, pray five times a day, and fast during the sunlight hours during the holy month of Ramadan. The first prayer is about 12:45 P.M. (lunch time in most U.S. organizations).

The situation is even less stable for the nation's most recent immigrants, comprised largely of Vietnamese, Cubans, and Haitians. As these new groups of immigrants come to the United States and as available jobs decrease, tolerance tends to give way to intolerance; nonviolence frequently gives way to violence. And the newest immigrants increasingly become the objects of prejudice and discrimination, especially the non-European ones. Furthermore, as the new immigrants concentrate in specific areas and form urban clusters or colonies, they become highly visible and in some cities very disliked by people of other ethnic groups with whom they compete for jobs, education, and social status. Each new immigrant group not only has its own language or dialect that tends to create a communication barrier, but it also has its own social and religious institutions that usually perpetuate intergroup solidarity and intragroup hostility.

Immigrants not only have to worry about how to protect themselves from their neighbors; many of them also try to separate themselves from African Americans and other American minorities. American minority groups, the objects of intense discrimination, often view foreign workers as hostile competitors. There is much basis in fact to this belief. African Americans and other minorities have in many instances had immigrants take their jobs. To keep the diversity pot boiling, some employers make a conscious effort to keep all the diverse groups separated along racial, nationality, or ethnic lines (Asher & Stephenson, 1990). A CEO said, "When the groups are fighting each other, they have little time, energy, or resources to organize into a single worker entity to fight oppressive job conditions."

The misfit between American managerial styles and traditional cultures of other nations pushes most foreign workers away from American job culture enclaves. Thus they may spend many years in the United States without becoming fully acculturated. These employees are seldom "ugly" foreigners, but they are almost always "invisible foreigners"—seen mainly on the job.

LAWS

In addition to laws that prohibit discrimination based on race, religion, national origin, and sex, there is one congressional act that specifically addresses the rights of alien workers: the Immigration Reform and Control Act of 1986. This act delineates the legal conditions that pertain to hiring aliens. Specifically, it is illegal to knowingly hire an undocumented alien. The act poses penalties in the forms of fines and imprisonment for employers and individuals within their organization who hire an unauthorized alien without complying with the statute. Thus, the employer has the obligation to verify that each person hired is legally qualified to work in the United States. The Immigration and Naturalization Service (INS), which is responsible for enforcement, can impose an initial fine ranging from $250 to $2,000 per illegal alien hired. A second violation can result in a fine ranging from $250 to $3,000. A continued disregard for the act is a criminal violation, with fines up to $10,000 and six months in prison.

SELECTED COURT CASES

Under Title VII, it is illegal to discriminate against people because of their national origin. However, there is relatively little case law pertaining to this protected class. Language requirements and dress and grooming codes have had the most litigation. For example, employers cannot require employees to speak English if it is not required for successful job performance. But they can require bilingual employees to speak English on the job (*Garcia v. Gloor,* 1980). On the one hand, employers do not have to provide native language tests for foreign workers (*Frontera v. Sindell,* 1975). On the other hand, labor unions must publish collective bargaining agreements in the languages of their foreign members in order to ensure adequate comprehension of the rights and responsibilities. Employers cannot legally use nationality as a job criterion when applicants are documented under the terms of the IRCA. Nor can employers favor one nationality over another, but they may give preference to U.S. citizens (*Espononza v. Farah Mfg. Co.,* 1973).

Employers can require their employees to adhere to specific dress and grooming codes if these codes do not discriminate on the basis of employees' nationality or sex. As an illustration, employers can require male employees and not female employees to wear neckties (*Fountain v. Safeway Stores,* 1977). Also, employers can specify hair length for males and that they be clean shaven (*Miller v. Missouri Pacific Railway,* 1976). In all instances, grooming and dress codes must be job-related and not just to comply with the employer's sense of socially correct appearance.

SPECIAL PROGRAMS

Until recently there were virtually no systematic programs to prepare American managers to optimize the skills of foreign workers. The basic assumption has been that all employees, foreign and indigenous, must adjust to the organization culture instead of vice versa. Successful cross-national interaction, in business or any other field, requires a detailed understanding of the specific cultures of the people involved. Culturally, there are many different ways of doing everything. And the "everything" that people do, which is what culture consists of, is multitudinous, indeed. Ideally, both parties involved in cross-national interactions would occupy central positions on the language and culture sensitivity continuums as suggested by Roger Shuy (1976):

| American managers only speak English | American managers speak only English but understand non-English | American managers speak and understand both English and non-English | Non-Americans speak and understand both their own language and English | Non-Americans speak only their own language but understand English | Non-Americans speak only their own language |

In terms of cultural sensitivity, a related continuum is as follows:

American managers understand only American culture	American managers understand American culture but are sensitive to foreign cultures	American managers understand and are sensitive to both American and foreign cultures	Non-Americans understand and are sensitive to both their own and American cultures	Non-Americans understand their own cultures but are sensitive to American culture	Non-Americans understand only their culture

TIPS AND TECHNIQUES

In most organizations, English is the only prescribed language. Employees whose first language is not English are expected to leave their native language at the door before entering the organization. This is especially harsh on immigrants. The theory behind the speak-English-only norm is obvious—it is believed that if immigrants speak only English they will be able to interact better with the other employees. Employers who support such behavior fail to understand—or dismiss it if they know it—that forced exposure to a new language can sometimes impede acquisition of communication skills in that language.

Not only are restrictive language norms unsound; they also are hard to enforce. A manager in charge of a work unit, for example, may prevent subordinates from speaking Spanish, but the result is likely to be silence. It is certainly no guarantee that fluent, idiomatic English will be spoken. In fact, the foreign employees may possess a very limited knowledge of the meanings of the English words that they are able to pronounce and attempt to use. Printing some of the organization's material in another language or languages is likely to facilitate communication. It is commonly done in consumer literature. And it can also be done to "sell" diversity.

English-only norms tend to make employees ashamed of their native language and cultural heritage. This is a not too subtle way to make other languages and cultures seem inferior. Culturally sensitive organizations provide employees from other countries with opportunities to teach American employees "foreign" words and cultures. Since communication is essential to good human relations, it is necessary for non-English-speaking employees to learn English—but not at the expense of their own language.

Dropping the first last name of a traditional Spanish employee's name would be considered very rude. For example, to address Manuel Maldonado-Denis as simply "Maldonado" without "Denis" would be considered a cultural blunder because the first last name is from the father's side of the family and the second is from the mother's. And both are equally important. In the United States, insisting on addressing people by all their names would be needlessly formal and, in the right circumstances, cold and unfriendly. Therefore, it is important to know each country's customs.

A Sample of Customs and Courtesies

Chinese. The Chinese are renowned for their good manners, hospitality, and humility. However, they do not like to be touched by strangers. A smile is much better received than a pat on the back, and it is impolite to exhibit physical familiarity with older persons or individuals with important positions. Either a nod or a slight bow is an acceptable greeting, but a handshake will suffice too. Chinese names consist of a one-syllable family name followed by a one- or two-syllable given name. The family name is always mentioned first. Thus Wang Fuming should be addressed as Mr. Wang, and Li Meili as Madam Li. Married women retain their maiden names. Chinese men and women who participate in social functions with foreigners attend because of their positions and usually do not bring their spouses. Strict punctuality is observed for business appointments and social occasions. And it is proper to arrive a few minutes before the specified time. It is customary for executives to present business cards.

In public and private places the Chinese expect people to conduct themselves with restraint, and to refrain from loud, boisterous behavior. They are taught to avoid self-centered conversations using the word "I." Nor do they single out co-workers as having unique qualities. It is considered rude to point with the index finger; the open hand should be used. Chinese women may cross their legs when seated but men seldom cross theirs. If they must beckon someone, Chinese are taught to do so with the palms down, not up.

Indians (East). Traditional values of modesty and humility are very important to most Indian people, particularly women. Public displays of affection are considered impolite, and females are taught to not wink or whistle in public. In fact it is impolite for males to whistle in public. Back-slapping is rude behavior. Most Indians believe love is divine, and therefore couples should express their love and affection only in privacy. Women cover their heads when entering sacred places. Normally, Indian women do not shake hands. Instead, the *namaste* (bending gently with palms together below the chin) is the common greeting. Men seldom touch women in formal or informal gatherings. Educated Indian women do shake hands with Westerners as a courtesy. It is proper to use the right hand for the *salaam* gesture of greeting and farewell. And it is polite to ask permission before taking leave of others. Beckoning is done with the palm turned down, and pointing is often done with the chin.

Generally, the right hand is used for eating and for giving and receiving objects. When in doubt, follow the host's lead. Men, elderly people, and children usually eat with the guests, and the women eat after them. The *namaste* gesture is the polite way to decline a helping. Traditionally, both single and married Indian women wear a *bindi* (red dot) on their foreheads. It is a sign of femininity, good posture, and gracefulness. After marriage the *bindi* is accompanied by a white powder on the upper forehead to signify that a woman is married and her husband is alive. Widows do not wear a *bindi*.

Business is usually conducted at a much more leisurely pace than Americans are used to. An exchange of pleasantries and a cup of tea are preludes to most business conversations. American business travelers need to be aware of, and sensitive to, the hospitality associated with doing business in India. A few basic religious beliefs and social customs merit brief mention. Hindus revere the cow, and thus do not eat beef. Many Hindus are in fact vegetarian, although their religion does not forbid the consumption of other forms of flesh. Alcohol is consumed (if at all) in moderation by Hindus, and orthodox Muslims do not drink alcohol. Muslims are forbidden by their religion to eat pork.

Japanese. The basic sense of family is so strongly a part of the traditional Japanese character that it is transferred to industry, government, bureaucracy, and national politics. Paternalistic industries are commonplace, and bureaucracies are extremely sensitive to citizen welfare and the integrity of the family structure. In many ways the entire Japanese society becomes a "national family." Nonfamily Japanese males in the community are the equivalent of uncles, and nonfamily Japanese females are treated like aunts.

To some extent Japanese adult roles match those found in many small conservative American communities. However, this kind of cross-national transposition is not reliable. Unlike Americans, who tend to view their role expectations as *obligations*, Japanese tend to view them as *an expression of gratitude*. For Japanese, duties fall into a hierarchy with two distinct categories. The highest level of adult obligations are *duties that can never be fully repaid:*

1. Duty to the law
2. Duty to one's parents, ancestors, and descendants
3. Duty to one's work

The second level consists of *duties that are to be fully repaid:*

4. Duty to one's name
5. Duty to the world (nonrelated others)

From this ranking it is understandable that the Japanese spend a considerable amount of energy preserving the family and home and striving for the best education possible in order to succeed as workers. Japanese parents and students are taught to place a high value on education. This commitment is seen in the willingness of families to undergo considerable, often drastic, financial hardship so that their children can receive the best education. Traditionally, Japanese students are dedicated scholars. Japanese students from kindergarten through higher education are almost never without a bag of books. In Japan, probably more than in any other postindustrial nation, the interdependence of the industrial technocracy and institutional education is recognized and supported.

The Japanese concepts of work and leisure differ from American concepts. The work ethic is very much a part of Japanese character; the Japanese seem to live to work, while U.S. citizens seem to work to live. Of course, these are generalizations, but it is fair to say that it is difficult to get Japanese to take leisure time. Typically, the Japanese do not take long vacations. Instead, they like to take a few vacation days here and there—usually in May, August, and early January—at the same time as their friends.

Koreans. Courtesy, formality, and modesty characterize the Koreans. Compliments are graciously denied, and reluctance to accept high honors is the mark of a socially correct person. Korean men greet their male friends by bowing slightly and shaking hands, either with the right hand or both hands. However, women rarely shake hands, which is a great honor for children. Custom dictates that one should pay complete attention to the person being greeted.

Koreans are particularly careful about touching in public older people and those of the opposite sex. Also, there is proper posture while standing or sitting. In informal situations visitors may cross their legs only with one knee over the other and with soles and toes pointed downward. It is impolite to cross the legs at all in formal situations. Feet should never be put on furniture, and hands should always remain in the sight of the person one is talking with. It is also impolite to not cover the mouth when yawning or using a toothpick. And both hands should be used for handing things to another person and for receiving objects.

Success depends on social contacts, and gifts frequently are given before asking for a favor. If one wishes to avoid an obligation, return gifts to the giver with a comment such as, "I am grateful but this is too much." Friendships are important as a prelude to long-term business dealings. Open criticism, public disagreement, and rude behavior are to be avoided because Koreans believe that no one has the right to lower the self-esteem of another. It is considered better to accept an injustice to preserve harmony than to assert one's individual rights.

Mexicans. The Mexican people have a high regard for the inner quality or spirit of the individual. A person's inner spirit represents his or her dignity, and any actions or words against it are considered disrespectful.

Also, the family is considered an important part of the individual's frame of reference. U.S. business personnel should learn to take discussions of the family with Mexican business personnel as seriously as they take their business discussions. Mexicans believe that one gets to know a person by knowing about his or her family.

The usual greeting is a handshake or a nod; longtime friends often embrace each other after a long absence. Mexicans stand closer to each other than North Americans when conversing. It is also common for friends to touch the other person's clothing during conversation. "No" can be spoken or indicated by moving the hand left to right (approximately 4–6 inches) with the index finger extended, palm outward. It is considered impolite to toss items to people. They should be handed. On the other hand, it is not impolite to beckon people with a "psst-psst" sound. If one beckons with a hand, it should be with a palm down, waving motion, taking care not to make it appear that you are waving them away. If someone sneezes, you should say *salud* (good health).

The father is the head of the family but the mother is responsible for running the household. The Mexican family is extended and a household sometimes includes other relatives besides the immediate family. Family responsibility supersedes all others. Parental approval of a boyfriend is still important, and single girls who go out alone after dark are considered persons of poor character. Chivalry is very much in vogue. On a bus, for instance, a gentleman is expected to give his seat to a woman. In routine conversation, Mexicans generally use more flowery and charming speech than North Americans. This is due largely to a high regard for the ability of the individual to be witty and charming in interpersonal conversation.

Another difference between Mexican and North American cultures is the concept of truth. Americans perceive truth in terms of reality and fact. Mexicans perceive truth in terms of building good interpersonal relations, that is, Mexicans would rather tell a visitor what they think makes the visitor happy even if they perceive the reality will not. "Untruths" are therefore socially acceptable in many subcultures in Mexico. This is in contrast to North Americans who consider telling an "untruth" to be a reflection of a person's moral character.

Time is another cultural concept on which Mexicans and most Eurocentric Americans tend to differ. Unlike U.S. citizens who conceptualize time in linear-spatial terms, Mexicans view time in a less linear fashion. Mexicans will do many things in one time frame, while Americans tend to have a set period of time to accomplish one goal. Mexicans use time with less constraints. They believe that what is not achieved today will be achieved tomorrow *(mañana)*. Consequently, Mexican workers place looser time constraints on business activities than their American counterparts. They also consider interruptions and delays as part of the normal business procedure.

Nigerians. Because of the diversity of customs, cultures, and dialects in Nigeria, the form of greetings varies throughout the country. However, they avoid using colloquial greetings and phrases such as "Hi" or "What's happening?" Also, dress varies throughout the country; in the Muslim north, men and women dress very conservatively, while non-Muslims in the east and west dress more casually. Individual Nigerians are very proud of their ethnic group and its unique cultural heritage. Because of the negative colonial connotations attached to the word *tribe,* many Nigerians prefer "ethnic group" to "tribe."

Managers are expected to be well dressed. Casual dress in many cases connotes a casual attitude, especially to European-trained Nigerians. Formal titles are used in conversation, especially the honorific titles of traditional leaders. In Nigeria, business of any consequence is consummated face to face. No worthwhile transactions can be completed either impersonally or quickly.

A word that U.S. managers and supervisors may hear often when dealing with employees who are Muslim is *Inshallah* (God willing). A Muslim "submits" to God's will. The use of the word is not a means of avoiding responsibility or making decisions, but merely a statement that only those things that God wills will happen. Americans who expect meetings to start on time are usually frustrated by Muslims who are not rushed. Eventually things do get done.

Portuguese. As a whole, the Portuguese people are serious and conservative in their dress and actions. Seldom are their conversations animated or loud. Women wear slacks and dresses, but long dresses are usually reserved for evening wear. And men work in suits. In offices and stores people are greeted politely and formally. A firm handshake is an acceptable greeting, and—as in all countries—a sincere smile is welcome. Portuguese shake hands when they meet and again when they part. It is impolite to yell when calling someone. Instead, the proper way is to extend an arm, palm down, and wave the fingers back and forth.

First names are used for friends, children, and youth; otherwise, Mr. or Miss or some other appropriate title is used before the family name.

The family is the center of Portuguese life. Portuguese children are taught to respect their elders, and this socialization extends to adults who respect persons older than themselves. They also respect authority and rank.

To show anger *(exaltarse)* in public will result in a loss of respect from those present. Furthermore, the Portuguese do not like to cause embarrassment to others and will do almost everything they can to avoid a conflict. But if their pride is hurt by someone else's action, the Portuguese will let the other person know about it. They are slow to anger, but will not let others abuse them.

Generally, the Portuguese do not stress punctuality in meetings, but they

expect visitors to be prompt. Most meetings are well organized and formal; friendly formality prevails in private interviews. A phrase frequently
used in conversations is *Se deus quizer* (If God so wills). The Portuguese
are likely to let things happen instead of trying to make things happen.
There are certain nuances that must be followed. For instance, it is rude
for a younger person to keep an older person waiting. A woman may
keep a man waiting, but a gentleman never makes a woman wait for him.
Portuguese women are accorded great respect and protection.

Business Styles

The North American socialization process tends to produce independent, free-wheeling business executives—many of whom are perceived
throughout the world as unpredictable, illogical, and insensitive. American
executives have a lot of discretion when making business deals. Conversely, non-Western decision-making is usually a group consensus process
that leaves little room for individual action. Consensus is achieved through
an elaborate, time-consuming process that unnerves most Westerners. U.S.
business executives are characterized by some foreign executives as being
obsessed with punctuality, action-oriented, inclined to develop shallow interpersonal relationships with their business colleagues, and extremely self-
centered. These behaviors are opposite of those exhibited by executives in
most other countries. The peoples of northern Europe are the closest to
kindred souls an American executive abroad can find—and they are not
extremely close kin.

When North American executives encounter employees from developing
nations who do not display "proper" deference, they often become hostile.
Organization consultants tell of an American manager of an engineering
company with operations in Nigeria. The poor fellow spent several days
in jail for shouting insults at and exchanging blows with his Nigerian co-
workers. When the precipitating events were sorted out, it was clear that
the problem was largely cross-cultural miscommunication. The Nigerians
displayed brusque behaviors—culturally acceptable in their country—
which the American interpreted as an insult.

Japanese managers are even more different from U.S. managers. Their
style of dealing evolves around problem identification, harmonious decision-making, and saving face. The Japanese action-orientation typically is
accompanied by a need to be very deliberate in negotiations so that they
can move on to the next project with few loose ends. Japanese executives
enter negotiations to ratify already reached agreements, while U.S. executives view negotiation sessions as opportunities to further define the deal.
The Japanese are loyal to their employers, and especially polite when dealing with foreigners. They are more concerned about the success of their
company than their own individual well-being. They should not be put in

a position of being required to admit failure or inefficacy. Unlike most U.S. executives, they are ill at ease working with abrasive, egotistical, or harsh individuals. Americans who feel uncomfortable with silence during negotiations tend to fill in the gaps with chit-chat; some Japanese managers have asked their U.S. co-workers how they can think and talk at the same time.

The Asian use of "yes" and "no" may cause confusion due to differences in the grammatical structure between English and many Asian languages. A "yes" to a negative question in the Asian grammatical syntax means a "no" in English. For example, the American manager asks his Asian colleague, "Haven't you finished the report?" His colleague answers "Yes," meaning, "Yes, I have not finished the report." One of the techniques used by traditional Asians to avoid confrontation is to blame themselves for the other person's mistake. The correct behavior for the second person is to say, "No, it is not your fault." This requires a degree of honesty and humility that American managers frequently do not exhibit.

Few executives throughout the world share the U.S. way of doing business in a hurry. From a non-U.S. perspective, time is not "lost" when it is used to get to know business acquaintances. Unlike the Western concept of linear time, many nations (particularly those in Latin America and Africa) have adopted the concept of cyclical or circular time—it cannot be lost, but merely continues into the future. Executives in most nations prefer to do business slowly and with friends, not strangers.

Training Immigrant Workers

Most U.S. employees believe that it is not only desirable but correct to tell their supervisors what they think, even when they disagree with them. Of course, not all workers do this, but many of those who do are not faulted for saying what they were thinking. U.S. culture, therefore, emphasizes face-to-face contact and confrontation, and it deemphasizes the importance of status differences. This is not the case in most other nations, where it is difficult for people to express their differences face-to-face and authority is strongly emphasized. This is particularly true of Third World peoples. To provide a minimum stress learning environment for foreign workers, the following teaching techniques are recommended by Thiederman (1991):

- Do not try to cover too much material at one time.
- Organize your thoughts and avoid extraneous materials.
- Use simple phrasing and words familiar to the employees. Avoid unnecessary jargon, slang, and idioms. When job-related jargon is used, provide a glossary.
- Speak slowly, distinctly, and in a nonpatronizing manner.

- Use extensive handouts, especially those with visual aids.
- Ask questions to encourage learning but do not force debate and interpersonal or intergroup competition.
- Allow employees who prefer to do so to ask written anonymous questions.
- If you must test for comprehension, avoid multiple choice questions. Allow quizzes to be self-graded and repeated.
- Recap the major points presented and frequently check to make sure the employees understand them.

In order to avoid national origin lawsuits, employers should do the following:

- Review recruiting and selection procedures to make sure they comply with the INS regulations.
- Require managers and supervisors to treat all ethnic groups fairly.
- Treat lawful aliens in the process of becoming U.S. citizens the same as U.S. citizens.
- Include nationality discrimination in the organization complaint procedure.

Accommodating Immigrant Employees

The unilateral effect of acculturation is vividly seen in instances when tradition-oriented immigrant employees forgo taking time off work to celebrate their native country holidays. For example, Muslim workers do not observe Friday as the day of rest and worship; Chinese do not take time off work in late January or early February to observe the Chinese New Year; Mexican employees do not miss work on December 12 to worship at the Shrine of the Virgin of Guadalupe. But these same individuals often must work during Christmas, Easter, Labor Day, and other American holidays to commemorate host country revered events.

Some culturally sensitive companies allow foreign workers to celebrate selected religious holidays by taking time off with pay. Other companies allow foreign workers to trade days off with pay to celebrate their native country holidays. For example, Chinese workers may opt to take the American New Year off without pay but be paid for being off a day during the Chinese New Year.

In addition to accommodations for holidays, a growing number of companies have expanded their cafeteria food selections to include foods preferred by immigrants. In doing so, they are cognizant that a variety of main courses are needed to avoid violating religious taboos; for instance, Hindus do not eat beef, and Muslims do not eat pork. Vegetarian and seafood selections are agreeable across cultures.

When the workplace has a large number of employees who speak the same foreign language, such as Spanish, some companies have bilingual business documents and reading materials. They also employ individuals who serve as translators for employees who have difficulty speaking or writing English. In a related area, whenever music is provided as background noise, care is taken to mix the music in order to appease diverse culture preferences. In summary, a conscious effort is made to accommodate all employees.

SIZING UP PEOPLE

1. There is no such thing as a "blank" look or an "uninterested" stare—all facial expressions convey some kind of message. The problem occurs when managers are unfamiliar with the culturally different ways people with whom they are interacting send facial messages. Describe a situation in which you incorrectly "read" a co-worker's or a subordinate's

facial expression. _____

_____

2. Sometimes people from other countries seem aloof: The more they are pressured to interact, the more they withdraw. But this is not unique to people from other countries. Recall a situation when you behaved that

way. Why did you withdraw? _____

_____

3. The peoples of some countries are more attractive to us than those of other countries. List the characteristics of foreigners that you like and those you dislike.

Like: _____

_____

Dislike: _____

_____

Part Two

Workplace Issues and Interventions

CHAPTER 7

Barriers to Cultural Diversity

Because managers and supervisors are creatures of culture, they tend to react to culturally different people in the same manner as their significant others. Therefore, prejudices found in the community are acted out in the workplace. Succinctly, prejudice is a conclusion drawn without adequate knowledge or evidence. The bigot blames members of out-groups for various misfortunes: floods, high taxes, inflation, wars, and, interestingly, bigotry. Such prejudgments are easier to make than objective judgments, which require more energy, knowledge, integrity, and time. In their efforts to make expedient decisions, bigots react to concepts rather than people.

However, as stressed throughout this book, it is behaviors, not attitudes, which create the major problems in managing diversity. There are many laws against discriminatory behaviors, but there are none against prejudicial attitudes. It is not what managers and supervisors think about diversity that hurts or helps employees but how they act out those thoughts. Some managers act out their prejudices by denying culturally different people equal employment opportunities. Contrary to popular writings, prejudices in the workplace are not limited to black-white conflicts and confrontations. There is prejudice against women, older workers, individuals with disabilities, foreign workers, and white workers—all the people who comprise the labor force.

A survey, conducted in 1993 by L. H. Research for the National Conference of Christians and Jews, found that black, Hispanic, and Asian Americans resent one another almost as much as they do whites (Holmes, 1994). This raises doubt about the strategy of merely hiring more minorities. Unless there is systematic training to help all employees—white and non-white—to accept each other, conflicts focusing on ethnicity will expand from within white groups to among the diverse groups. No ethnic group has a monopoly on prejudice.

DIVERSITY-RELATED ATTITUDES

A diversity-related attitude is a degree of readiness to behave in a given manner toward culturally different people. Much could be added to this definition to make it more scientifically precise, but it is adequate for this discussion. There are three major implications of the definition.

1. A diversity-related attitude is a *degree of readiness.* This is a vague statement. However, when cast in the perspective of a manager's ability to perceive certain employees, his or her quickness to respond to them, motivation to respond to them, and experience in responding to them, the degree of readiness can stand the test of further scrutiny.

2. A diversity-related attitude is a degree of readiness *to behave in a given manner.* An attitude is not an overt response. It is a response, to be sure, but an implicit or mental one. Therefore, an attitude is a readiness to act, not an act itself. The crucial diversity question that arises is: "Under what conditions does an attitude elicit overt expression in the workplace?" Even the most general answer to this question must include at least two variables: A diversity-related attitude is likely to result in overt expression in direct proportion to organization rewards and in inverse proportion to organization sanctions or penalties.

Although behavior cannot always be predicted on the basis of whether it will be rewarded or sanctioned, it is probable that employer recognition significantly encourages acceptance of diversity. Overt behavior is likely when there is a sufficient degree of readiness. Some employees act out their antidiversity attitudes no matter how negatively management reacts to them. One of these employees said, "I know what I should do, but I don't believe in this equality crap. *Those people* don't deserve my respect." Technically, his resistance had not lowered to a crucial threshold in order for the change to occur. It is generally assumed in psychological experiments that when most variables in a situation are held constant, the degree of acceptance of diversity is a function of motivation, the desire to achieve the goal. Thus, there are talkers, doers, and talkers who are doers.

3. A negative diversity-related attitude is a degree of readiness *to behave in a given manner toward culturally different people.* This refers to any individuals or groups considered by the actors to be inferior to them or a threat to the status quo.

How Attitudes Are Formed

Attitudes are learned. Attitudes are learned; they are not innate. John, a CEO testifying at a racial discrimination hearing in which he was the defendant, said, "I'm not a racist. . . . I don't socialize with black people by choice. I have never been comfortable with them, but I hire on the basis of ability, not race." There was evidence to the contrary. John's discomfort with blacks was not innate. His sister recalled that when he was in the third grade, John befriended a black classmate. His mother told him not to play with black children because "they are dirty and will steal from you." Research studies have detected racial attitudes in children as young as three years old (Lasker, 1929). But these attitudes are not very well developed until about age ten or eleven. Young children begin to use hate words before they fully understand their connotations. John was such a child.

The most insidious prejudices are negative attitudes directed toward groups of people. They take the form of assumptions or generalizations about all or most members of a particular group ("You know how those people are!"). This kind of in-group versus out-group hostility disrupts work unit interactions and subverts organization effectiveness. The behaviors, customs, and values of out-group people are labeled *strange* or *weird*.

Employee attitudes of acceptance of culturally different co-workers are learned in much the same manner rejection is inculcated. They most often learn as children to reject culturally different people. Thus, difference becomes a synonym for "inferior." In the insightful words of Carl Jung (1968): "We still attribute to the other fellow all the evil and inferior qualities that we do not like to recognize in ourselves, and therefore have to criticize and attack him, when all that has happened is that an inferior soul has emigrated from one person to another. The world is still full of *bêtes noires* and scapegoats, just as it formerly teemed with witches and werewolves" (p. 65).

Researchers have also found that as children grow older, they tend to forget that they were instructed in attitudes by their parents and significant other people (Horowitz & Horowitz, 1938). Around the age of ten, most children regard their attitudes toward culturally different people as being innate. Seldom do they recall being coached. *Social amnesia* develops, and elaborate rationalizations are presented to account for learned attitudes, with the result that most people believe that they came by their attitudes "naturally."

Attitudes are learned mainly from other people. We learn most of our attitudes from other people. As ego-deflating as it may be to accept, it is a fact that a few people invent attitudes for most people. An attitude about racial diversity, for example, is a complex perceptual invention, and most people are not perceptually creative. Consider a seemingly simple perception made by a Cuban supervisor: "That man is an African American, and therefore, he is not as good as me." Such a straightforward attitude as this—including the man and his racial label—requires considerable rationalizing. People who perceive African Americans as inferior have to think beyond individual African Americans, who may be adequate by every objective standard, in order to define the racial group "African Americans" as inferior.

The superiority or inferiority of a group (as contrasted to that of an individual) is not obvious; not many casual observers can perceive significant group differences. Besides, there are more differences within racial or ethnic groups than between them. Most employees bring their racial baggage (hatred) to work with them—bags packed by other people. And very much like children, they were molded and shaped by peer pressure. A white clerk said to his friend who watched him harass a Mexican-American co-worker, "Sam, if we ain't better than a greaser, who are we better than?"

There are other reasons for assuming that attitudes are learned mainly from other people. Autobiographies and case histories corroborate such learnings. An individual's attitudes tend to be those of his or her relatives, office mates, and friends. Certainly, employees can develop attitudes independently of their relatives and friends, but their relatives and friends are the foremost determinants of the initial diversity attitudes. The tendency of most employees to hold the same attitudes toward cultural diversity as their significant others is so consistent as to make independent acquisition unlikely. The key concept is "significant others." In order for diversity to be embraced, managers and supervisors promoting it must be perceived by subordinates as the most significant others in that activity.

Diversity-related attitudes are learned mainly from people who have high or low prestige. In a typical experiment employees respond to questions pertaining to diversity in the workplace. Then they are told the answers given by 98 percent of the nation's leading CEOs, or the majority of their own reference group. Later they are retested. In most cases the retest scores move significantly in the direction of the CEOs or the reference group (Festinger, 1950). There are, of course, exceptions. Some employees will not shift their attitudes to match those of an admired person if the attitudes attributed to the latter are diametrically opposed to theirs.

The second part of the hypothesis is that people tend to adopt attitudes opposite of people whom they perceive as having low prestige or status. Such attitudes are likely to be held for one of two reasons: (1) certain people have low prestige because they are members of "inferior" groups or (2) certain people are members of the employee's in-group but they are considered "losers"—people not likely to rise in the hierarchy.

Once attitudes have been learned, they are reinforced. After they are formed, attitudes serve various motives such as economic or nationalistic ones. The economic motives that reinforce antidiversity attitudes are obvious. In the short run, it is economically advantageous for one group to keep another group out of certain kinds of jobs or out of an organization entirely. This is the age-old process of reducing the competition. The questions that economic interpretations of diversity-related attitudes fail to answer are "Why are repressive methods used against some minorities (e.g., Chinese) but not others (e.g., Japanese)?" and "Why are certain attitudes enforced even to the point of lowering productivity?" Some critics of diversity seem willing to discount or waste human resources even if this negatively affects survival of the organization.

How Attitudes Are Changed

There are several ways in which antidiversity attitudes are changed. Administrators who are aware of the following processes are better able to manage diversity.

Attitudes are seldom changed by logic. It is difficult to find circumstances in which antidiversity attitude change has come about as a result of logical argument or additional information (Siperstein, Bak & Gottlieb, 1977; Wilson & Alcorn, 1969). When employees who hold antidiversity attitudes are confronted by supervisors with logic or with new information, they usually do not change their beliefs. Instead, they tend to hide their attitudes and pretend to have been converted, particularly if their supervisors are monitoring the training. Prodiversity information alone is seldom enough. Therefore, not simply *what* is said but also *who* said it is an important variable influencing whether an argument or information will change attitudes.

There is also the general finding that prodiversity attitudes acquired by logical arguments are seldom acted out very logically (Hafner & Marcus, 1979). For example, male managers' attitudes toward female employees may be tolerant during diversity training but show very little carryover into the workforce. They give lip service to being equal opportunity employers but maintain dual standards for male and female subordinates—with the females having to be better qualified than their male peers to be appointed to certain positions.

Not only is there little evidence that important antidiversity attitudes are changed by logical-information inputs, but there is considerable evidence that a great amount of information, particularly on controversial topics, actually hardens or freezes antidiversity attitudes. Opponents of diversity look for other sources to support their beliefs, such as biblical passages or antidiversity research findings. Techniques such as an exceedingly emotional appeal or carefully crafted experiential exercises focusing on cultural diversity often are more effective than highly structured scientific lectures. What is true and what is personally desirable are not always the same. Most attitudes such as those supporting racism, sexism, and ageism are seldom initially formed by logic; nor are they frequently altered by logic. Recipients of new information have several options open to them.

1. They can fail to hear, see, or correctly interpret the new information.
2. They can receive the information accurately but deny its validity so as to keep intact the integrity of their existing beliefs.
3. They can shift their existing opinions to accommodate the new information in a way to adopt both prodiversity and antidiversity perspectives—a famous middle ground.
4. They can abandon their antidiversity beliefs and accept the diversity mandate.

Antidiversity attitudes are not always changed when training and work environments are desegregated (Beamer, 1992; Cox & Blake, 1991). Merely placing culturally diverse people together in training or job situations can sometimes be counterproductive. The participants may observe members of the out-group responding in stereotypical ways (e.g., women crying when frustrated; ethnic minorities behaving as inarticulate, ingratiating people; older workers falling asleep during lectures). Attitudes can be formed or changed by personal experience (1) if the attitudes are not in conflict with more powerful motives; (2) if the experiences are carefully selected to place the participants in peer, egalitarian relationships; and (3) if the attitudes to be changed involve perceptions that are so simple as to be obvious examples of empirical contradiction. That is, all participants are placed in a win-win situation in which there are no losers when the diversity initiative is completed.

Employee Resistance

There are two main approaches to diversity-related attitude change. Both approaches center on communication. The *formal attitude-change approach* is based on learning theories and assumes that people are rational, information-processing beings who can be motivated to listen to a message, hear its content, and incorporate the learnings when it is advantageous to do so. The means of change is formal, structured communication, and the reason for change is either actual or expected reward for embracing diversity. The *group dynamics approach,* based on Kurt Lewin's (1951) field theory orientation, assumes that employees are social beings who need culturally diverse co-workers in order to realistically adjust to environmental changes.

The amount of attitude change depends on employees' initial position regarding diversity, their attention to the message and to the communicator, their understanding of the message, and their acceptance of the message. Depending on the motivational bases for employees' antidiversity attitudes, acceptance of diversity will be positively affected by diversity activities that provide tangible pay-offs. It is seldom enough for CEOs to merely urge their subordinates to embrace diversity because it is "the right thing to do." Efforts to bring about attitudinal and behavioral changes can and often do result in strong resistance from employees. Alvin Zander (1950) outlined several reasons for this resistance:

1. *Resistance to diversity initiatives can be expected if the changes are not clear to the employees.* Most people want to know exactly what they must do. It is not enough for managers to say, "The change is necessary because of new laws (policies)" or "It's what we ought to do."

2. *Different people will see different meanings in the proposed changes.* There is a tendency for employees to see in the proposed changes the things they want to see. Minorities and women may see job opportunities, while white males may see "reverse discrimination" (Gross, 1978). Complete information can be distorted just as easily as incomplete information, especially if employees feel insecure.

3. *Resistance can be expected when employees in supervisory positions are caught between strong forces pushing them to make changes and strong opposing forces pulling them to maintain the status quo.* Administrative coups must be thwarted. CEOs must make the pay-off to implement diversity greater than the pay-off to oppose it. However, opponents must not be made to "lose face" during the change process.

4. *Resistance can be expected to increase to the degree that employees influenced by the changes have pressure put on them to change and it will decrease to the degree they are actually involved in planning the diversity initiatives.* It is true that employee behavior can be mandated, but it is also true that forcing people to embrace diversity leads to recalcitrant behaviors (e.g., sabotage, character assassinations, resignations). Decision-making should be shared.

5. *Resistance can be expected if the changes are made on personal grounds rather than impersonal requirements or sanctions.* After employees have had a chance to discuss the changes, if they still resist the program, then it is not prudent for the manager to plead, "I think you should implement the diversity plan." Who really cares what he or she thinks? A better approach is for the manager to say, "This plan is consistent with the company's diversity objectives." The changes should be grounded in organizational objectives and commitments.

6. *Resistance can be expected if the changes ignore the organization culture.* There are informal as well as formal norms within every organization. An effective change will neither ignore old customs nor abruptly create new ones. Timing is important. However, this does not mean that plans to implement diversity must drag on for months or years.

IMPLEMENTING DIVERSITY TRAINING

Before implementing a cultural diversity training program, Gemson (1991) recommended that employers consider the following questions:

- Is the CEO supportive of the initiative?
- How is the concern for diversity training perceived by the employees?

- What are the goals for the training? Are they realistic?
- Is the training targeted for all employees?
- Is the training mandatory or voluntary? Why?
- Is the trainer credible to your organization?
- Does the trainer have enough information about the work site?
- Will the training facilitate different learning styles?
- Will the training focus on issues familiar to your employees?

Michael Mobley and Tamara Payne (1992) cautioned that employee backlash to diversity training programs occurs when one or more of the following things happen:

- Trainees use their own psychological issues, that is, trust or affection needs, to divert the training.
- Trainers impose their own political agendas to support special interest groups (i.e., blacks or women or Hispanics).
- Timing is wrong—the training is too brief or too late or too reactive to specific incidents that occurred in the organization prior to the training.
- Trainers do not adequately distinguish among affirmative action, valuing diversity, and managing diversity.
- Training is used to provide remedial intervention instead of proactive strategies for change.
- Training supports some but not all diversity initiatives within the organization.
- Training forces people to divulge psychologically painful feelings but does not effect helpful closure.
- Trainers do not respect individual styles of learning.
- Training is too shallow or too deep.
- Resource materials are outdated.
- Trainers do not model the behaviors they encourage the trainees to adopt, that is, diversity trainer teams are not culturally diverse.
- Training does not engage each participant.

With the preceding information in mind, employers should carefully contract with outside consultants for diversity training or assign it to in-house diversity experts.

Diversity Training Activities

In order to establish a supportive learning environment, the trainer and trainees may elect to adopt norms similar to the following: (1) Everyone who is here belongs here as long as he or she does not try to hurt other people. (2) What is true for each person is determined by his or her life experiences. (3) The first purpose is to get in touch with our feelings about diversity. (4) The second purpose is to make contact with each other. (5) We will try to be as honest as possible and to express ourselves as we really are. (6) What we say in this training is confidential; no one will repeat anything said here outside the workshop. (7) Everyone in the group needs to take part in some way in group decisions.

The trainer should not get upset when the participants withdraw during group activities. Some people feel uncomfortable in group interactions and others will use any excuse for not cooperating. There are also instances when employees will be confused by an exercise and withdraw. Of course, some individuals may believe that an activity is not related to their needs. When this happens, the trainer should not become defensive. Instead, he or she should ask the withdrawing individuals to identify ways they might approach the task differently, that is, to act as observers and give the rest of the group feedback, or alter the task to accommodate their concerns.

Now for a discussion of specific training techniques and activities.

Lectures are best when they are short, less formal, and well organized and well delivered. Lecturers should remember that most trainee attention spans are short, and for this reason lectures should involve trainees through interest-catching illustrations, make provision for trainee involvement, and not attempt to present too much information in a short period of time. Several other factors affect the quality of the lecture, including room conditions, backgrounds of the employees, and the tone and voice of the speaker. When a lecture is meant to spark discussion, the lecturer should not cover the points he or she wishes the trainees to develop.

Generally the lecture method of teaching is most effective for clarifying issues, expanding knowledge beyond the trainees' available resources, sharing personal experiences, and giving instructions. The lecture method has the advantages of allowing the trainer to bring specific ideas into immediate focus and to draw on his or her own experiences. It facilitates covering a large amount of material with a large number of trainees, helps trainees develop listening skills, and can supplement assigned readings. Disadvantages of the lecture method include the fact that it tends to be a one-way process, with employees passively listening. Lectures also hinder the learning of individuals who are not effective listeners or note-takers, may be repetitious for some employees, may limit the pace of learning to the pace of the speaker, may evolve around the interest of the lecturer rather than the trainees, tend to cause trainees to accept the trainer as the final authority, and are inadequate for teaching diversity skills and attitudes. An effective lecturer:

• Gets the attention of the trainees from the beginning.
• Makes clear the purpose of the lecture.

- Follows a clear organizational pattern (e.g., tells trainees what will be told, tells them, and tells them what was told [repeats main ideas]).
- Clearly indicates the point of view from which the material is presented.
- Periodically checks to see if the trainees are understanding the presentation.
- Relates the lecture to previous learnings.
- When possible, uses multisensory aids to clarify important points.
- Uses helpful examples, including humor.
- Projects interest and knowledge of subject in a warm, friendly manner.
- Allows for audience feedback.

Discussions may begin spontaneously or be planned by the trainer. In either case, sufficient time should be allowed for discussions. It is also imperative for the trainer to be familiar with the subjects being discussed. Groups of more than fifteen should be divided into small subgroups in order to permit each trainee the opportunity to actively participate. Whenever possible, the participants should be seated so that they can see each other. Trainers should not become unnerved by silence during discussions. Initially, employees may be reluctant to speak their feelings. If the trainer is to be an effective discussion leader, several behaviors are worth learning. He or she:

- Encourages trainees to do most of the talking.
- Provides an opportunity for all trainees to speak, and tactfully discourages those who are dominating the conversation.
- Corrects misunderstandings and misinformation through the use of brief, concise comments.
- Keeps the discussants on the topic.
- Tries to prevent trainees from physically and verbally abusing each other.
- Ends the discussion while interest is still at a high peak.

Effective discussion groups have been proven to:

- Result in above average achievement on tests focusing on diversity issues.
- Foster positive attitudes toward cultural diversity.
- Reduce anxiety levels of employees undergoing diversity activities.
- Raise or maintain high levels of employee self-concepts.

Advantages of discussion groups are: employees can become actively involved in the process of learning; participants pool their individual information and gain broader insights; individuals learn to organize facts, ask insightful questions, think reflectively on relationships with and among their personal ideas and the ideas of other persons; and participants can test, alter, and improve their beliefs and values. Discussion groups have disadvantages also. The process can be frustrating if meetings end with questions but no agreement about solutions. Discussions can degenerate into attacks on personalities of group members. This intervention strategy requires discussion skills on the part of all participants. If the trainer or group facilitator does not maintain an open mind, the process is not likely to be democratic. Also, a few members of the group can dominate the discussion, causing the other members to be bored. Effective group discussions include the following trainer behaviors:

- Assures a common knowledge base and understanding of small group discussion.
- Does not judge trainee answers in terms of right or wrong.
- Enables trainees to reach some positive end or purpose, for example, alternative solutions or group consensus.
- Provides time for trainee feedback to the trainer.

Similar concerns are implicit in the other strategies that follow, but these will not be spelled out in as much detail as they have been for lectures and discussions. Above all else it is important for the trainer to:

- Know why a particular strategy is used.
- Know the advantages and disadvantages of the strategy.
- Provide ample instructions, material, and time for the activities.
- Relate the activity to a diversity purpose.
- Supervise carefully the trainees' activities.
- Assist trainees in evaluating the effectiveness of their efforts.

Brainstorming is an effective way of generating ideas. In order for brainstorming to succeed, an uninhibited atmosphere, spontaneity, and teamwork are required. There are four basic principles of brainstorming:

1. Criticism is not allowed (adverse judgment of ideas is withheld until all ideas are stated).
2. "Freewheeling" is encouraged (the wilder the idea, the better).
3. Quantity is wanted.
4. Combination and improvement of previous ideas are desirable.

After all the ideas have been recorded and categorized, the trainees evaluate them (using group-determined criteria), and unworkable ideas are discarded.

Panel discussions are widely used but often poorly done. The trainer should:

1. Select an appropriate or relevant topic so that each panelist will be able to make a contribution.

2. Select participants with different backgrounds or experiences so that the topic will be approached from many different perspectives.

3. Select a moderator (or do it her/himself) who is able to (a) introduce the topic, (b) keep panelists on the topic, (c) prevent monopolization by any single panel member, (d) keep track of the time, (e) end the discussion in time to summarize the discussion before the question and answer period, (f) accept questions from the audience and then direct them to the appropriate panelists, and (g) stop the question-answer period in time for the final summary.

Classroom demonstrations are useful only when the trainer makes sure that the trainees understand the procedure. This is best accomplished in a step-by-step breakdown of the activity. Thus there should be sufficient class time for the demonstration. The demonstration should be in an area that permits all trainees to see and hear the demonstrator. It is important that questions are solicited and answered. Where possible, bibliographies and other handouts should be used.

Work groups have the advantage of allowing, through a division of labor, the participants to investigate thoroughly an aspect of a subject and, by sharing their research, become familiar with the total subject. Each subgroup must be familiar with its purpose and the research steps to be taken. A team leader may be appointed by the trainer or one may emerge spontaneously. The trainer becomes a resource for the groups, checking their progress and clarifying areas of confusion. Group reports should be presented in different forms so as to minimize boredom during the show and tell period.

Buzz groups—small groups of three to six trainees—are formed for information discussion of issues, with the trainer being available if the groups need clarification of points. Buzz groups should not be used if the trainees are unfamiliar with the topic. Each group may, at the trainer's discretion, have a leader and a recorder. The best buzz groups are thoroughly briefed on the topic, either orally or in written assignments. Furthermore, buzz groups may all be assigned the same topic or they may be given different topics. When the groups have completed their task, they should be brought together again in a large group to share relevant points.

Problem analysis through on-the-spot reaction works best when participants feel free to share their feelings without the benefit of much time to collect their thoughts. By allowing themselves to be placed on the spot, the trainees are able to see a wide range of reactions and, ideally, alternative ways of viewing a situation. Answers that trigger negative reactions or laughter can serve as the basis for subsequent trainer lectures.

Role-playing should be done in friendly, supportive environments. Initial role-playing should not focus on situations that are personally threatening to the participants. In most instances, it is better to let the trainees volunteer for role-playing rather than to draft them. When possible, the trainer should give each player written instructions. In any case, instructions—written or oral—should clearly spell out who each individual is to portray and how he or she is supposed to feel at the outset of role-playing. Each player should be given a few minutes alone to get into the mood of his or her role. Once the role-play begins, it should be allowed to continue until it begins to drag. After the role-play, the trainer should lead a two-part discussion. Part 1 should focus only on the events surrounding the role-play. During Part 2 the trainees are encouraged to relate the role-play to their own lives.

Dramatization—acting without rehearsal or script—differs from role-play in that in the former activity, the outcome of the situation is determined in advance. In both dramatization and role-play, the participants must be at ease with each other and the trainer. In order for dramatizations to be effective, the trainer should:

1. Clearly delineate the situation to be portrayed and the outcome of the situation.
2. Allow reluctant trainees the option of not participating.
3. Give the actors a brief period to get themselves psychologically ready for their parts.
4. Stop the dramatization when the purpose of the activity has been realized or the trainees are hopelessly floundering.
5. Lead a discussion focusing on the effects of the dramatization.

Films are excellent for supplementing training presentations. They should be planned into the lesson, and all films should be previewed. The trainees should know the reason why the film is to be shown, and should evaluate the film for future use.

WHITE MALES, TOO

Frequently during the process of preparing employees for diversity, employers and diversity trainers are insensitive to the emotional needs and plight of white males. The foremost research studies focusing on diversity training have been conducted in counselor education programs (Hardiman, 1982; Helms, 1984; Ponterroto, 1988). Acknowledging a paucity of research describing psychosocial adjustment patterns of white male counselors, Haresh Sabnani and associates (1991) integrated several models of white racial consciousness to postulate six stages of adjustment white males typically go through during successful diversity training:

Stage 1: They realize that they do not have an adequate awareness of self as a racial being.

Stage 2: Their cultural awareness is heightened through interaction with members of other cultural groups.

Stage 3: They begin to seriously question their beliefs regarding diversity issues. This is a period of intrapersonal conflict.

Stage 4: They adopt a prominority stance.

Stage 5: Realizing they may have overreacted during Stage 4, many participants adopt a prowhite, antiminority stance.

Stage 6: They learn to be propeople, neither antiminority nor antiwhite.

It is important to note that many white males enter diversity already at Stage 6. They can be valuable facilitators during the training. When properly done, diversity training helps white males—and all other participants—gain better understanding of their cultural conditioning, including negative stereotypes of and prejudicial attitudes about minorities and women. In most instances, this leads to internal conflict between the desire to maintain the status quo and the need not to be perceived by their supervisors and co-workers as obstructionists.

The conflict is heightened when white males learn about the cultural heritage and contributions of minority groups and women. Denial, guilt, anger, and values ambiguity are typical responses during the middle passage to cultural literacy. It is common for guilt-stricken white trainees to become prominority. Fewer white males become profeminist, however. When the pendulum swings the other way, white males retreat to whiteness. For most of them this is a period of information and they will experience digestion and redefinition of self. In the best case scenario, white males undergoing diversity training learn to accept themselves and peoples of other cultures as co-workers of equal human worth.

Employers must not rely exclusively on training to prevent or abate all problems centering on diversity (Evans, 1992). When training is used as a "quick fix," the gains tend to be short-lived. To be optimally effective, training must be long-term and appropriate (Jones, 1989). The question all employers must answer is this: "What will you do if, after employees undergo diversity training, some of them are still behaving in discriminatory ways?"

RUSH TO CONFLICT

Mary Alice Bordo was told by Paul Smith, her supervisor, to revise the company's affirmative action plan and send it to Alex Sumpter, the CEO, who would hand deliver it to the regional EEO office. She pulled together a team of employees and they diligently revised the plan to incorporate current laws and court-approved procedures. After proof reading and correcting the plan, Mary Alice gave it to Alberto, a Hispanic administrative assistant in her office.

"Drop what you're doing and hand deliver this to Mr. Sumpter," she ordered Alberto.

"Can't it wait?" he asked. "I'm almost finished with the last assignment you gave me. Can't you get someone else to do it?"

Mary Alice frowned and stared at Alberto. He did not look at her. Here we go, again, she said to herself. I tell him what to do and he doesn't do it.

"I'm the boss in this office, Alberto, You can either do what I tell you or start looking for another job, *pachuco*," she snapped.

Glaring at Mary Alice, Alberto yelled, "What you need is a good man to teach you some manners. I'm a man, not a boy. You don't give me respect. If you were my woman, I would . . ."

"That's it! You're fired, you bean eater," Mary Alice screamed as she walked quickly out the office door.

What really happened between Mary Alice, a white female who worked very hard to succeed in the company and prove to the white males that she had what it took to be a supervisor, and Alberto, a tradition-oriented Mexican American whose cultural conditioning dictates that women defer to men? If you were Mary Alice's manager and she gave you Alberto's termination papers, what would do you do? How could diversity training possibly have prevented this situation?

HUMAN RELATIONS BEHAVIOR STYLE

This questionnaire is designed to measure your human relations style. There are no right or wrong answers. For the results to be meaningful, you must answer each question truthfully.

After each statement are three possible behaviors. Place a number "3" beside the behavior you would *most likely make,* a "2" beside the behavior you would *next likely make,* and a "1" beside the behavior you would *least likely make.*

1. When leading a team meeting, I would:
   ____(1) Keep focused on the agenda.
   ____(2) Focus on each team member's feelings and help each person express his or her emotional reactions to the issues.
   ____(3) Focus on the different positions team members take and how they deal with each other.

2. A major objective of an administrator is:

_____(4) To maintain a climate in which organization goals can be achieved.

_____(5) To promote the efficient operation of her or his job.

_____(6) To help subordinates better understand themselves.

3. When a strong disagreement occurs between me and a colleague for another ethnic group about work to be done, I would:

_____(7) Listen to the person and try to understand his or her point of view.

_____(8) Ask other people familiar with the work to mediate the dispute.

_____(9) Compliment my colleague for asking his or her question about the work.

4. In evaluating ethnic minority team members' job performance, I would:

_____(10) Involve all team members in setting goals and evaluating individual performances.

_____(11) Try to objectively assess each person's accomplishments by using standardized instruments.

_____(12) Allow each ethnic group person to determine her or his own goals and performance standards.

5. When two employees from different ethnic groups get into an argument, I would:

_____(13) Help them deal with their feelings as a conflict resolution strategy.

_____(14) Encourage other workers to help resolve the argument.

_____(15) Allow both persons to express their views but keep the focus on company regulations.

6. The best way to motivate women employees who are not doing their job properly is to:

_____(16) Point out to them the importance of the job and their responsibilities.

_____(17) Try to get to know them better so that I can motivate them.

_____(18) Show them how their low performance is adversely affecting themselves and their co-workers.

7. The most important element in judging my professional performance is:

_____(19) My technical skills and ability.

_____(20) How I get along with my colleagues and help them to get work done.

_____(21) Success in accomplishing goals that I set for myself.

8. In dealing with diversity issues, I:

___(22) Deal with such issues only when they disturb the organization's atmosphere.

___(23) Encourage all of my subordinates to understand the history and cultural conditioning of ethnic minorities and women.

___(24) Help each subordinate understand his or her own personal attitudes toward ethnic minority groups and women.

9. My foremost goal as a manager or supervisor is to:

___(25) Make sure that all of my subordinates have clear knowledge of their health plan.

___(26) Help employees work effectively in groups and use this relationship to achieve organization goals.

___(27) Help each employee become responsible for his or her own career development.

10. The difficulty with being an administrator is that:

___(28) It is hard for me to handle all the job-related details.

___(29) I do not have enough time to really get to know my subordinates as individuals.

___(30) It is hard for me to keep in touch with all of my subordinates.

SCORING INSTRUCTIONS

1. Transfer your answers to the scoring columns, placing a 1, 2, or 3 beside each question number.

A	B	C
(1)___	(2)___	(3)___
A	B	C
(4)___	(5)___	(6)___
A	B	C
(7)___	(8)___	(9)___
A	B	C
(10)___	(11)___	(12)___
A	B	C
(13)___	(14)___	(15)___
A	B	C
(16)___	(17)___	(18)___
A	B	C
(19)___	(20)___	(21)___

A	B	C
(22)____	(23)____	(24)____
A	B	C
(25)____	(26)____	(27)____
A	B	C
(28)____	(29)____	(30)____
Total____	Total____	Total____

2. Add up your totals for each column. The three totals combined should equal 60.

3. Mark your score for each column on the bar graph below.

A. Organizational

_____

_____

B. Individual

_____

_____

C. Group

_____

_____

0   5   10   15   20   25   30

See the Appendix for interpretation of your scores.

CHAPTER 8

Communication in Organizations

Communication is a process by which a person sends a message—verbal or nonverbal or behavioral stimuli—to someone with the conscious intent of evoking a response. In reality, "one cannot not communicate" (Watzlawick, Beavin & Jackson, 1967, p. 49). All human behavior is potentially a communication. The focus in this book is on behavior that is informative—any behavior, intentional or unintentional, interpreted by another person. Most of what is communicated is not interpreted as it was intended. Thus, *effective communication* is the process in which the receiver interprets the message in the same way intended by the sender. This is extremely difficult to do across cultures. An unknown author summarized the difficulty thusly: "I know you believe you understand what you think I said, but I am not sure you realize that what you heard is not what I meant!"

THE COMMUNICATION PROCESS

The overarching element of the manager-subordinate communication process is empathy. Subordinates are influenced to achieve organization goals when their supervisors project empathic credibility. Whether they come of their own free will or are coerced, most employees enter the diversity process with preconceived notions of what is interpersonally satisfying. Consequently, unless through communication managers and supervisors are able to establish rapport with subordinates, much of the diversity initiative will fail or will be inappropriately carried out. We cannot separate communication from culture. There have been numerous attempts to explain the importance of *intercultural communication, trans-*

cultural communication, and *interracial communication* (Gudykunst & Ting-Toomey, 1988; Heikal, 1980; Kim, 1984; Rich, 1974). Also important is *cross-national communication:* a subset of intercultural communication across societal boundaries between individuals who differ in ethnicity.

There are at least five barriers to accurate communication of organization initiatives (Barna, 1976). First, language differences impede accurate communication. Second, nonverbal communication is frequently less articulate and more emotional. Third, cultural stereotypes distort meanings. Fourth, most people tend to evaluate what others say and do as being either good or bad. Fifth, a high level of anxiety, which characterizes diversity-related interactions, tends to distort meanings. The most effective managers are skilled in intercultural communication (Arrendondo-Dowd & Gonsalves, 1980; Schroeder & Ibrahim, 1982; Sundberg, 1981). By the very nature of their jobs all managers and supervisors should be concerned with successfully managing diversity. However, this is a complex task that requires an understanding of human relations. Verbal and nonverbal communications are integral aspects of all organization behaviors.

Communication constitutes the basic process of human interaction. Most definitions of human communication include explicit or implicit references to a dynamic, irreversible process. Equally important, it is a symbolic process that allows employees to transcend their physical limitations. That is, through communication (symbolic interaction) they are able to recall their past diversity-related experiences, analyze their present situation, and predict their future. Without symbolization each employee would be trapped in his or her own skin, unable to communicate personal experiences to others.

Through communication, diversity problems can be described, solutions can be discovered, and plans can be devised. Usually the CEO must send the first message in a diversity initiative communication: "Help me. I can't solve these problems alone." Most administrators are reluctant to admit they need help. But only after telling that they are in need of help will their subordinates adopt the helper role. Edward Hall (1959) said that culture and communication are synonymous. Communication is imbued with culture. Language embodies culture and therefore cultural diversity lives in language.

VERBAL COMMUNICATION

People of similar cultures agree that certain sounds, grunts, and gibberings made with their tongues, teeth, throats, lungs, and lips systematically stand for specified things or conditions. All people utter sounds in hope that the person who receives them will be in common agreement about their meaning. Dean Barnlund (1989) summarized this process in eloquent terms: "These symbols, these fragile and arbitrary sounds, scratches and gestures, make it possible, vicariously, for one person to enter and glimpse the subjective world of another—and, on some occasions, to participate in the richness and subtlety of another's view of events" (p. 97). Indeed, words are what make us human; their value is transcendent. At the same time, words are full of human relations traps. Their meanings can be distorted and, when this occurs, an individual may experience physical pain and psychological misery beyond all reason. In extreme cases, distortion of words has cost employees productivity and, in some cases, their jobs.

The language of a culture describes and determines the identity of the individual worker (Giles & Edwards, 1983). The European languages, as an illustration, ascribe private identity to individuals. These languages have only one pronoun for the first and second person such as "I" and "Thou." In Japanese, there is no single word equivalent for "I" or "Thou." The Japanese first- and second-person pronouns are expressed differently, depending on the situation of the moment: whether one is speaking with a male or female; whether the other person is on a higher or lower social level; whether one is speaking in public or private; whether one is writing or speaking. Identity is public, based on a series of interrelationships. In Asian and African cultures the self is a collective or group identity. The self does not create but instead is created by social situations.

Language and Culture Are Inseparable

The relationship between language and culture forms the basis for the language paradigm of cross-cultural communication. Philip Harris and Robert Moran (1986) concluded that there is a consensus among scholars that culture and language are inseparable. Ruthellen Josselson (1992) said the learning of language is the first act of embeddedness in a culture:

How we speak, our form of communication, ever after denotes our connection to culture. In a large sense, our language expresses our embeddedness in one nation or another, our accent within that language identifies our social class or place of origin, and our choice of vocabulary links us to certain subgroups. We "speak" from our place within a society. (p. 180)

Thus, language is inherently cultural. L. E. Sarbaugh and Nobleza Asuncion-Lande (1983) defined language as "a culturally defined, rule-governed system of shared arbitrary symbols used to transmit [and elicit] meaning" (p. 242). Each of us learns and uses language as we do because of our individual and cultural backgrounds. According to Joyce Valdes (1986), the language learner must first be made aware of his or her status as a cultural being. The inseparability of language and culture may be demonstrated by modern views of language, which Anderson (1993) said are moving toward understanding it as the tool with which a culture creates its reality. As children learn the code (language) of their culture, they also learn its values, beliefs, perceptions, and norms. For example, the words "man" and "woman" illustrate this point. "Woman" is derived from "wif-man," defined as an annex to "man." The dominant role of males is inherent in this word.

Cultures devise symbols to label things around them. Important things are given specific names and less important things are given general names. Different cultures may have different meanings for the same symbol or word. Many words are culture-based and have no direct translation. Semantics become quite relevant when one tries to translate from one language to another. Many times, much of the meaning of words and phrases are lost in translation. " 'Out of sight, out of mind,' when translated into Russian [by computer], then back again into English, became 'invisible maniac' " (Peter, 1977, p. 100).

As another illustration, Anna Wierzbicka (1992) discussed the Polish verb *tesknic* in her study of cross-cultural emotions. *Tesknic* is hard to translate into English equivalents. One can come close by using the English words "homesick," "long," "miss," "pine," and "nostalgia." Therefore the word *tesknic* can mean all these terms. And one can also say, "But all these terms mean something different in English." Yes, this is true. English terms are more compartmentalized and broken down for exclusive use in certain situations. The Polish, however, use the word *tesknic* to mean all these terms and more. It is culturally determined how a word is used in a sentence.

Sometimes cultural orientation can render a direct translation into nonsensical results (Samovar, Porter & Jain, 1981). Values are inherent in the decoding of the message by members of different cultures (Bateson, 1966). Consequently, it is very difficult, if not impossible, to communicate across cultures without a conscious effort to find a common ground of experience and meaning in the codes.

Another related issue is the accuracy of language used by persons outside a culture to describe it. Consider how the word *African* is used. The reference group *Africans* is technically correct. Socially and culturally, however, the term is a nondescript generalization: Africa is a continent. A citizen of Nigeria who is a member of the Ibo tribe is not the same as a Kenyan, Egyptian, or South African—all who also may be classified as "Africans." In Swahili language there are three main racial-social groups: *Mafrika* (black Africans); *Mhindi* (Asians and Indians); and *Mzungu* (Europeans or all white persons). In Japanese there are two broad groups of people: *Nihon jin* (the Japanese) and *Gai jin* (Westerners or white foreigners); there are no specific words for other peoples.

The ability to communicate with other people requires words to have basically the same meanings. Symbols are arbitrary and sometimes can have several diverse meanings. For example, according to Larry Samovar and associates (1981), "linguists have estimated that the 500 most often used words in the English language can produce over 14,000 meanings" (p. 140). Every person decides what a symbol or word means based on his or her personal experiences and background, and people have similar meanings in language only to the extent they have similar experiences. Mary Kutch (1992) cautioned that our native language has a strong influence on the way we react to and deal with new experiences. The more dissimilar individuals or cultural experiences are, the more difficult mutual understanding will be among them.

The phenomenon of the process of intercultural communication relates to the interconnectedness of actions, events, states, and relations of the persons, objects, and abstractions associated with them (Asuncion-Lande, 1983). Consider the following example of the necessity of commonality of experience for mutual understanding: A young man from England tells his American female co-worker that he "will knock her up at noon." He is not making a sexual reference to getting her pregnant as American English would tend to indicate. Rather, he is specifying the hour at which he will meet her for a prearranged activity. Although both British and Americans speak English, they have different language usages and they frequently do not understand each other. The central point of the illustration is that language functions not simply as a device for reporting experiences, but it also is a way of defining experiences for its speakers. Meanings are not so much discovered in experience as imposed upon it. Consequently, each employee's experiences in culturally diverse situations will have a tremendous influence on the meanings of them communicated in language.

Commonality of experience aids in communication across cultural environments. Josselson (1992) concluded that the commonness of cultural experience or embeddedness is a component of mutuality. She wrote: "Embeddedness can also be a link to mutuality, as when we say, 'He speaks my language' " (p. 180). This expression means that people share enough similarity in their embeddedness to establish a groundwork for mutuality. However, embeddedness requires one to learn social conventions beyond language. This means that to effectively communicate across cultural boundaries, employees must find a way to share experiences that will enhance their understanding of the symbols used.

Argots as Barriers

During the course of sharing experiences or work, people talk and communicate their cultures to each other. Ideally, they will discover differences, ask questions, offer support, and share emotions and feelings. This is the crossroad of communication. In diversity workshops the participants make decisions about each other—about each other's culture. Sometimes these decisions breed dislike, fear, and distrust. Vocabulary, syntax, idioms, slang, and dialects cause difficulty. Employees struggling to understand co-workers who use a different language experience firsthand the difficulty in crossing cultural barriers. According to LaRay Barna (1976), the situation is exacerbated when an employee learning a new language clings to his or her own meaning of a word or phrase, regardless of the cultural connotation or context. The infinite variations of one word can make it extremely difficult to clearly communicate in a new language. In addition, native languages can impede communication by forcing people to think in certain ways (Farb, 1973).

Some language symbols are used specifically to make it difficult for outsiders to understand. This may help ethnic minorities survive. This notion is demonstrated by a subculture's use of a specialized linguistic code: *argot*. Argot is a special vocabulary and idiom of a particular social group or class. "Argots are more than specialized forms of language, they reflect a way of life. . . . They are keys to attitudes, to evaluations of men and society, to modes of thinking, to social organization and to technology" (Maurer, 1950, p. 269). Samovar et al. (1981) listed several needs that are met by the use of argots. First, they aid in the subculture's self-defense. "Because many subcultures function in a hostile environment, members of the subculture use argot as a device for communicating with each other in a manner that makes it difficult for outsiders to understand or detect the code" (p. 140). The use of Yiddish by Jews to communicate when Nazis were present during pogroms in Europe is a vivid example of a survival use of argot.

A second major function of argots is to assert a subculture's solidarity and cohesiveness by a unified communication code. This is illustrated in the world of the "tramp" and "hobo." These people were set apart from the main culture and yet they developed a type of in-group solidarity with its own argot: a "yap," for example, was a newcomer; a "tool" was a pickpocket; a "paper" was a railroad ticket; to be "oiled" was to be intoxicated; and to "lace" was to hit someone.

The third function of argots is to help a group establish itself as a real, viable social entity. This use is demonstrated by the "San Francisco drug language" developed by a group of individuals who met to use drugs. Argot helped them become more than just a disparate group of people. Some of their terms included "Bernice" for cocaine, "hay" for marijuana, "heat" for police, "pipe" for a large vein, "roach" for the butt of a marijuana cigarette, "octagon" for a square person, "lightning" for achieving a high, and "head" for a heavy drug use.

Argots can cause communication problems outside of a subculture when some of the terms become common in the dominant culture. The words that make up argots are constantly changing, and this makes many of them outmoded. Furthermore, there are regional argot differences. It takes very little imagination to see the difficulty of employees from one culture trying to communicate in their argot with employees of another culture (Sarbaugh & Asuncion-Lande, 1983).

Words are helpful, harmful, or neutral in their effect. To use an analogy, words are like a sharp ax—invaluable for cutting through barriers but also capable of injuring the people behind the barriers. For this reason, numerous writers have advised managers and supervisors that words and their meanings will to a great extent determine how successful or unsuccessful they will be in relating to their subordinates. On the one hand, the use of a jargon is often a major factor that subverts effective communication even when an attempt is made to manage diversity. On the other hand, the use of precise technical terms may be equally as confusing and alarming. The clerk who is told that she has a "translucent self," even when other terms are appended, may still come away with the idea that she has a terrible disease.

By now it should be clear that it is hard work to communicate with people from other cultures. Managers frequently are unaware that their subordinates verbally say one thing or "nothing" while their bodies communicate the opposite (Davis & Skupier, 1982). It is customary, for instance, for Asians to sense another person's feelings rather than for the person with the feelings to express them verbally (Marshall, 1979). There is ample research that notes that a considerable amount of communication is the outgrowth of nonverbal behavior and not words (Davis & Skupier, 1982; Kim, 1984; Mehrabian, 1972; Watzlawick, Beavin & Jackson, 1967; Wolfgang, 1985).

NONVERBAL COMMUNICATION

Only about 20 to 30 percent of what is communicated in conversation is verbal (Birdwhistell, 1970; Mehrabian & Wiener, 1967; Samovar, Porter & Jain, 1981). Even so, nonverbal communication should never be considered a total substitute for words unless the employee has a hearing impairment. Nonverbal communication is commonly called "body language." Technically, it is the science of kinesics (Hall, 1959). This science includes the study of reflexive and nonreflexive movements of a part or all of the body used by a person to communicate a message. People use several kinds of body language.

Gestures and Movement

There are approximately one hundred thousand discrete gestures that have meaning to peoples around the world. These gestures are produced by facial expressions, postures, movements of the arms, hands, fingers, feet, legs, and so forth. Gestures are essential in face-to-face communication because they accentuate words. It is now accepted in psychology that facial expressions of emotions are universal (Ekman & Friesen, 1986; Ekman et al., 1987). In a seminal study Ekman et al. (1987) found that agreement in judgment of facial expressions of emotions was very high among subjects in Estonia, Germany, Greece, Hong Kong, Italy, Japan, Scotland, Sumatra, Turkey, and the United States. But it is important to remember that although facial expressions of emotion are universal in evoked muscular displays for particular emotions, they are also culturally variable in terms of display rules. All people learn culturally acceptable rules for communication.

In the United States a common way to call a waiter or waitress is to point upward with a forefinger. In Asia this is how people call a dog or another animal. To get the attention of a waiter in Japan, one should extend the arm upward palm down, and flutter the fingers; in the Middle East clap your hands; and in Africa gently knock on the table. Americans hold a thumb up as a gesture meaning "okay"; in Japan it means money; in Ghana and Iran it is a vulgar gesture, equivalent to raising the middle finger in the United States. Nodding the head implies agreement in the United States, but a slight upward nod means "no" in Greece. In Brazil it is a sign of seduction when a man nods to a woman.

Different cultures teach their members to move their body trunks differently (Curt, 1980). Nordic Anglo and Asian cultures move their body trunks as if they were one unit. Conversely, non-Nordic cultures—particularly Latino and African cultures—move their trunks as if they were made up of several parts. These differences are especially noticeable in dance. Anglos tend to dance with rigid, methodical motions, while Latins and Africans tend to dance with more fluid, free-flowing movement. Neither culture is more rhythmical; they merely learn to express themselves differently.

Body movements may be the most expressive of the modes of nonverbal communication. Kenneth Johnson (1971) discussed meanings of elaborate systems of body movements in the African-American culture. For example, the way that some African Americans walk away from an authority figure after a reprimand can reveal their attitude about the situation. A displeased person walks differently than a pleased one. A member of another culture may not notice, but if the authority figure who just delivered the reprimand is an African American, he or she very well may instruct the displeased individual to come back and walk away "right."

White males learn to walk on the balls of the feet with quick strides. The message is competence and confidence. Young black males also learn a walk to communicate the same message, but it is accomplished through different motions. The walk is much slower with only one arm swinging (as opposed to both for the white male), and a slight limp may be effected. When white males meet to talk, boundaries usually remain fairly rigid. In comparison, the boundaries of a group of black males will usually be fluid and flexible. For example, a gesture of turning around with one's back to the group and walking a few steps away before turning back around and returning is sometimes used by African Americans to affirm agreement with a particular point. African Americans in an audience may lean forward in their seat to show interest or concern about what is being said and then shift to partially expose their backs to the speaker. This gesture conveys understanding and strong agreement. African-American females sometimes put their weight on a leg positioned to the back and place a hand on one hip to exhibit hostility or aggression.

Shaking the head left and right means "no" in most countries of the world. But among some Arabs and in parts of Bulgaria, Greece, Turkey, and Yugoslavia, a person says "no" by tossing the head to the side. In some traditional Chinese cultures, people sometimes widen their eyes to show anger, and scratch their ears and cheeks to express happiness. The Japanese show little nonverbal communication and their culture encourages little communication of information. In a study of interpersonal attraction (McGinley, Blau & Takai, 1984), Japanese students rated a young model most attractive when she smiled while exhibiting limb-inward or closed body positions. American students rated the same model most interpersonally attractive when she smiled while exhibiting limb-outward or open body positions. Other research indicates that astute observers can successfully detect lies of their ethnic group members by interpreting their body movements without hearing any spoken words. The same facile ability does not usually exist between cultures.

Manner of Speaking

The tone of an individual's voice and the placing of oral emphasis are closely related to gestures. Specifically, the manner of speaking includes the quality, volume, pitch, and duration of speech. Relatedly, how a message is delivered will favorably or unfavorably influence the recipients. There are mixed results in emotional speech. An emotional speaker is likely to be judged by Western standards as being assertive, self-assured, and tough-minded, while a calm, objective speaker is likely to be seen as more trustworthy, honest, and people-oriented (Pearce & Conklin, 1971; Scherer, London & Wolf, 1973). However, a manager's ability to correctly use his or her voice to communicate understanding is only half the communication problem. The subordinates must be able to decode the message (Hall, 1980).

Zones of Territory

Hall (1959) coined the word *proxemics* to describe human zones of spatial territory and how they are used. Zones of movement increase as intimacy decreases. That is, the more space available without other persons present, the more movement is likely to occur. Each culture has zones of appropriate distance. At near or far distances more attention is paid to the speaker's physical appearance, while at the intermediate distance more attention is paid to the content of the speech (Albert & Dobbs, 1970; Heslin & Patterson, 1982).

In informal gatherings, a distance of six to eighteen inches is considered too close for the average North American male, whereas this distance does not cause discomfort for the average North American female. In one study, middle-class whites stood farther apart during interpersonal interactions than lower-class African Americans or Puerto Ricans (Aiello & Jones, 1971). In another study, Mexican Americans stood closer together than Anglos or African Americans (Baxter, 1970). Among lower-class African Americans, Anglos, and Puerto Ricans, females of all ethnic groups stood closer together than males (Jones, 1971). When our zones of territory are invaded or we invade the territory of others, we communicate our discomfort or apologize for the intrusion.

The nature of most American business interactions requires managers and supervisors to invade the intimate zones of subordinates even when such an invasion is uncomfortable. Physical comfort zones vary from country to country, and the space allowed for interactions is also important. In informal gatherings, people of Anglo countries tend to require more territory than those of non-Anglo countries. South Americans stand much closer than North Americans. During a conversation between a North American and a South American, the rhetoric of nonverbal communication is attraction-repulsion. Arabs stand even closer than South Americans. Many Americans are literally pushed around the room by people from countries in which closer contact is acceptable.

Researchers have identified Latin Americans, Africans, Arabs, and Southern Europeans as "contact" cultures; and Asians, Pakistanis, East Indians, and Northern Europeans as "noncontact" cultures. In the former cultures, people face each other more directly; there is a progressive decline in the frequency of contact from Central America to South America. The most extreme differences exist between Colombians and Costa Ricans.

Eye Contact

Most North Americans are taught not to stare at other people (Kelley & True, 1980). Instead, they learn to acknowledge another person's presence through deliberate and polite inattention. That is, they look only long enough to make it clear that they see the other person and then look away. Through body language individuals conditioned to respond in this manner say, "I know you are here, but I will not intrude on your privacy or embarrass you with my stare." Managers are taught to stare at subordinates—

even if it embarrasses them. In most Third World countries, continuously looking at someone in the eyes is considered rude behavior. Good taste requires looking at someone only long enough to establish contact and then looking away.

In some Far East countries, it is impolite to look at the other person at all during conversation. And in England the polite listener stares attentively at the speaker and blinks occasionally to signal interest. In Israel it is common for an individual to stare at the other person from head to toe. The lack of eye contact, the blinking of eyes, and staring at the total body are all subject to misinterpretation by culturally uninformed or insensitive persons. Lack of eye contact may be incorrectly perceived as a lack of interest, blinking may be misinterpreted as a gesture of intimacy, and head-to-toe staring could be taken as a precursor to physical aggression.

Facial Expressions

Facial expressions may be the least culture-specific nonverbal method of communication. It is generally accepted that a smile means a person is happy or wants to appear happy. Biting the lip, yawning, and grimacing also have highly predictable meanings for most cultures. However, there are cultural restraints to facial expressions. In Japan, for example, it is considered disrespectful for an individual to betray his or her feelings of grief or pain. There is an elaborate code that requires an individual to deny any outward expression of anger, grief, or pain. He or she must display the opposite feeling through smiling. Only with training and practice can a genuine smile and the "mask" of the smile be differentiated by members of other cultures (Morbach, 1973).

Touching

The sense of touch conveys acceptance or rejection, warmth or coldness, positive or negative feelings (Barcorn & Dixon, 1984; Suiter & Goodyear, 1985; Willison & Masson, 1988). Little of the manager's contact with subordinates requires touching. But in some situations the touch of a supervisor can be helpful. Sensitive hands can be soothing to an employee, help relieve tension and fear, instill confidence and courage, and communicate understanding and a desire to help.

In terms of body movement, Hispanics touch each other more than Anglos or African Americans (Baxter, 1970). There is much more physical contact between members of the same sex in Asian, Arab, and Latin American countries than in North America. In Mexico men greet each other with an *abrazo* (embrace), and women frequently kiss. Touching—hugging, patting each other on the back—is an important way of communicating in Mexico. At least one study concluded that Hispanic fathers touch their sons more than Anglo and African American fathers touch their sons (Pollack & Menacker, 1971). From research studies we can extrapolate several recommendations for managers who have Third World culture subordinates: (1) Do not attempt to maintain eye contact with workers who consistently avoid it; forcing eye contact may be interpreted by the employee as a loss of respect or impropriety of the manager. (2) Chairs should be placed less than two feet apart between the manager and the subordinate. (3) Placing an arm on the shoulder of a male or shaking hands may increase discomfort.

As noted earlier, touching has many cultural meanings. It may communicate power and authority to another person. It may suggest the wish to become intimate with another person. Or it may imply that the toucher wants to get the other person's attention, support, or empathy. It may be a salutation or farewell. Therefore a touch can soothe, control, or give directions. In the workplace *it should never be used to harass another person*.

The determinants for appropriate touching often include location and timing. In North American culture it is acceptable for girls to hold hands, but not for boys. In Africa or the Middle East, however, it is an accepted sign of friendship for males to hold hands. Some degree of touching upon greeting is considered proper in most cultures. In Germany it is expected that people will shake hands at almost every meeting. In the United States handshaking is very common but not required. Males are taught that a firm handshake can command respect. American workers often joke about different types of handshakes: the pump, the grip, the limp palm, and the dead fish. African-American males often use a "slap" handshake or a "soul" handshake to affirm agreement on a particular subject (Johnson, 1971). Other variations would be the "high-five" and "low-five," both of which have been adopted by peoples of many cultural backgrounds.

Listening

Effective communication does not occur unless effective listening also occurs. Interviews on the job are designed to get and give information. It is during the interview that a manager's or supervisor's listening skills become crucial to problem solving. In order to conduct a good interview, they must familiarize themselves with the purposes of specific interviews and methods of conducting effective interviews, including things to look for during the interview.

Movement

Most managers and supervisors do not learn how to give verbal feedback and elicit employee conversation. Nor are they systematically taught to understand how various cultures use movement and the arts (music, dance, drama, and visual arts) in communication. Africans, Latin Europeans, and Latin Americans use movement and the arts as modes of communication. Kofi Gbekobu (1984) pointed out that to Africans the arts, similar to religious beliefs and practices, are part of the whole life. According to Curt Sachs (1937), art is the recreation of things heard and seen, and gives form and substance to intangible and irrational perceptions. But if they are to be helpful, managers must learn to fit how people move and say and do things into a total social and cultural context (Allan, 1987; Turner, 1969). Inability to do this will cause the manager to misinterpret a worker's movement, to attribute meaning that was not intended. This caution notwithstanding, it is true that African Americans in particular, more frequently than do nonblacks, perceive the environment and respond to it with movement (Hanna, 1984; Pasteur & Toldson, 1982).

CULTURAL IMPERATIVES

Individuals learn the norms and rules of interaction through the language socialization process. In this process, they learn culturally appropriate worldviews and beliefs which, in turn, validate their sense of cultural identity and lend credence to their role identities. In every culture, in most situations, there are special forms of words, or types of conversation, which are thought to be appropriate. Anglo Americans prefer directness; Third World peoples regard openness as a form of weakness or treachery, and they try to not allow the outside world to penetrate their thoughts. The direct verbal style embodies and invokes the speakers' true intentions in terms of their wants, needs, and desires in the discourse process. The indirect verbal style, in contrast, refers to verbal messages that camouflage and conceal the true intentions of the parties in terms of their needs and goals.

The episode structure of conversations can vary greatly between cultures. For example, Third World cultures have a period of chit-chat for several minutes before talking business. As noted earlier, cultural differences are not only reflected in verbal language but also in nonverbal language. For example, disagreement is communicated by a head-shake in Western countries, but by a head-toss in Greece and Southern Italy. Learned patterns of discussion also vary among cultures. Wilma Longstreet (1978) related an incident that illustrates this point. During a seminar comprised of black, white, and Asian students, a heated debate occurred. Suddenly, the black students were all talking at once; the white and Asian students had yielded the floor to them. Then the black students angrily demanded to know why the other students were not talking. Upon review it was evident the white students were more comfortable with the "you-take-a-turn-then-another-takes-a-turn" communication process; and the Asians were more comfortable with first thinking, or reflecting, before talking.

Deference to a high-status person also varies greatly among cultures. An equally important variable is age. Third World peoples defer more to older people than Anglo Americans.

Phil Downing . . . was involved in the setting up of a branch of his company that was merging with an existing Japanese counterpart. He seemed to get along very well with the executive colleagues assigned to work with him, one of whom had recently been elected chairman of the board when his grandfather retired. Over several weeks' discussion, they had generally laid out some working policies and agreed on strategies that would bring new directions needed for development. Several days later . . . the young chairman's grandfather happened to drop in. He began to comment on how the company had been formed and had been built up by traditional practices, talking about some of the policies the young executives had recently discarded. Phil expected the new chairman to explain some of the new innovative and developmental policies they had both agreed upon. However, the young man said nothing; instead, he just nodded and agreed with his grandfather. Phil was bewildered and frustrated . . . and he started to protest. The atmosphere in the room became immediately tense. . . . A week later the Japanese company withdrew from the negotiations. (Brislin et al., 1986, pp. 155–56)

The issue of "giving face," especially to people with high status, is important in collectivistic cultures. The young chairman of the Japanese company was giving his grandfather "face" by agreeing with him. This did not, however, negate any of the negotiations he had with Phil. Phil obviously did not understand this, and he violated the expectation of giving face. By protesting and disagreeing with the grandfather, Phil not only failed to give face to the grandfather; he also threatened the grandfather's "face."

Further, there is great variance between cultures regarding the use of silence. Euro-Americans tend to be very talkative. They usually become uncomfortable with silence. Native Americans, however, have a very different regard for the spoken word. Most Native American cultures believe that the sign of a great individual is not in his or her ability to talk, but in his or her ability to remain silent. Similarly, Japanese students learn that the most valuable aspects of life are acquired by experience, not by discussion. This is a lesson of Zen Buddhism that has had a large influence on the shaping of Asian cultures. A Zen proverb states, "He who knows does not speak and he who speaks does not know." Following this injunction of silence, Asians learn to listen not only to what is said but also to what is not said. Sometimes the most important part of a message is not spoken.

Christine Bennett (1990) succinctly captured the salient differences be-

Table 8.1
Contrasting Values, Beliefs, and Behaviors

	High Context	Low Context
Time	**Polychronic**	**Monochronic**
	Flexible schedules, parallel activities. Last minute plan changes are common. Time is less tangible.	Rigid schedules, singular, linear activities. Time is more tangible.
Space & Tempo	**High Sync**	**Low Sync**
	Move in harmony with others and with nature. Social rhythm is highly developed.	Harmony in movement and nature has low priority. Social rhythm is undeveloped.
Reasoning	**Comprehensive Logic**	**Linear Logic**
	Knowledge is gained through intuitions and contemplation. Feelings have precedence.	Knowledge is gained through analytic reasoning. Words have precedence.
Verbal Messages	**Restricted Codes**	**Elaborate Codes**
	Greater reliance on non-verbal and contextual cues. Overall emotional quality is more important than particular words.	Greater reliance on verbal communication. Little importance given to feelings.
Social Roles	**Tight Social Structure**	**Loose Social Structure**
	Behavior is predictable conforming to role expectations.	Behavior is unpredictable, frequently does not conform to role expectations.
Interpersonal Relations	**Group is Paramount**	**Individual is Paramount**
	Status distinctions are clear between insiders and outsiders. Human interactions are emotionally based, group oriented.	Status distinctions are subtle between insiders and outsiders. Human interactions are oriented to individuals.
Social Organization	**Personalized Law and Authority**	**Procedural Law and Authority**
	Oral agreements are binding. Friends make things happen. Authority figures are personally responsible for the actions of their subordinates.	Written procedures, laws, and policies are more important than oral agreements. Authority figures are responsible for their own survival.

tween *high-context* and *low-context* cultures. (See Table 8.1.) High-context peoples are collectivistic and low-context peoples are individualistic. The headings in the left margin of the table (Time, Space & Tempo, Reasoning, Verbal Messages, Social Roles, Interpersonal Relations, and Social Organization) are generic, English reference terms with which to categorize the two cultural contexts. Examples of high-context cultures are African, Asian, Hispanic, and American Indian. Examples of low-context cultures are Anglo-Saxon and Germanic.

Basically, there are six aspects of culture that determine how employees react to each other in the workplace: (1) the nature of reality and truth, (2) the nature of time, (3) the nature of space, (4) the nature of human nature, (5) the nature of human activity, and (6) the nature of human relationships (Schein, 1992).

The Nature of Reality and Truth

Every culture has a set of shared assumptions about the meaning of reality and how one determines what is real. Western-oriented cultures tend to define reality empirically by applying the concepts of science and rationality. Conversely, non-Western cultures, particularly Third World cultures, generally determine reality subjectively. From this latter perspective, there is no clear distinction between mind and body—spirits can determine human events. Third World peoples are high-context (Hall, 1976) and multiple causal in perceptions (Maruyama, 1974), whereas Western peoples are low-context and unidirectional in perceptions.

In high-context, multiple causal cultures social reality can be understood out of context: meanings may vary, categories may change, and causality is ambiguous. In low-context, undirectional cultures events cannot be understood out of context: meanings do not vary, categories do not change, and causality cannot be ambiguously established. Depending on their cultural beliefs, employees are either comfortable or uncomfortable with ambiguity and uncertainty. For example, a low-context manager is likely to have difficulty accepting as sincere the statement of a high-context Hispanic who believes that the quality of her work is deteriorating because a neighbor put a curse on her. Conversely, she will have difficulty accepting his admonishment: "Curses aren't real and they can't affect your work."

The Nature of Time

Cultural assumptions determine how time is defined, measured, and valued. Therefore it is cultural belief that determines whether an employee is "late," "early," or "on time"; whether someone has "wasted time" or has "enough time."

Time is a fundamental symbolic category that we use for talking about the orderliness of social life. In a modern organization, just as in an agrarian society, time appears to impose a structure of work days, calendars, careers, and life-cycles that we learn and live in as a part of our cultures. This temporal order has an "already made" character of naturalness to it, a model of "the way things are." (Dubinskas, 1988, p. 14)

Westerners, including North Americans, are *monochronic*—people who compartmentalize activities into appointments and do only one thing at a time. They are linear in thinking, sequential in behavior, clock-oriented, and work-oriented. Southern European, Middle East, Third World, and

Native American peoples are *polychronic*—they are not bound by a clock. They do many things at the same time, are circular in behavior and repetitive in speech, and time is not of essence. Polychronic employees driven by monochronic job requirements, as an illustration, often receive low performance ratings from monochronic supervisors. Relatedly, Native American, Mediterranean, African, Asian, and Carribean peoples have a preference for right hemisphere of the brain activities, while Anglo Americans and Western Europeans are left-hemisphere peoples (Trotter, 1979).

The Nature of Space

Space is an integral aspect of power and social relationships. It has both physical and social meanings. In the United States there are four kinds of "normal distance," within which there are "very near" and "very far" comfort zones (Hall, 1966).

Intimacy distance. People who are intimate with each other consider contact and touching as being very near. Six to eighteen inches is very far.

Personal distance. Most Anglo Americans consider eighteen to thirty inches near enough for personal conversations, even in crowded places. When this space is lessened, Anglo Americans back away so as not to be too close.

Social distance. Social distance allows an individual to talk to several people at once, as in a training session. Four to seven feet is near; seven to twelve feet is considered far.

Public distance. Banquets, keynote speeches, and similar activities occur within public distance. Twelve to twenty-five feet is near; beyond twenty-five feet is far. Anglo Americans tend to prefer greater distances for personal and social interactions than Third World peoples.

The Nature of Human Nature

The relationship between nature and humans of Western cultures is radically different from that of most Third World cultures. Third World cultures perceive humans as a part of nature. For example, traditional Asians and Africans believe that people and nature must be in total harmony because they are eternally inseparable. Thus, people must adapt themselves to their natural surroundings. Western cultures see humans as subjects whose object is nature and therefore humans can and must utilize and dominate the environment. The Euro-American mode of living is characterized by confrontation with and exploitation of the external world. Consequently, Euro-Americans are frequently at war with nature. The conquest of the physical world is the dominant goal of Western peoples, particularly those in business and industry. John Condon (1985) described the American relationship with nature as a "master-slave relationship . . .

with man the master of nature" (p. 103). This formidable and sometimes reckless drive to control the physical world is diametrically opposed to the adaptive attitude of Third World peoples (Stewart, 1971).

The Nature of Human Activity

Basic to human functioning are assumptions about appropriate ways for people to act in relation to their environment. Depending on their culture, most employees can be classified as having a *doing* orientation or a *being* orientation (Kluckholm & Strodtbeck, 1961). As a whole, American workers are doers—they are taught to "get things done," "do something about it," and "not be outdone." Africans, Arabs, Hispanics, and Native American workers are more fatalistic—things will get done if God wills it. Thus, they focus more on being content with their place in the workplace. Asians and American Indians tend to seek harmony with their environment by developing their unique capabilities to be in perfect union with it.

The Nature of Human Relationships

In individualistic cultures people are taught to take care of themselves and their immediate family; in collectivistic cultures people belong to in-groups or collectivities that look after them in exchange for loyalty (Hofstede & Bond, 1986). On the one hand, collectivistic cultures are characterized by interpersonal ties that permanently unite human beings in family and clan. The individual is conditioned to interdependence. On the other hand, individualistic cultures are characterized by temporary ties among closely related people. Having no permanent base in family and clan, each individual's orientation toward life and environment is self-reliance. That is to say, individuals are conditioned to think for themselves, to make their own decisions, and to carve out their own future by their own initiative.

The "we" identity has precedence in collectivistic cultures over the "I" identity, which takes precedence in individualistic cultures. Individualistic cultures promote "self-realization" for their members, while collectivistic cultures, in contrast, require that individuals fit into the group. Employees from individualistic cultures form specific friendships, whereas those from collectivistic cultures form friendships that are predetermined by stable relationships formed early in life. Donald Cushman and Sarah King (1986) illustrated the differences in friendships in individualistic and collectivistic cultures when they described friendship patterns in the United States and Japan:

Japanese follow two types of friendship formation sequences: *tsukiai*, or interpersonal relationships cultivated and maintained as a result of social obligation; and personal friends or class relationships that develop from mutual liking, attraction, interests or common values. Interpersonal relationships based on mutual liking, attraction, interests, values, or personal friends are usually among same sex school-mates and usually last a lifetime. The number of close friends one has is small, but those friends serve the important function of allowing one to talk freely about a broad range of mutual interest while being at ease. . . . [North] Americans follow a single type of friendship formation sequence, when a [North] American meets another who has as part of his/her real self-concept some attribute that is admired, then one attempts to initiate a friend relationship. Such a relationship appears to have three underlying dimensions: trust, self-concept support and helping behavior. Trust refers to a relationship based on authenticity; self-concept support refers to a relationship based upon respect for one's social and psychological identity; helping behavior refers to a relationship based on reciprocal assistance in time of need. (p. 48)

COMMUNICATION ACROSS CULTURES

Managers and supervisors can effectively communicate with culturally diverse employees, according to George Simons (1989), by trying to under-stand each individual, his or her personality, his or her cultural back-ground, and the workplace situation. Jawaharlal Nehru (1950) provided the following advice for achieving such understanding:

If we seek to understand a people, we have to try to put ourselves, as far as we can, in that particular historical and cultural background. . . . It is not easy for a person of one country to enter into the background of another country. So there is great irritation, because one fact that seems obvious to us is not immediately accepted by the other party or doesn't seem obvious to him at all. . . . But that extreme irritation will go when we think . . . that he is just differently conditioned and simply can't get out of that condition. . . . One has to recognize that whatever the future may hold, countries and peoples differ in their approach and their ways, in their approach to life and their ways of living and thinking. In order to under-stand them we have to understand their way of life and approach. If we wish to convince them, we have to use their language as far as we can, not language in the narrow sense of the word, but the language of the mind. That is one necessity. Something that goes even much further than that is not the appeal to logic and reason, but some kind of emotional awareness of the other people. (pp. 48–49)

There are likely to be problems that grow out of diversity initiatives. The following proven, basic ground rules can be a solid foundation upon which CEOs can build diversity programs: (1) Do not avoid the issue of diversity. In most organizations it is a puzzle that must be solved. And, like any puzzle, it can be solved only if all the pieces are in place. (2) Know what all employees under your supervision bring with them to the diversity table that can help nourish their co-workers and the organization. (3) Model diversity by being actively involved in diversity activities. (4) Do not tolerate the pernicious isms—racism, sexism, ageism, handicappism.

Jeffrey Goldstein and Marjorie Leopold (1990) elaborated on those suggestions. Managers and supervisors must also be aware of their silent mind. Numerous writers have described how our "silent mind" works—how we talk to ourselves about ourselves and other people. Actually, this is a subconscious level of awareness that triggers automatic or habitual feelings and behaviors. As an illustration, a manager who avoids telling an African-American employee that she is doing a poor job in certain tasks may be engaging in silent mind talk such as: "She is incompetent but she is also a physically menacing person. I won't talk to her or even look at her." In yet another example, Paul, a personnel officer, has just hired a Puerto Rican female for a job she is not qualified to do. During the interview, he disregarded her job application and listened to his silent mind: "Wow, this is a physically attractive woman. I would really like to know her better. Those dark brown eyes, full lips, and curvaceous body will look good in the sales department." It is imperative that a manager's silent mind focuses on culturally appropriate behaviors.

The door to diversity must swing both ways: majority-group and minority-group employees must learn to co-exist in organization climates foreign to them. All employees must learn written and unwritten rules of diversity. Succinctly, they must *understand the role of each player in the cultural diversity drama*. It usually is what the role of the protected class person is to be: He or she is the individual to be helped. However, in contrast to the role of the culturally different employee, the roles of majority-group employees are not always as clear. Questions that they often ask in their silent mind are "What is expected of me?" "What are my limits?" In other words, "Where do the minority employees' roles end and my role begin?" Actually, these are questions protected class people ask too. Once all employees have answers to these questions, they can effectively interact with each other. Without answers nobody will know what to expect in the diversity initiative and probably everybody will refuse to commit themselves to it.

Listen to what others say. Although total silence is not recommended in the interaction with an employee, neither is nonstop talking. Talking is one way of relieving anxiety, but excessive talking creates anxiety in the person to whom one is speaking. Effective listening requires paying careful attention to not only the spoken words but also the speaker's body language. Managers and supervisors can obtain a great deal of information by observing employees' facial expressions and body movement. They should also pay attention to how an employee talks (i.e., inflections and pauses).

Organize your thoughts and make sense of the many perceptions that may be running through the subordinates' minds. Some of these thoughts may be "I am uncomfortable with this diversity stuff." "She is asking me to do something I am afraid to do." "That is not what I want to do."

"What will my friends think of this?" "I am embarrassed talking about this." "Will my co-workers accept me?" It is imperative that managers learn to sort out and deal with the disquieting feelings of the moment and carefully discuss them with subordinates. It is not uncommon for people under stress to jump from one subject to another. Therefore, it is helpful for employees to be encouraged to state their feelings and to make their points clearly, serially, and coherently.

Wait for reaction once something has been presented to employees. This is more effective than skipping from one concern to another. Waiting for a reaction means more than listening to the words. It also means, where possible, observing the other person's body reaction.

Keep an open mind. This is more than being receptive to subordinates' ideas. It is being willing to question one's own values and perceptions. Just because a manager is a professional does not mean that he or she automatically knows what is best for achieving diversity.

Make sure of the communication. Once an agreement has been made regarding the subject under discussion, every attempt should be made to ensure that the subordinates' understanding and the manager's understanding are the same. The best helping strategies will crumble if all parties are not operating from the same reference points.

Avoiding Diversity Mine Fields

Managers must move quickly but carefully to their diversity objectives. Much of what must be traversed is uncharted and full of potentially explosive situations that can emotionally and economically destroy employees. Therefore the following suggestions may prevent such disasters. Many managers unknowingly use inappropriate names for individuals and groups. That is, they do not think about the connotations of the words they use to describe culturally different people. A general rule of thumb is to:

• Pronounce employees' names correctly. When in doubt, ask them for the correct pronunciation.

• Use proper titles of respect: "Mr.," "Mrs.," "Doctor."

• Call employees by their proper name; avoid slang such as "girl," "boy," "honey," "dear," "guy," "ace," "fella," "babe," "stud," "chief," "mama," "sweetheart." When in doubt, ask people if they are offended by the slang.

Anything that demeans or degrades another person is inappropriate. In fact, it demeans and degrades both the offender and the offended person. Us-them dichotomies delude people into believing us/we are right, good, deserving but them/they are wrong, bad, undeserving.

COMFORT ZONE QUESTIONS

The following questions will help you conceptualize how you react to culturally different people in a job-related situation.

1. What type of culturally different workers are you uncomfortable around or disturbed by in some way?

_____

_____

2. When dealing with those workers, what conflict situations do you encounter?

_____

_____

3. When in social activities attended by ethnic minorities how do you interact with them? What is your comfortable social distance when interacting with them?

_____

_____

4. What physical characteristics do you find attractive and unattractive in culturally different peoples?

_____

_____

IRRITATING COMMUNICATION HABITS

Below are listed fifty communication habits that are distinctly irritating to many people during conversations. Some of these habits are unconscious, some purposeful, some trivial, some important, some remediable, some deeply rooted in the personality of the person. (1) Place an X before the habits listed that irritate you when they are practiced by others. (2) Place an I before the habits which characterize your behavior. Some statements may elicit both marks.

_____ 1. He doesn't give me a chance to talk. I never get a chance to tell my problems.

_____ 2. She interrupts me when I talk.

_____ 3. He never looks at me when I talk. I don't know whether he's listening or not.

_____ 4. She makes me feel that I'm wasting her time. She doodles or draws pictures all the time.

_____ 5. He continually fidgets with a pencil, a paper, or something, looking at it and examining it as if studying it rather than listening to me.

_____ 6. She paces back and forth as if impatient with the way I am telling my story.

_____ 7. He has such a poker face and manner that I never know whether he's listening or whether he understands me.

_____ 8. She treats me like a child, ignoring me while taking several incoming phone calls.

_____ 9. He never smiles; I'm afraid to talk to him.

_____10. She asks questions as if she doubted everything I say.

_____11. He always gets me off the subject with his questions and comments.

_____12. Whenever I make a suggestion, she throws cold water on it. I've quit making suggestions.

_____13. He always tries to get ahead of me by prestating my point or prefinishing my sentence.

_____14. She rephrases what I say in such a way that she puts words into my mouth that I didn't mean.

_____15. He talks me around into a corner and makes me feel like a fool.

_____16. She frequently answers a question with another question, and usually it's one I can't answer. It embarrasses me.

_____17. Occasionally he asks a question about what I have just told him that shows he wasn't listening. For example, just after I finish telling him about a problem he might then ask, "Let's see, what was it you wanted to talk to me about?"

_____18. She always takes notes when I am talking. I get so worried about what she is writing, and so worried about how I am saying things that I forget what I was saying.

_____19. He argues with everything I say—even before I have a chance to state my case.

_____20. Everything I say reminds her of an experience she has had or an event that she has heard about recently. I get frustrated when she continually interrupts to say, "That reminds me. . . ."

_____21. He sits there picking hangnails or clipping fingernails or cleaning his nails or cleaning his glasses, etc. I know he can't do that and listen too.

_____22. He rummages through the papers on his desk or through his desk drawers instead of listening.

_____23. She twitches and turns constantly, just waiting for me to stop so that she can take over.

_____24. When I have a good idea, he says, "Oh, yes, I've been thinking about that for some time."

_____25. Whenever I talk to him, he swings around and looks out the window.

_____26. She smiles all the time, even when I am telling her about a serious problem of mine.

_____27. She stares at me as if trying to outstare me.

_____28. He looks at me as if appraising me. I begin to wonder if I have a smudge on my face, or tear in my coat, etc.

_____29. He looks me in the eye too much—unnaturally long at times. It's just not normal.

_____30. She overdoes trying to show me she's following what I'm saying—too many nods of her head, or "Mm-hm's," and "Uh-huh's."

_____31. He inserts humorous remarks when I am trying to be serious.

_____32. After apparently listening, she may say, "It looks to me as though your problem is . . . ," and what she suggests usually isn't my problem at all.

_____33. She has bad breath and sits too close to me. It gets nauseating.

_____34. He blows smoke in my face. It almost makes me dizzy at times.

_____35. She asks personal questions when other people are in the same office or room with us.

_____36. He frequently looks at his watch or the clock while I am talking.

_____37. She closes her eyes, rests her head on her hand, as if resting.

_____38. He doesn't put down what he is doing when I am in his office and turn his attention to me completely.

_____39. She doesn't seem to take personal interest in me. She is completely withdrawn and distant.

_____40. He always makes some remark that indicates that he is doing me a favor in seeing me.

_____41. She acts as if I should know how to solve the problem and not bother her.

_____42. He is always rushed for time and makes comments about his "busy day." He won't sit still.

_____43. He walks away when I am talking and often stands with his back to me.

_____44. He passes the buck on diversity-related problems. "We'll have to think about it," he'll say.

_____45. He says he has to go to another meeting, but only after we talk a while.

_____46. He acts as if he knows it all, frequently citing incidents in which he was the hero.

_____47. She says something and then denies it at the next meeting we have.

_____48. She tries to avoid seeing me—as if she doesn't want to talk to me about any problems.

_____49. If several people are in the room, she looks at someone other than the person who is talking.

_____50. He asks questions that demand agreement with him. For example, he makes a statement and then says, "Don't you think so?" or "Don't you agree?"

CHAPTER 9

Words That Hurt

No one can deny that Americans are changing their environment with fantastic rapidity. The implications of these changes defy even the best scholars. Only one thing seems certain: Wherever we are going, we are going with great speed. In the past century the speed of communication has increased by a factor of 10^7, the speed of travel by 10^2, the speed of data handling by 10^6, energy resources by 10^3, power of weapons by 10^6, and the ability to control diseases by 10^2. We are a nation of mobicentric people. Our lives are centered on motion—arriving, doing, and becoming. One out of every five Americans changes his or her residence every year. The implication is clear: To adjust to this new form of existence, people have to learn to develop relationships quickly. Along with mobility comes the challenge to find a few people with whom we can be intimate (Jennings, 1970).

NEW PARADIGMS

There are four basic sources in our society for change: technology, diffusion, structural developments, and the relationship of the United States to the rest of the world. The basic technological changes are likely to grow out of new biomedical engineering, the computer, and better utilization of human resources. Diffusion of goods and privileges in society can do much to equalize health, education, and welfare opportunities for all people. Structural developments—especially in politics, education, and industry—have already moved us into a postindustrial society. The newness of scientific breakthroughs is seen in the following statistics:

1. Approximately 90 percent of all scientific achievements have been made in the twentieth century.
2. The gross national product of goods and services in the technologically advanced nations of the world is increasing.
3. Until the nineteenth century, the speed of transportation never exceeded twenty miles per hour. Today rockets carry astronauts at more than twenty thousand miles per hour, and the speed of some airplanes exceeds the speed of sound.
4. The number of scientific journals and articles is doubling every fifteen years, with a current output in excess of 20 million pages per year.

New Relationships

In their book *The Year 2000,* Herman Kahn and Anthony Wiener (1967) identified what they called "the basic long-term manifold trend." They warned that, as humans gain technological power over the world and become more affluent, alienation—cynicism, emotional distance, and hostility—rather than contentment will characterize our lives. The most important contribution of "people" is that they attempt to bring some order into the chaos of predictions about the future. The major flaw in such studies is that they plan in such detail that they close future options. They leave nothing for future generations to control. It seems wiser to allow for realistic options that can be exercised by future generations.

Moving further into the future is not likely to be without negative consequences. However, these consequences need not be as negative as some people imagine. The world is becoming a global culture, but this fact alone is neither good nor bad. By providing an extended range of common experiences through the facility of transmission-shared symbols and attitudes, the societies of the world are becoming more similar in norms and behavior. It seems unlikely, however, that a single political ideology will prevail. As cultural boundaries blur between nations and within nations, the need for greater cross-cultural understanding increases. New paradigms are being developed in business and industry to convey relationships between individuals of differing cultures that did not exist prior to the twentieth century.

Paradigm is a pattern or model (Harman, 1988). In *Organization Transformation: A New Paradigm* Beverly Fletcher (1990) defined paradigm as a functional way of viewing the world, a conceptual framework or guide for making sense of things, and a way to define truth and reality. Examination of the elements that pertain to multiculturalism within the workplace can offer useful knowledge of processes that must take place for organizations to survive and better function in an emerging global economy (Gundykunst & Ting-Toomey, 1988). Some paradigms are difficult to change; others shift almost immediately. About thirty years ago the phrase "Made in Japan" connoted something inferior—cheaply constructed, disposable, small, low-tech. Today the phrase means quality—well-constructed, permanent, various sizes, high-tech.

With the development of paradigms encompassing the broad field of cross-cultural communication, differences and similarities among cultural groups emerge. The fact that almost every employee in American organizations is faced with communication situations encompassed by intercultural or intracultural paradigms highlights the need for more research in this area. Most businesses and industries recognize the need for expanding language skills beyond the native tongue. As this need is met, paradigm shifts are inevitable. The acquisition of language skills, however, is only the first step in communicating effectively with peoples of other cultures. In retrospect, it appears that even when the native tongue is the same, if employees are from different ethnic or geographical backgrounds, the potential for miscommunication is still great. Axioms, slang, regional accents and jargon, ethnic prejudices, and culturally unique patterns of nonverbal communication all contribute to problems in achieving cross-cultural communication. The following facts about paradigms are important:

• Paradigms are never complete and never identical.
• Paradigms can be wrong.
• Paradigms can limit behavior.
• Paradigms of self come from the "social mirror"—the reflection of significant other people's responses to us.
• When paradigms change, related behaviors and attitudes usually change too.

As transportation and communication get faster, the planet seems to shrink, merging cultures and throwing peoples from varying cultures together. This blending makes it necessary to find ways to coexist and to eventually develop interdependent relationships. Communication is the basis for the development of such relationships, and verbal communication elicits the most immediate understandable response from other people. Thus verbal communication is of utmost importance because it is an avenue to human encounters and a means to learn the unknown values of another culture (Brislin, 1981).

When Cultures Clash

English has become the international business language (Kameda, 1992). This occurrence has many benefits for Americans but it presents problems for the peoples of other cultures. The fact that some people can speak the English language does not mean that they are fluent in *American* English. As linguists point out, English is one of the most difficult languages for people in other countries to learn because there are so many forms of like-sounding words. Different American accents are confusing enough for novices without them having to sort out the various meanings of colloquial "sayings" that are indigenous to a particular geographical location. Consider the sayings "Cool," "Right on," and "Righteous." Most people learning to speak English would think they are being told, respectively: (1) the temperature, (2) that they should keep going straight ahead (right on) in a direction, and (3) that they have encountered a religious person.

Learning when to interpret and think metaphorically and when to follow the literal translation can be difficult even for people whose native language is English. These are encounters of a cultural kind not replicated in any other part of the globe. Consequently, it is easy to imagine how difficult it is to conduct conversations free of misinterpretations across cultures. All too often when Americans encounter someone for whom English is a second language, they focus too much on the foreigner's mispronunciations and misuses of English without giving the outsider guidance to become more proficient in English. Interestingly, peoples of other countries as a whole do a better job learning English than Americans do learning foreign languages.

Barriers to Paradigm Shifts

The information "niches of the mind" are universal to all cultures but the way that they are organized differs by culture or subculture (Stewart & Bennett, 1991). And culturally bound experiences, values, and beliefs slant abstract thoughts and change the meanings of specific words or phrases of a particular language. This is also true of corporate cultures, which have become a topic of great interest in the past decade. Business executives realize that a strong corporate culture coupled with effective business strategies can be powerful tools for organization success. The concept of corporate culture involves the basic assumptions, values, norms, and language that guide employees' behaviors within a company. It is a product of long-term social learning and reflects what has worked in the past. For this reason corporate culture is not an easy thing to change.

If new business strategies need to be implemented, cultural road-blocks often arise if the employees believe the company's current culture is incompatible with the new strategies. On a broader scale, corporate culture affects an organization's national excellence as well as its global business strategies. Comparisons of American and Japanese management styles reveal that much of the success of Japanese companies can be explained by their strong corporate cultures emphasizing employee participation, open communication, security, and equality (Cummings & Huse, 1989). They utilize a high-context style of relating and communicating. There is growing evidence that North American companies are becoming more successful by emulating selective Japanese companies and developing internal corporate cultures that emphasize human values and life-long human resources development. This often requires paradigm changes.

The meanings of the word *deep* illustrate how spoken language can change things about an entire corporate culture. For example, the abstract meanings of the word "deep" in American English, Chinese, and Japanese languages vary greatly. Most Western philosophies of life were taken from the Greeks, including the old American proverb, "Still waters run deep," which refers to a quiet, thoughtful person. The use of the word *deep* to refer to wise leaders with a broad knowledge base was first used by ancient Greek philosophers (Snell, 1953). In China and Japan a wise leader is "great" or "valuable." This metaphor is very prevalent throughout East Asian cultures. Asians use horizontal terms to describe size, rank, and multiplicity, and they do not use the term "deep" as it is used in Western cultures. In this paradigm East Asians concentrate more on external roles and relationships than on the depth of thought itself. This tendency to think on a horizontal plane is an extension of a sense of community. Ergo, East Asian language facilitates the larger social body rather than focusing on the psychology of individuals (Stewart & Bennett, 1991). Western corporate cultures tend to be the opposite; they conceptualize individuals on vertical planes.

A study was recently conducted on the marital satisfaction between Australian and German couples with nationality being the manipulated variable (Halford, Hahlweg & Dunne, 1990). The researchers observed Australian couples who reported that they were happily married and compared their perceptions to Australian couples who were "troubled." They then repeated this process for German couples. The researchers were looking for conflict differences across cultures. One finding proved especially interesting and pertinent to studies of cross-cultural verbal communication. The "happy German couples" experienced about the same number of verbal coercive escalations as the "unhappy Australians." The researchers hypothesized that a marriage between an Australian and a German might be fraught with the potential for conflict and misinterpretation. Cross-cultural business interactions often encounter similar differences in communication styles among employees.

RACIST LANGUAGE

Verbal misunderstandings are frequently the beginning of problems between culturally different employees. Most employees fear things and people who are different and they often verbally strike out or physically lash out in an aggressive manner to protect themselves. This is actually a defensive mechanism designed to protect boundaries. Aggressive discourse occurs as dominant-group members verbalize negative feelings toward minority-group members, and vice versa. Compared with other forms of discrimination, verbal attacks appear to be less harmful. However, though they differ from physical violence, the consequences of hateful words are no less painful (Donaldson et al., 1988; Maggio, 1988; Petrini, 1993). For example, if CEOs used epithets to describe blacks it would be "only" words, but the effect of the words would be very real and extremely negative in emotional consequences. Ultimately, the words would probably trigger behavior consistent with the epithets. If a manager chooses not to hire a minority applicant, the decision and motivation are expressed in words, but the result, unemployment for the job applicant, is concrete evidence that the verbalization did not end in words.

If newspapers and broadcast medias present stories biased against minorities, the results are more than simply "bad reporting" (Donaldson, Geneva & Van Dyk, 1988). The stories may, for example, influence legislative decisions to cut social programs or a city's decision to increase police surveillance in minority neighborhoods. The stories also may perpetuate prejudices that form the basis for discriminatory acts, such as decisions not to hire minorities, not to allow them equal access to housing, and to treat minority workers with disrespect solely because they belong to an out-group. Indeed, although the texts and talk of such stories may seem harmless, they usually have very real and very harmful consequences.

The links between language and discourse on the one hand and discrimination and racism or sexism on the other hand are complex and varied. A dominant group has many ways to exert, consolidate, and legitimize its power and thus maintain control. Control over language and discourse in the workplace is vital for either maintaining or reducing cultural oppression. This is borne out in newsletters, memorandums, corporate meetings, job interviews, news announcements, and other forms of communication. Words are not without social consequences.

Symbolic Racism

Even more pervasive than overt racism, symbolic racism allows for subtlety, indirectness, and implication (Donaldson, Geneva & Van Dyk, 1988). Whereas slurs, epithets, graffiti, or even old movies may be clearly racist in their tone, most of today's racism is more sophisticated, less obvious. As an illustration, few bigoted politicians publicly utter explicit racial slurs. Instead, they vent their hatred through "innocent" stories, perhaps telling about a black neighbor's unkempt lawn or a Turkish immigrant worker poorly cleaning an office. The reality of such conversations is that through implication they impute negative behaviors or characteristics to the target group. More often than not these derogations are prefaced with "I have nothing against them. . . . Some of my friends are . . ." or a similar caveat. The fact is, however, the target group is defamed.

Ethnic attitudes, prejudice in particular, are not individual aberrations or pathological exceptions. Instead, they are structurally rooted and have socially shared cognitions. The absence of positive conversations about particular minorities can usually be correlated to the absence or underrepresentation of these individuals in the workplaces in question. The representation of minorities in negative symbols tends to parallel the attitudes of the majority of employees. A review of symbolism pertaining to African Americans cogently describes the pernicious aspects of words.

Negroes a.k.a. African Americans

From dictionaries, encyclopedias, and other word-defining sources we learn that the derivation of the word *Negro* is from Latin. Phobena Nelson's (1962) analysis of its historical usages leads to a better understanding of current meanings given to "Negro":

The most ancient names for so-called black people are Neheru, or Nubian; Ethiopian and Moor from ancient Egypt, the Negrito from West Africa. All of the above are native African words. "Negro" is probably the oldest as Negritas are the oldest known branch of the human race. "Negro" comes from the River Niger. "Niger" found its way into Latin. . . . Black and colored, like white, are on the other hand, European words. Ethiopian and Moor were popularly used to describe the so-called blacks until 1500. Shakespeare used "Negro" only once and used it synonymously with Moor. (p. 40)

Thus, through the ages, particular groups of humankind have been distinguished from others not only by geographical location but also by skin pigmentation. And, in terms of common usage, a Negro is usually defined as a person having black or dark skin pigmentation. Color, coupled with other physical characteristics, categorizes the people referred to as being members of the Negro race. Technically, "race" refers to a subdivision of humankind, the members of which are distinguished by possession of similar combinations of anatomical features, usually due to heredity (Hooton, 1938). For academic convenience, anthropologists classify present-day peoples into three or more major divisions, including Mongoloid, Negroid, and Caucasoid. And most anthropologists readily admit that their categories of race are not absolute truths uncovered from an analysis of the creation of *Homo sapiens*. Having freed themselves from the task of supplying dogmatic, categoric revelations, most anthropologists further agree that no race is "pure" and that all people are of the same genus and species (Foster, 1953).

Realizing that there are discrepancies in racial classifications, many researchers preface their findings with an acknowledgment that human races exist only in the imagination of the classifiers and that the purity of groups is, at most, dubious. At this point, biologically and genetically, a Negro by any name is but another human being. And depending upon their geographical location, Negroes by any other name could be the same as all other people in their specific environment. But in actual practice, in our present American society, a Negro by any other name probably still would be denied certain employment opportunities.

Sociologists and anthropologists have attributed many characteristics to people called "Negroes" or "blacks" or "African Americans." But the lack of consensus is not unique to sociologists and anthropologists. Charles Mangum (1940) noted that although several states once defined Negroes with respect to limitations in marriage, education, sex, and so forth, there has never been an adequate legal definition of Negroes in the United States. For several years, individuals who desired a more exacting definition found the concept used by the United States Bureau of Census to be adequate:

A person of mixed white and Negro blood . . . no matter how small the percentage of Negro blood [is Negro]. . . . Both black and mulatto persons are . . . Negroes, without distinction. A person of mixed Indian blood very definitely predominates and he is universally accepted in the community as an indian. Mixtures of non-white races are reported according to the race of the father, except that Negro-Indian are reported as Negro. (Murray, 1958, p. 175)

Often, therefore, when in doubt, researchers classified a person as being "Negro." As a result, the total number of Negroes at any given time was subject to enormous subjective fluctuations. Dark-skinned Hispanics and Portuguese have at times been counted as black Americans. Blood types are no longer used to identify racial groups.

Using a historical approach, we may relate the course of early American events in which Africans become slaves, then freed people, and, finally, legal citizens. And to further update the progression of historical events, we may cite the 1964 Civil Rights Act as additional evidence of equal rights and opportunities for African Americans. It could now be concluded by some naïve observers that an African American by any other name is indistinguishable from other Americans. But in social practice, labels are libels. Or in the jargon of advertising, most African Americans are still defined as "Brand X" and not a "Trade Name." The past and present negative definitions of the word *Negro* would make it difficult, if not impossible, for many Americans to give it positive meanings. By current definitions the words *African Americans denote* dark skin. Also by current definition, they *connote* inferiority.

Gordon Allport (1954) reminded us that because words are symbolic and stand for what we agree they stand for, definitions are a matter of social convention and do not necessarily have a relation to objects. S. I. Hayakawa (1941) was but one of many who cautioned Americans to remember that the word is not the thing. Words are but language symbols that we arbitrarily use to stand for something. There is nothing about the physical beings whom we call African Americans that logically or necessarily requires that designation. But once a language symbol is given it implicitly conveys attitudes. In fact, Alfred Lindesmith and Anselm Strauss (1950) stated that a language symbol does not merely stand for something else. It also indicates the significance of things for human behavior, and the meaning organizes our behavior toward the thing symbolized.

Connotative meanings, according to David Krech, Richard Crutchfield, and Egerton Ballachy (1962), refer to the wider penumbra of action tendencies and feelings that cluster about a word. Or stated another way, understanding of meanings does not come through dealing with words alone but rather with the things for which words stand. Charles Ogden and Ivor Richard's (1963) classic work on meanings of meanings urges us to find the referent: "Confusion and misunderstanding arises whenever we use words for which the referent is not clearly specified and may be particularly dangerous in the case of emotionally toned symbols which may signify different things to different people" (p. 76).

"African American" is an emotionally toned symbol that does indeed signify different things to different people. The negative reaction potential of the words in the workplace may be equated to a red flag and bull situation or to the cry of "fire" in a crowded theater. Many Euro-American workers, continuing the illustration, have suffered stress attacks upon being told that some previously "white" jobs will be occupied by African Americans. In an extreme sense, there are times when "African American" or "black American" erroneously becomes a synonym for "rapist," "thief," "murderer," or some other socially defined scoundrel. We can safely conclude that the word *African American* has many connotative meanings—some positive, others negative. Of utmost importance is the fact that the meaning of the word depends greatly upon the processes of socialization. As discussed in earlier chapters, we learn to define and respond to people. Therefore, the words *African American,* the individual African American, and the group African Americans all elicit intricate sociopsychological responses in the workplace.

Although the oft-quoted "man or woman in the street" may firmly believe in the racial inferiority of African Americans, current scientific evidence indicates that no race is superior to another. While lacking in scientific corroboration, racists are amply supplied with nonscientific superiority-inferiority definitions of the situation. A significant trend in social interaction is that groupings of people for many reasons (primarily ethnocentric) claim racial superiority over others. Of course, these claims are made by both majority and minority groups. Overt confrontation of these claims may not debilitate minority groups. Yet, in most instances, the majority group emerges as "superiors."

The Word Becomes the Thing

When most workers think or see black, they either consciously or subconsciously think that black is the antonym of white. More often than not, white is associated with everything that is "good"—with Christ and the angels, with cleanliness and virtue. On the other hand, through the ages black has been associated with all that is "bad." A review of the literature reveals that black, at various times, has stood for dirt, sin, and the devil. Metaphoric usages of black as evil and white as goodness are abundantly sprinkled throughout the Bible; are ingrained into the writings of ancient and contemporary literature; and, indeed, are woven into almost every entwining thread of the symbolism in which American history is clothed. Or we can find similar usages in our dictionaries, ranging from "white hope" to "white wash," from "black arts" to "black-mail."

The Bible's central theme of good (white) and evil (black) is cogent enough to become a chief source of reference for racial bigots. While the Bible's imagery is not quite equaled by Chaucer or Milton, Shakespeare does, according to Harold Issacs (1963), offer suitable competition. The king in Shakespeare's *Love's Labor Lost*, for example, cried: "O paradox! Black is the badge of hell, the hue of dungeons, and the shade of night." In yet another condemning tone, Shakespeare had Macbeth cry out: "The devil damn thee black"—the symbolic joining of sin and the devil with blackness.

The raising of "white" and debasement of "black" has been marked deep on the minds of all through time and every white person has more or less unconsciously imbibed it as nourishment for his self-esteem. Like the English child in Blake's poem, he was already the color of angels, while the black man could only yearn after whiteness, whether of character, soul or skin, and hope that by becoming "like" the white man—whether on earth or in heaven—he would come at last to be loved. This arrangement of things was communicated to all in our culture by all its modes and means, passed by osmosis through all the membranes of class, caste, and color of relationships, caressingly and painlessly injected into our children by their school texts and, even more, their story books. (Issacs, 1963, p. 76)

Accordingly, black Americans become a contrast of white Americans. They become the opposite race, the enemy. As a result, in the 1950s and 1960s when black Americans moved into neighborhoods occupied by whites, sociologists used the war terminology "invasion." And reflecting their superiority, when whites moved into neighborhoods occupied by blacks, this was usually called "integration." Less subtle than definitions of changing neighborhoods, Melvin Tumin (1958) concluded that no matter how he divided a sample of white respondents—whether by education, income, occupation, or whatever—he found that a majority of them viewed blacks as being inferior to whites in certain essential regards, such as intelligence, morality, responsibility, and ambition.

Of course, many of the views from the "outside, looking in" are positive views. There are people who accept or reject African Americans on their merit and not prejudicially. Yet the continuing unequal employment opportunities for blacks in America suggest that many employers will have a difficult time moving from theories of diversity to workplace practices.

HATE IN THE WORKPLACE

Racism is the cause of tremendous hostility within the workplace. In some organizations, racial, sexual, and other derogatory remarks are transmitted through high-tech machines—hate mail and hate faxes are commonplace. In other organizations they are transmitted the old-fashioned way—scribbled on desks and lockers. These incidents have been occurring at a high rate in the last few years (Solomon, 1992). One has to ask: Why do racism, sexism, and the other isms still exist in the workplace? The answer is simple: Societal negative attitudes found in the workplace are exacerbated during times of rapid immigration, socioeconomic privations, and high unemployment. The workplace is ripe for ethnoviolent conflict (Ehrlich, 1992).

Events such as urban riots reflect the precipitous, explosive nature of human relationships between ethnic groups as a by-product of economic recession. Further, increased diversity—on and off the job—brings discomfort and anxiety to many employees. Fear of an unknown economic future, competition for jobs and housing, and competition for sexual partners are some of the reasons for animosity among workers. When people are fearful about their future, particularly their economic survival, they look for scapegoats. This, in turn, leads to an escalation of hate words, which in turn leads to hate crimes.

From 1990 to 1991 there was a 31 percent increase in attacks on gay people in five major U.S. cities (Solomon, 1992). Anti-Semitic incidents reached the highest level since the Anti-Defamation League began its annual monitoring of hate crimes—an 11 percent increase from 1990. In Los Angeles County alone, where the first human relations commission was established in 1944 to promote understanding among ethnic groups, hate crimes (which are classified legally as violations of the law, based on the victim's background—ethnicity, gender, sexual orientation, etc.) increased 22 percent. African Americans, Hispanics, homosexual males, and Jews were the primary targets of most of those hate crimes. Some specific examples include the following:

• An African-American employee of an East Coast company took the day off to celebrate Martin Luther King, Jr. Day. Upon returning to work, he discovered a note that had been scribbled on his desk calendar: "Kill four more, get four more days off."

• An elderly Jewish employee in an East Coast electronics firm was told face-to-face by another employee that the new boss was about to design microwave ovens large enough for people to walk into.

• Fifteen employees in a West Coast public utilities corporation marched in a gay pride parade with the company's logo. When they returned to work, they were greeted by hundreds of E-mail letters, one of which read: "If I had been anywhere near the gay pride march and had an axe, I would have axed you people."

These examples do not illustrate violence punishable by law, but they certainly exhibit intolerant, hurtful attitudes that could destroy the effectiveness of a work environment. There are stereotypes of various racial and ethnic groups around the world. So powerful are these images that personal knowledge of friends and public figures may not change them. "The fiery Spaniard, hearty German, inscrutable Asian, conservative Briton, and exuberant Italian are just a few examples. Less complimentary are the cold Dane, sleepy Mexican, and miserly Scot" (IABC, 1982, p. 5). Employees who talk about racial, ethnic, and gender stereotypes are usually aware of the dysfunctional nature of words, images, and situations that suggest that all or most members of a particular group are the same. As noted throughout this book, stereotypes lead to assumptions that are unsupportable. And negative stereotypes are offensive; they cloud the fact that all human attributes are found in all ethnic groups. The growing hate directed at foreign nationals illustrates this point.

Negative beliefs about foreign nationals are often influenced by news media presentations. The choice of villain is "dependent to a great degree on the headline events that attract public interest, and the villain of the hour in America has changed frequently" (Shaheen, 1984, p. 11). For example, in 1986 news stories about the U.S. air strikes against Libya painted a "mad dog" image of Libyan leader Moammar Khadafy in the minds of many Americans. The fallout of that negative press accrued to countless Arabs working in America. Even today, because of the war against Iraq, Arabs are believed by many Americans to be barbaric, uncultured, lascivious people. Similar images are projected to other foreign workers whose countries have been associated with hostile actions against U.S. citizens.

Derogatory Ethnic Labels

No utterance can convey hatred for an individual based on his or her membership in a group as quickly or as vividly as a derogatory ethnic label (DEL). In the United States words such as "nigger" and "chink" are in this category. DELs have such great impact that their use in face-to-face interactions between members of different ethnic groups often precipitate violence. As volatile as they are, DELs are used with considerable regularity in the workplace. There are DELs for members of every ethnic group in the United States. The list includes beaner, camel jockey, chink, frog, kikes, gook, Jap, peckawood, spic, wop, nigger (Donaldson, Geneva & Van Dyk, 1988). There are more than one thousand terms for American ethnic groups and many of them are derogatory.

Muzafer Sherif and Carolyn Sherif's (1953) classic field studies showed that DELs are espoused when hostilities between groups escalate, even when the groups are arbitrarily formed. Teon Van Dijk (1984) identified DELs as an important element in the formulation and diffusion of ethnic prejudice. Among his many conclusions, the following three are especially relevant to the workplace:

1. Majority-group members use stories to place themselves in the victim role and thereby justify their prejudiced views.
2. Majority-group members tend to present themselves to interviewers in a positive light.
3. Majority-group members often explicitly communicate tolerance while implicitly conveying prejudice.

Such findings explain subtle, underlying hostilities that persist long after overt discriminatory acts have ceased (Guthrie, 1976; Jones, 1980; White, 1984).

Why DELs Are Used

In *The Nature of Prejudice* Allport (1954) briefly discussed the role of labels in prejudice. He postulated that labels provide a basis for grouping humans into separate categories. Labels necessarily imply similarities among people within a given category and differences between themselves and members of other groups. Quite simply, without a labeled group there would be no object of general hatred (prejudice). Labels encourage thinking in terms of in-groups and out-groups. Employee in-groups and out-groups use group labels to accentuate the similarities between their own members and the differences between themselves and members of other groups (Allen & Wilder, 1979; Quattrone & Jones, 1980). The use of ethnic labels, therefore, may promote workplace prejudices simply by enhancing the negative perception of out-group individuals as being like each other and unlike in-group members. Thus, by facilitating categorization and emphasizing differences between culturally different workers, DELs increase the potential for hostility in the workplace toward the employees to whom negative labels are applied.

DELs have other properties in addition to encouraging categorization.

Primarily, they symbolize all the negative, stereotypical beliefs associated with the group. Because DELs have the power to communicate all the negative beliefs about a group in a single word, they are especially potent communicative devices. Words have the power to make a concept appear to be natural throughout the world. For example, there are many negative beliefs about blacks in the United States, but the term *nigger* crystallizes these beliefs into a concept or prototype that has a sense of concrete reality to peoples throughout the world.

Essentially, the DEL is a cultural legitimization of a negative conception of members of a particular out-group. The mere existence of a term implies at least some cultural sanctioning of it. DELs also allow members of an out-group to be referred to without making reference to their national or cultural affiliation and heritage, thereby eliminating their patriotism, heroism, and other positive characteristics. In this way, out-group members are dehumanized, not recognized as human beings from a geographic location or with a national affiliation, but rather as fundamentally genetically, different subhuman creatures. Of course, not all minority out-groups are viewed in totally negative ways. As an illustration, with the U.S. corporate quest to emulate Japanese management and productivity, the Japanese are no longer viewed as inferior workers.

Demoralization Through DELs

Geneva Smitherman (1977) pointed out that "nigger" is an element of "black semantics," which she defined as "the totality of idioms, terms and expressions that are commonly used by black Americans" (pp. 42–43). Given that "nigger" is a DEL when applied by out-group members, one possible explanation of in-group usage of the term may be that African Americans who use the epithet accept the negative stereotypical view of themselves (Allen, 1983). This acceptance then contributes to their demoralization. Most employees are exposed to this particular pervasive DEL through television, parents, and peers.

In *Doby's Gone* Ann Petry (1971) wrote from the perspective of a young black girl who suffered from racially biased verbal harassment (e.g., "nigger girl") by her white schoolmates. The girl's reaction is described first as rejection, then dejection, and eventually anger and rage. These feelings, along with helplessness and self-depreciation, are typically described in literature as responses to the communication of institutionalized racism (Grier & Cobbs, 1968; Wright, 1940). Demeaning and hurtful labels that begin in childhood are brought to the workplace by oppressors and the oppressed.

Sexist Language

A discussion of hate language would not be complete without some attention to sexist language. The permeation of sexism in the workplace, as well as the larger society, projects attitudes of male superiority and female inferiority. Often males use language that is diminishing to females without realizing the implications of the words. An example of this is calling an adult female "girl." This happens frequently in the workplace, even though a girl is an immature female, a child. The same implication pertains to "boy" when used for male adults. Many of the terms used to denote gender carry behavioral expectations, stereotypes, and norms that are inappropriate in the work environment.

Sara Shute (1981) cautioned that changing sexist language will not in itself eliminate sexism. She theorized that sexism can only be eliminated by changing people's attitudes and requiring equal treatment such as equal pay for equal work. Changing "sexist" language to "nonsexist" language requires considerable effort that often does not produce tangible results. This brings to fore the dilemma of whether it is best to change behavior first, assuming attitudes will follow; or if attitude change has a more salient effect on changing behavior. There are schools of thought that support both strategies, just as there are people who disagree with Shute's premise that eliminating sexist language would not eliminate sexism. It would, some people argue, be at least a first step in the direction of acknowledging equality for females.

Many employers have substituted asexual workplace words and phrases for "man-words." For example, they sanction words such as *people, human beings,* and *human race* rather than *mankind.* Instead of *man-hours,* new terms include *total hours, staff-hours,* and *working hours.* This allows the communication to overtly include both male and female employees. Relatedly, managers and supervisors are beginning in large numbers to respect females by avoiding patronizing tones. They also avoid portraying women as typically weak, helpless, or hysterical; or men as typically strong, brave, or rational. The more sensitive administrators avoid all nonsexist language. Using phrases such as "just like a man" or "just like a woman" perpetuates stereotypes. Stereotypical beliefs about where men and women "belong" in the workforce, in turn, can lead to unequal employment practices. Consider, as an illustration, the terms *the executive* and *lady executive* or *the manager* and *woman manager.* Similarly, men become the oddities when labels such as *male secretary* or *male nurse* are used. This distinction suggests that certain jobs or responsibilities are reserved for men and other jobs are for women.

SUMMARY

Managers can help curtail and prevent discrimination based on race, color, gender, and national origin by implementing bias-free written and spoken language in the workplace. Some additional tips for doing this are listed below.

Identify people by race, color, gender, and ethnic origin only when this identification is appropriate. Unless there is a very good business-related justification, it is inappropriate to identify people by race, color, gender, and ethnic origin (e.g., "Mary Adams, a female African-American engineer, has been with the company for five years"). If this statement is part of an affirmative action report, identifying Mary's gender and race is appropriate. Otherwise, it is inappropriate.

Avoid using words and phrases that may be unoffensive to you but can offend other people (e.g., "culturally deprived" or "culturally disadvantaged"). These terms imply inferiority. The term *culturally different* does not have such a connotation. "Nonwhite" implies that white is the normative standard. So too does a "nonblack" or "non-Hispanic."

The use of the term *Third World* is acceptable. However, when referring to specific peoples, use their national identity (e.g., Nigerians, Mexicans, Chinese). The same principle pertains to American Indians and peoples with Hispanic surnames.

The language used in business communications should *include* all employees rather than *exclude* some of them (Maggio, 1988; Petrini, 1993). And communications describing employees should pertain to their job skills, not their color, age, race, sex, or national origin. Employees are not the jobs they do; nor are they their physical condition. Thus, instead of "disabled welder," for example, Joe becomes a "welder with a disability."

For those individuals who demur when they are chastised for using inflammatory words, the courts have been consistent when adjudicating such cases: Words are not neutral—people associate words with feelings and behaviors. Some words have the capacity to pierce the psyche of the listeners and strip away their sense of worthwhileness (Flynn, 1992). Hence, words may be the ultimate stealth weapon that can wound quickly and mortally with rapier-like precision. Predictions have been made that by the end of this decade the majority of new hires for companies in the United States will no longer be white males (Kennedy & Everest, 1991). Even if this prediction is not accurate, it is essential for employers to embrace inclusive paradigms.

Is Silence Golden?

Imagine that you are attending a meeting to discuss your organization's strategic plan for the next fiscal year. Several of the participants arrive early and begin teasing each other about various problems in implementing the current strategic plan. Quickly, the conversation turns to sports.

"If we were a football team, some of us would be waived," Chuck laughed.

"Yeah," Bob chimed in. "Except for you, Joe, the rest of us would have to sit on the bench."

Feeling good about his successful record to date, Joe beamed, "I guess it's in the blood."

"Either it's in the blood or you're the boss' bastard son," Bob responded angrily. "Since you spooks were spirited into this company with the affirmative action quotas, it's hard for us white people to get good assignments. There are too many of you people on the team."

An uncomfortable silence engulfs the group. Chuck is embarrassed, Bob is angry, and Joe is surprised. Bob had shown a side of himself that Joe did not believe he had. After all, it was Bob who bent over backwards to make sure Joe not only learned his job; he is also Joe's "best friend" in the company.

"I'll just forget you said that," Joe turns to Bob.

Bob glares at him and replies, "That's mighty black of you. You people take and take. I can't give any more." He then storms out of the room.

What happened? If you were Chuck, what would you say to Bob and Joe? What are the advantages and disadvantages of your decision? Which paradigms are operative in this scenario?

WORDS FOR THOUGHT

1. When you were a child, what kind of people were you socialized to believe were "like you"?

_____

_____

_____

2. When you were a child, what kind of people were you socialized to believe were "not like you?"

_____

_____

_____

3. What slang terms do some of your friends use for the following people?

A. Black Americans _____

B. American Indians _____

C. Mexican Americans _____

D. Italian Americans _____

E. Polish Americans _____

F. Jews _____

G. Catholics _____

H. Poor Whites _____

I. Homosexuals _____

J. Arabs _____

4. What is your stereotype of the following executives?

A. Males _____

B. Females _____

5. What epithets do you consider offensive when they are used to describe your race, ethnic group, and gender?

_____

_____

_____

CHAPTER 10

Cross-Cultural Conflict

Cultural diversity changes the workplace by providing new human resources and managerial challenges to employers. As the United States experiences shortages of skilled workers, most organizations will have to find
ways to optimally utilize multicultural workers. This often entails dealing
with employees who have different attitudes toward time, status and roles,
relationships, responsibility, decision-making, and technology (Goldstein
& Leopold, 1990). To effectively manage diversity, managers and supervisors must be aware of the values, motivations, communication styles, attitudes, and needs of their employees (Foxman & Polsky, 1989). This is a
Herculean task even for people trained in intercultural relations. And as
the nation's workforce is reshaped with respect to age, sex, racial composition, and national origin, the challenge to managers and supervisors is
magnified (Abbasi & Hollman, 1991).

SEEDBED FOR CONFLICT

When demographics change and the demand for labor becomes greater
than the once traditional labor pool can provide, cultural diversity becomes a formidable activity for employers. This does not necessarily mean
the new labor pool is incapable of meeting the needs of employers, but it
does mean that in some instances extensive job training strategies must be
implemented. The shortage of skilled workers and the increase of employees' diverse cultural backgrounds are reasons corporations like Apple
Computers, Southwestern Bell, Corning Inc., and Quaker Oats have implemented programs that focus on diversity issues rather than following the
traditional corporate practice of ignoring existing cultural differences (Nel-

ton, 1991). Success in the global marketplace and maximization of human resources are synchronous (Leonard, 1991).

Changing technologies and the global marketplace require organizations to adapt or lose their competitive edge. Indeed, the survival of businesses and industries are dependent on how well they manage cultural diversity (Sue, 1991). The seedbed for intercultural conflict is the public school system. The quality of today's elementary and secondary schools foreshadows the workforce of the future. Because the public schools prepare most of the workforce, if they falter, business and industry will reap a deficient crop of employees. Some employers have opted to do more than lament the general deficiency in high school and college graduates. They are initiating programs to supplement the education of the graduates (Jones, 1989). Interestingly, education is usually the first institution blamed for economic crises, and it is also seen as the key to future national survival (Jones-Wilson, 1990).

School is a major arena where people are exposed to cultural diversity and conflict. It is there where attitudes are shaped, reinforced, or changed. And the process starts early. Children in day care centers and kindergarten classes are exposed daily to cultural differences. The preponderance of data indicates that our school systems are not adequately preparing students for cultural diversity. A discomforting paradox is that within two decades, if the current pattern continues, 48 percent of the public school student population will be ethnic minority children, but less than 3 percent of the teachers will be minorities. Surveys conducted by the Carnegie Foundation (1988) note that most of the white, middle-class teachers wanted to develop positive relations with students of color but did not. Instead, increased alienation occurred as the gap between the educators' and the students' values and lifestyles widened. The gap also widens when those students enter the workforce.

Even though each employee is shaped by his or her ethnic and racial group, managers must not forget that each person is unique. When confronted by employees who are culturally different, effective managers become aware of the nuances of individuality. Work environments in which the majority of employees are from the same ethnic group often create the illusion that all employees are alike, therein distorting individual uniqueness and causing workplace identity conflicts (Goldstein & Leopold, 1990).

Cross-cultural differences and multicultural conflicts are convoluted because of the multiple identities found within cultures. Examples of multiple identities include Catholic African Americans and Hispanic homosexuals. Also, cross-cultural differences due to geographic location may have little to do with race. For example, inner-city poverty-stricken people suffer from low income more so than racial discrimination. Amy Reynolds and Rachelle Pope (1991) explored the complexities of multiple identities such as when an individual belongs to more than one minority group. They concluded that little attention tends to be given to differences within multiple identity groups. It is important to be aware of the diversity within ethnic groups as well as between them.

Understanding the history of an ethnic group, the current stage of its national and social identities, and its relationships with other groups is critical to recognizing and resolving cross-cultural conflict. Specifically, an ethnic group's reasons for coming to the United States can provide valid data pertaining to intercultural conflict. Some ethnic groups are still searching for freedom from religious persecution that drove them from their homeland, or escape from ethnic group prescription, or job opportunities not available in their native country. For others, however, migration was a way to survive political oppression. And others—Africans—are trying to extricate from their lives a history of being kidnapped and sold as chattel property. The relocation of more than four hundred American Indian sovereign nations adds yet another issue to intergroup conflict. Indeed, employees bring their cultural histories to the workplace.

CAUSES OF CROSS-CULTURAL CONFLICT

There are many causes of cross-cultural conflict, including, but not limited to, language and communication barriers, racism, sexism, and ageism. As discussed in previous chapters, language is the basic form of communication and it is also the primary cause of cross-cultural conflict. Because language is representative of culture, conflict is precipitated. When an employee's language is ignored or devalued, an intrinsic part of his or her identity is also ignored or devalued (Campbell, 1991). According to Henderson (1989), the following barriers to cross-cultural communication must be bridged: (1) language differences, (2) differences in emotional and articulate forms of nonverbal communication, (3) cultural stereotypes that distort meanings, (4) evaluating the content of speech as either good or bad, and (5) high levels of anxiety that distort meanings.

The ability to exchange ideas is a primary vehicle for managing business negotiations, expediting decision-making, and evaluating employees' performances. Language differences are communicated in sentence structure, word meanings, and tense. Inadvertent workplace conflict can arise when job-related materials are incorrectly translated from one language to another (Hersey & Blanchard, 1993). Language can also lead to group stereotyping, nonacceptance of certain employees, and individual alienation. As an illustration, some Americans believe that a European accent (e.g., French or British English) is more urbane and desirable than Spanish or the Middle Eastern accents (Fernandez, 1991). Third World employees with above average intelligence are often considered "stupid" by their Anglo co-workers if they are unable to communicate fluently in English.

Many of those same Anglo workers are graduates of remedial employment training programs. But because English is their native language, their supervisors perceived them as being "trainable" instead of stupid.

Cross-cultural differences in the workforce exist among all employees—CEOs, support staff, supervisors, and other workers. No one is exempt from cultural differences or conflicts that grow out of them. One of the dangers in managing cross-cultural differences is the assumption that all individuals within an ethnic or nationality group are the same (Nelson, 1985). Several factors affect the attributions or judgments managers and supervisors make about their subordinates, including stereotypes and ethnocentrism. It is important to note that not all stereotypes are negative. Positive stereotypes may facilitate cultural acceptance.

Positive stereotypes could include, for example, the assumption that Hispanics are religious, that Asians are polite and loyal, and that African Americans are strong people. Obviously these stereotypes can also be benign degradations (Beamer, 1992). Examples of blatantly negative stereotypes include beliefs such as most Native Americans are alcoholics, most African Americans are lazy, most Hispanic males are macho, most Asians are inscrutable, and most white males are racists. When perpetuated in the workplace, negative stereotypes can destroy employee unity, greatly diminish productivity, and ultimately disintegrate an organization's viability. The subscripts of organization conflict are replete with stories of racism, sexism, and the other isms described in this book.

Contrary to popular notion, a large number of Americans believe the race, gender, age, nationality, and disability stereotypes depicted in the news media. It is not so much the belief in the veracity of stereotypes that perpetuates them but the need of oppressors to convince denigrated peoples of their inferiority in order to legitimate their own superiority. Indeed, the conflicts that center on diversity are mainly about power—getting it and keeping it. This kind of conflict is a *zero-sum game* of survival—someone must win and someone must lose. In most instances, the losers are ethnic minorities and women—members of the so-called protected class. When this happens, organizations appear to be places of affirmative inaction. The best scenario in conflict resolution is a *nonzero-sum game* in which all employees win or, if the conflict is not resolved, they all lose something of value.

It is worth repeating the admonitions woven throughout previous chapters: It is behavior, not attitudes, which triggers conflict. Unchecked discriminatory behaviors usually lead to conflict (Dickens & Dickens, 1991). And conflict raises the barrier of cultural differences between groups or individuals. When this happens, both minority-group and majority-group employees misperceive their opportunities to cooperate. In the fray, disgruntled employees often believe that the most qualified individuals (people like themselves) are not selected to fill vacancies. Specifically, the selection process is believed to be based on gender and color, instead of talent, with unqualified or the least qualified people being selected to fill affirmative action or, depending on one's perspective, infirmative action quotas. The absence of some groups and the large number of other groups in managerial positions are seen as signs of discrimination. Usually, innocent job occupants bear the brunt of such inflammatory innuendoes or character assassinations.

OPENING THE DIALOGUE

Oppressed employees are almost always expected to communicate to their manager or supervisor their condition. But most oppressed employees are hesitant to admit that they need help. Only after being told by significant other co-workers that they need help do they comfortably adopt the role of help seekers. It is no secret that administrators have power over their subordinates. Managers and supervisors who are authoritarian and dominating are the most difficult persons to tell about grievances. Those who are democratic encourage such disclosures. Most employee communications follow the classic power flow interaction process:

1. Communication flows more readily laterally between administrators or between subordinates than either downward from managers and supervisors to subordinates or upward from subordinates to managers and supervisors.
2. More communication of diversity problems goes from subordinates to managers and supervisors than from managers and supervisors to subordinates.
3. Subordinates are more cautious than managers and supervisors about the messages they send.
4. Managers, supervisors, and subordinates incorrectly assume the extent that their problems are understood by each other.
5. Most employees tend to avoid filing formal complaints.

Part of the administrator's dilemma is that he or she must be sufficiently detached from subordinates to exercise sound judgment and at the same time have enough rapport with and concern for aggrieved employees to provide sensitive, empathic support. It is possible for an administrator to suppress on the conscious level emotional responses while counseling angry subordinates. But this detachment does not remove the stress and concern hidden in the unconscious domain of the mind. The pathological process of detachment that produces mature administrators also has the tendency to produce cynical problem solvers. Helping subordinates report civil rights violations or tell about other abuses requires more than a receptive listener. Managers who believe that the structured interview is the only effective method for ascertaining facts and perceptions do not understand the process of telling and eliciting information.

It has long been said in casework, reiterated against the sometime practice of subjecting the client to a barrage of ready-made questions, that the client should be allowed to tell his story in his own way. Particularly at the beginning this is true, because the client may feel an urgency to do just that, to pour out what *he* sees and thinks and feels because it is his problem and because he has lived with it and mulled it within himself for days or perhaps months. Moreover, it is his own way that gives both caseworker and client not just the objective facts of the problem but the grasp of its significance. To the client who is ready and able to give out with what troubles him, the caseworker's nods and murmur of understanding—any of those nonverbal ways by which we indicate response—may be all the client needs in his first experience of telling and being heard out. (Perlman, 1957, p. 142)

Employee Resistance

Norman Hill (1981) stated that many employees do not tell what is actually troubling them until they are certain a manager or supervisor is really going to listen to them. In many cases, Barbara Okun (1992) cautioned, the initially stated problems obscure more pervasive underlying ones. This is often indicative that the employees do not trust supervisors, or they do not understand or acknowledge the real issues. This led Amy Barkin (1986) to advise administrators to be judicious in their efforts to help troubled subordinates focus on the most pressing problems. She recommended that when an employee chooses not to discuss a conflict situation, any negative consequences that can come from the avoidance should be communicated. While supervisors must be supportive and allow a "reasonable period of time" for problem abatement, the critical point to remember is that supervisors do not help employees or the organization by neglecting problems. Nor do problems go away or resolve themselves if given ample time. *Time solves nothing, people solve problems.* Many factors such as written policy, precedent, and the nature of the organization culture determine what is a reasonable period of time for employees to work things out. If after a reasonable period of time employees continue to have work-related diversity problems, the supervisor should assume a more active role.

It is common for supervisors to be confronted with resistance and hostility from employees during efforts to resolve conflict. Sonnenstuhl and O'Donnell (1980) were correct: "No matter how excellent a company's . . . prevention program, some employees refuse to recognize the existence of a problem" (p. 36). Resistance is not always bad. Actually it is a necessary part of the change and growth process. Indeed, conflict is a natural and inevitable aspect of life (Evans, 1992). Thus, resistance can be therapeutic rather than something to be feared and avoided (Okun, 1992). Carl Anderson and Susan Stewart (1983) concluded that a healthy amount of conflict can be a positive force; it can energize an organization. And resistance to change may be a sign of good mental health, without which there would be deadly compliance to every sensory input. In a similar vein, Joseph Follman (1978) theorized that conflicted employees will invariably deny that they have a problem, at least until the symptoms can no longer be denied.

On the one hand, employers should not minimize the fact that many employees do not report conflicts because they fear such disclosure will cost them their jobs. On the other hand, the fact that a troubled employee is being offered assistance by his or her supervisor may encourage other employees to come forth. Too much employee resistance will subvert diversity initiatives and create other job crises. Most employees will seek problem resolution when it will save their jobs. Supervisors rarely get sustained, rancorous employee resistance if they are honest and sincere in attempting to help troubled persons to become more effective employees (Wilson, 1962). In essence, managers and supervisors must be more than disciplinarians. They must be effective counselors.

Employee Needs

Few employees know exactly how they feel about what is bothering them until they have communicated sufficient data to someone else—a supervisor or a co-worker. To tell what they are feeling about job-related problems is in itself a relief for most workers, but telling is not enough. An adjustment or resolution must occur. Typical questions raised by employees include the following:

- What is wrong here?
- What's going to happen to me?
- What can I (you) do to help?

The words of Paul Tournier (1957) sum up the process of helping a troubled colleague communicate: "Through information I can understand a case, only through communication shall I be able to understand a person" (p. 25). Comments such as "I imagine that this is not easy for you to talk about" or "Go on, I'm listening" may be enough encouragement for reticent employees. Others will need direct questions to help them focus their conversation. One of the most difficult and important administrator roles is that of communicator. It is even more difficult when a friend is involved. The first rule of communication is that the manager or supervisor should understand the subordinate's values. The second rule is that the manager or supervisor should adapt his or her communicative behavior to the subordinate's value systems. This implies respect for different gender and cultural values, but it does not mean "talking down" to or patronizing people. Effective administrators are effective listeners.

Listening skills. Perhaps the single most important thing a manager or supervisor can do to open the dialogue is to listen carefully and let subordinates tell their complaints. The greatest block to interpersonal communication is the inability to listen intently. Managers and supervisors who counsel aggrieved employees should be aware of the normal propensity of people to talk rather than listen. Numerous studies have documented that the average manager or supervisor in a counseling interview will talk about 85 percent of the time (Steinmetz, 1969). In order for managers to really listen to employees, they must let them do about 90 percent of the talking (Wilson, 1962).

Sometimes the communication process will break down between managers and their subordinates. This is especially true when there are job-related conflicts and confrontations. If racial, gender, and disability issues are also involved in the communication break-down, the conflict is even more heated. All conflict has the following characteristics: (1) Two or more individuals must interact. (2) The interaction centers on imagined or real mutually exclusive goals or values. (3) In the interaction one party will win by defeating, suppressing, or reducing the power or ability of the other party to achieve the desired goals or values.

Unlike cooperation, a form of interaction in which two or more individuals or groups work together toward a common end, conflict is rivalrous interaction that emphasizes the differences between people and minimizes their similarities. Conflict is intermittent and personal. Even though every organization contains many factors that lead to conflict, efficient functioning requires that it be controlled. If left unchecked, conflict can destroy the stability and eventually the very existence of an organization. Societies such as ours, with many different subcultures, create special problems for managers committed to workforce assimilation. Most workers belong to different groups and are expected to conform to different and often contradictory norms. When these norms contradict one another, such as when minority subculture norms contradict organization norms, workers are forced to make a choice between them. What will a black separatist do when offered a supervisory position in a white work unit? Or what will a white separatist do when offered promotion in a unit headed by a black supervisor? Conformity to one set of norms is frequently tantamount to violation of another. Minimizing the importance of a conflict situation or denying that it exists may be expedient but this will only allow the conflict to simmer and escalate. The more effective managers engage in the following conflict resolution behaviors:

1. They are sensitive to the egos and self-esteem of all parties involved in the conflict. Thus they try to not publicly embarrass or criticize subordinates, which would result in a "loss of face" for them.
2. They do not let the conflict drag on for a long time. To do so would increase stress and hostility among the parties.
3. They focus on *what* is right instead of *who* is right. In any conflict involving two individuals, for example, there are at least three truths: A's truth, B's truth, and *the* truth.

The best resolution to diversity-related problems is to "beat the problems" rather than beat the employees. Thus managers as counselors must ferret out the needs of all conflicting parties, discover the nature of the conflict, and, whenever possible, help all parties win something.

CONFLICT RESOLUTION

Conflict resolution of employee diversity-related problems—racial, gender, age, physical ability, national origin discrimination—almost always affects job performance. And whenever an employee's problems affect his or her job performance, it should become a concern of the organization in general and his or her supervisor in particular (Wilson, 1962). Excluding the stressed subordinate, the supervisor has the most to gain when such problems are resolved expeditiously and in an equitable manner. When subordinates are free of inordinate conflict job efficiency is maintained or improved. This is an important aspect of managing diversity.

In order to be optimally effective, managers and supervisors must be culturally proactive rather than reactive. They are "in a critical position to observe and intervene in a 'preventive' capacity, i.e., before the employee becomes overwhelmed by his or her problems and the work becomes seriously impaired" (Barkin, 1986, p. 3). From this vantage point, most managers and supervisors are in strategic positions to observe a diminution in an employee's job performance. In some organizations the much needed interventions seldom happen before major altercations erupt because few administrators possess the counseling skills needed to serve as effective diversity counselors (Hill, 1981; Steinmetz, 1969; Wilson, 1962). A strong case could be made for the premise that, diversity training notwithstanding, counseling skills and proven strategies for organization change are seldom taught to managers and supervisors in a systematic manner.

If an individual was learning to swim, the instructor would first give him helpful tips on how to stay afloat—to tread water while learning more sophisticated methods of swimming. Unfortunately, most trainees in diversity workshops, in-service programs, and university management courses are seldom given much more than disparate data about counseling that tend to drown them in guilt or anger and therein cause them to disdain further lessons. That is, they are seldom taught to be competent counselors in the diversity workplace. This is a major reason most managers and supervisors shun the role of counselor. They do not want to be embarrassed by displaying their lack of training.

At a minimum, administrators must understand basic principles of human behavior in the workplace. Managers and supervisors who lack this information and corresponding intervention skills tend to "look the other way" when diversity problems occur.

Any intervention a supervisor makes with one employee will ultimately affect all of his or her subordinates. Therefore conflict resolution is necessarily a systems approach. Along with such interventions also comes the requirement for administrators to be knowledgeable about human relations concepts such as coping, adapting, and changing. This necessarily means carefully analyzing the organization's culture in order to help all employees cope with the changes inherent in incorporating diversity into the workplace. Employers must adopt operations, procedures, and policies that accommodate a heterogeneous labor force. This is not a linear project with a termination point or date. On the contrary, managing diversity is a continuous process. Consequently, the counseling skills needed to resolve conflict require continuous updating.

Obsolete Paradigms

It is evident from numerous studies that the old paradigms of discipline, suspension, and discharge as the only means to handle employees' problems are inappropriate. Of course, these actions are still viable and, in some instances, necessary. But they are seldom the most expeditious way to handle conflicts centering on diversity issues. Today's workers do not as a whole respond positively to behavior modification interventions. While it is true that such interventions can mediate the effects of poor job performance, it is also true that they do not deal with the causes of conflict (e.g., feelings of rejection, jealousy, hatred, etc.).

"Good employees don't stop being good employees without reason" (Levesque, 1988, p. 456). It is not unusual for individuals who were once described by their supervisors as "good workers" to be guilty of racial discrimination or sexual harassment, for example. Their reprimanded behavior is for a reason. Therefore, discipline, suspension, or discharge without counseling is seldom effective. Skillful counseling before discipline or suspension often makes discharge unnecessary. The financial cost alone of discipline and cases adjudicated in courts, arbitration, and compliance agencies are much more time-consuming, expensive, and organizationally disruptive than one-on-one or small-group counseling.

During conflict resolution, effective administrators are able to elicit trust and respect from their subordinates (Bittle, 1985; Lewis & Lewis, 1986; Okun, 1992). These administrators have learned to do the following things when counseling victims and perpetrators of diversity-related problems:

1. Clearly define the behaviors in question.
2. Specify acceptable behaviors.
3. Listen patiently, attentively, and actively to all parties of a conflict.
4. Focus on behaviors, not personalities.
5. Criticize inappropriate behavior but never an individual's personhood (i.e., say "I will not tolerate this behavior because it is against company policy [state or federal laws]" instead of "I will not tolerate you").
6. Never argue while trying to counsel employees.
7. Use a problem-solving approach, with mutual goal-setting.
8. End each counseling session with a concrete plan for further action.
9. Follow through and monitor agreements and directives.

It is important for organizations to include diversity as an aspect of career progression. That is, employees must be told that they cannot be promoted out of diversity. From this perspective, diversity is an integral aspect of career planning that traditionally has been "a deliberate process for becoming aware of self, opportunities, constraints, choices and goals; and for programming work, education and related developmental experiences to provide the direction, timing and sequence of steps to attain a specific career goal" (Gutteridge & Otte, 1983, p. 22). Successful career counseling as an aspect of managing diversity can facilitate the interdependence of the human resources in an organization. This is a more efficient use of human resources. It can improve morale and employee loyalty. Equally important, people are elevated to the same level of importance as inventory and equipment.

CHANGE THE GAME, NOT THE PLAYERS

Michael Maccoby (1977) described four prototypes of managers: the *craftsman*, the *jungle fighter*, the *company man*, and the *gamesman*. Each is very much present in organizations undergoing diversity acculturation. Also, one person may play multiple roles. Craftsmen are traditionalists who value the Protestant work ethic and its commitment to quality. They are builders and creators of things and structures. As a whole, they are quiet and mild-mannered with a propensity to be authoritarian and impatient with people unlike themselves. They value their individuality more than teamwork and, consequently, seldom rise to senior management positions.

Jungle fighters believe in survival and success at almost any cost. They thrive on the zero-sum game of relationships in which some people must win and others must lose. Jungle fighters are wheeler-dealers and sometimes empire builders. In their struggle for survival, they perceive their colleagues to be either for them or against them. Enemies are expendable. Jungle fighters seldom mentor others because they are afraid to impart knowledge that can be used against them.

Company men, sometimes called organization men, are individuals who gain their sense of organization identity from associating with people who are powerful. They tend to be loyal, cooperative team players whose behavior is a reflection of their CEO or manager. They are malleable team players but generally ineffective leaders. Their foremost goal is to survive with a minimum of conflict. In reality, many of them are passive-aggressive personality types.

The gamesmen thrive on challenges and competition. Above all else, they like to be winners—but not at any cost. Unlike jungle fighters, they are judicious in using destructive strategies. They are socially facile—glib, articulate, and charming. Gamesmen are innovators and visionaries who seek new approaches and strategies to achieve organizational goals. Like the craftsmen, they value excellence.

Audrey Edwards (1991) described another version of managers as conceptualized by Iris Randall: D style, I style, C style, and S style. While present in all cultures, she stated that some styles are more prominent in particular cultures. D, or dominant, managers make decisions rapidly. They are interested in immediate results. Their behavior is well structured and their communication is succinct. Euro-Americans, particularly white males, tend to behave this way. I style people, or influencers, are good at influencing and persuading other people to get things done. They are the organization cheerleaders: "I can, you can, we can make a difference." They are consummate actors who like people and applause. African Americans, Hispanics, and women tend to be I style managers.

C, or cautious, managers are more reserved than most administrators. They seldom rush to judgment. Taught not to be conformative, they carefully weigh options before speaking. Asians tend to behave this way. S, or steady, managers are good team players who have a high tolerance for long deliberations. Further, they readily defer to the person in charge. Native Americans tend to behave this way. S types feel more comfortable following strong leaders, whereas D types act as if they are strong leaders.

Problem Solving

If a business is managed poorly, it loses profits and eventually fails. If cultural conflicts are handled poorly, valuable employees are lost. Avoiding financial and human resources losses tests the leadership mettle of managers. Central to conflict resolution is mastering the processes of problem solving, the dynamics of which are threefold:

1. The facts that constitute the problem must be understood. Facts almost always consist of both objective reality and subjective reactions.
2. The facts must be thought through. They must be probed into, reorganized, and turned over in order for distressed employees to grasp as much of the total configuration as possible.
3. A decision must be made that will result in resolving or alleviating the problem. This usually involves a change in behavior and, if possible, attitude.

Succinctly, the three operations of problem solving are fact-finding, analysis of facts, and implementation of conclusions. For the maximum effectiveness, the people involved in the conflict must be fully involved in the efforts to solve their own problems. It is possible for a manager to define the problem and prescribe solutions, but when this happens the self-responsibility of the employees involved in the conflict is weakened. It is always better if the employees who have problems are able to assist in bringing about the resolution.

A problem cannot be solved if the necessary information is missing. A manager may want to understand his or her subordinates' conflicts but be unable to do so because some of the data are missing or distorted. In some situations administrators are not privy to all the information. In other instances, the information may have been misinterpreted. Like any puzzle, missing pieces of information in a human relations problem will render it insolvable.

Information alone is seldom enough. Too much information can freeze negative attitudes and reinforce dysfunctional behavior. Conditioned by organization and peer group norms, contradictory information may cause a manager to say to a complainant, "I understand what you have said but I don't believe it." For example, a sexist supervisor may disregard documentation of a female's abilities to do male-oriented jobs. An individual with delusions of male superiority is not likely to believe reports documenting female competence in "male" jobs. Thus, in order to be helpful, information must be believed by the manager.

Sensitivity is the capacity to identify and empathize with the values, aspirations, and feelings of subordinates. Today, more than ever, we need culturally sensitive administrators. Without being able to see employees as they see themselves, to dispel fears of cultural differences, and to communicate with their subordinates, managers will turn their organizations into socially and psychologically destructive battlefields. If they are unable to put themselves in the minds of their subordinates, there will be little help for the aggrieved persons. To quote Karl Menninger (1930):

When a trout rising to a fly gets hooked on a line and finds himself unable to swim about freely, he begins with a fight which results in struggles and splashes and sometimes an escape. Often, of course, the situation is too tough for him. Sometimes he masters his difficulties; sometimes they are too much for him. His struggles are all that the world sees and it naturally misunderstands them. It is hard for a free fish to understand what is happening to a hooked one. (p. 3)

It is precisely this understanding that forms the raison d'être of conflict resolution—that is, for a psychologically mature human being to counsel, care for, or facilitate solutions for workers in conflict or who feel uncomfortable with themselves, other employees, the job environment, or any combination of these.

Frequently, managers are problems themselves or causes of problems. As noted earlier, the ability of managers to achieve and maintain a condition of objectivity when dealing with their subordinates' problems is important in the conflict resolution process. If a manager gets wrapped up in his or her own inner world, he or she will not be able to perceive clearly the feelings of others. The challenge to administrators is awesome: They must empathize with subordinates but not to the point of losing their objectivity.

The manager must consciously focus on feelings. Even when employees resist these efforts, the manager must do so in such a way as to communicate, "If you do not understand or agree with my perceptions, I will not reject you." Facts alone are relatively ineffective in altering deep-seated stress. Besides, facts include accounts and events seen and felt by all parties in a dispute. For this reason, all parties must be allowed and, if necessary, encouraged to express their feelings so that the manager can focus on the same issues.

In many instances, aggrieved workers do not know how they really feel about their situation until they have communicated these feelings to someone else. Distressed workers may only be aware of internal discomforts. Providing opportunities for them to tell how they feel is usually the first step in isolating negative feelings and related behaviors. They may have previously communicated internal discomforts by arguing with, laughing at, or avoiding contact with other workers. Talking about negative feelings can provide a better view of them and a better chance for managing them. While allowing an employee to "tell" is a valuable technique in resolving problems, it is only a first step. Telling should be related to some end and not merely an end in itself. Solutions must be sought. To quote William Glasser (1965):

In their unsuccessful effort to fulfill their needs, no matter what behavior they chose, all [distressed workers] have a common characteristic: They deny the reality of the world around them. Some break the law, denying the rules of society; some claim their neighbors are plotting against them, denying the improbability of such behavior. Some are afraid of crowded places, close quarters, airplanes, or elevators, yet they freely admit the irrationality of their fears. Millions drink to blot out the inadequacy they feel but that need not exist if they could learn to be different. . . . Therapy will be successful when they are able to give up denying the world and to recognize that reality not only exists but that they must fulfill their needs within its framework. (pp. 174, 179)

Perhaps the major distinction lies between *talking about* a problem and *talking through it*. In the first instance, usually nothing more than random talk, free association of ideas, occurs. In the second instance, more structured thinking occurs: a problem is acknowledged, its implications and related behaviors examined, and solutions pondered. Talking through a problem excites all the body processes, often causing increased heartbeat and sweating. The whole person gets caught up in it.

It is imperative that distressed workers focus on problems that can be solved. This is by far the most efficient use of one's energies. For example, an older worker who focuses on his age, a woman on her gender, and a Hispanic on his ethnicity are all wasting valuable time and energy, as they cannot alter those things. However, if they focused on ageism, sexism, and, racism, then something constructive is possible. Managers must also focus on problems that have the potential of being solved. Some of the questions to be answered by managers and supervisors during this process are:

• What is the problem? (Who did what, when, where, what happened?)
• Who senses (feels) the problem? (Only the aggrieved, co-workers, supervisors?)
• How are you personally affected? (Emotionally, socially, economically, professionally?)
• What was the immediate cause for what happened?
• What organization rules and regulations pertain to the problem?
• Who can act to resolve this problem?
• What do you want to happen?
• What are your options?
• What will you do?

Beyond Talk

For people who keep score during conflict, there are four basic scores: win-win, win-lose, lose-win, and lose-lose. When the parties involved in the conflict *cooperate* to achieve something of value to each of them, they both win. In this instance, conflict is a positive growth process. If winning is more important than cooperating, there are likely to be winners and losers. This can occur through *competition* or *adaptation*. In competition, one party tries to overpower the other; during adaptation, one party surrenders his or her goals to maintain or establish a positive relationship with the other. Through *avoidance* the conflict is allowed to simmer. When this happens, both parties lose.

In summary, effective conflict resolution consists of the following factors. All parties involved in the dispute must be respected. Further, they must be encouraged to openly discuss the situation. The individual trying to resolve or mediate the dispute must give each party unconditional regard and listen carefully to each person's story without prematurely reaching a conclusion. This will require tolerance for different styles of storytelling and culturally different ways of reacting to conflict. The mediator must carefully determine the specific issues involved and, in concert with the disputing parties, determine if a common ground can be found upon which a positive resolution can occur. As noted earlier, in the best case scenario the resolution of a conflict will be a win-win situation. The mediator should adopt the philosophy to do maximum good or, if that is not possible, to do minimum harm. A general rule of thumb is that the individuals involved in a dispute should not be more conflicted after the intervention. Jeffery Goldstein and Marjorie Leopold (1990), drawing on Anti-Defamation League literature, recommend the following guidelines for managing cross-cultural conflicts:

1. Do not avoid the issue; bring it out and talk about it. Discussions should be open-ended and shared in a safe environment, without prying.

2. Each individual comes from a unique background. All employees should understand as much of those backgrounds as possible.

3. Use tact and respect during discussions of ethnic, cultural, racial, or gender conflict. Look for commonalities so that understanding can be mutual.

4. Stay within the organization's equal employment opportunity guidelines. Under no circumstances should managers tolerate sexism or racism within the organization.

5. Mediate between an individual's personal and organization needs. Employees must often make choices between their personal lifestyles and the organizational culture. While it may be personally satisfying, bigotry has no place in an organization.

6. Discuss and explain the unwritten rules of the company or organization so that the corporate culture can be better understood.

7. Encourage all employees to interact with each other in order to infuse diversity.

By now it should be evident that resolution of diversity problems should not be left to the whims of individual managers. All employees should be able to get redress for their grievances. Care must be taken to not place the burden of conflict resolution on minorities and women. The benefits that accrue to organizations that successfully manage diversity are quantifiable (Foxman & Polsky, 1989). However, if conflicts are ignored, employee problems such as lateness, absenteeism, poor job performances, wrongful dismissals, sexual harassment, and racial discrimination are likely to increase (Evans, 1992). When correctly done, conflict resolution will be a win-win process.

DON'T TALK TO ME

A national clothing manufacturing company has a Hispanic workforce that talks exclusively in Spanish in the lunch and break rooms. The non-Spanish speaking employees are overtly hostile toward the Hispanics. The company is moving into international markets and has initiated relationships with foreign companies, especially those in Spanish-speaking countries. In order to be more competitive, the company has implemented a mandatory language program for all managers and supervisors to learn Spanish. George, an African-American supervisor, refuses to attend the workshops, stating that his job description does not include learning another language. If you were George's boss, what would you do? What would you say to him?

ELOISA

Eloisa, an American Indian, is employed as a stock clerk in the Docile Company. She is a well-trained and valuable employee. However, she has a reputation for being overly aggressive and is sometimes verbally abusive to her white co-workers. When a white employee from her department was promoted, Eloisa stopped talking to all of her co-workers. She no longer participates in the company's informal social activities. Her co-workers have reciprocated by ignoring Eloisa. The warehouse is no longer a "fun place to work," as Eloisa once described it. If you were her supervisor, what would you do to resolve the conflict?

CONFLICT-MANAGEMENT STYLE SURVEY

[Developed by Marc Robert. Reprinted from J. W. Pfeiffer & C. D. Goldstein (Eds.). *The 1982 Annual for Facilitators, Trainers, and Consultants.* San Diego, CA: Pfeiffer & Company, 1982. Used with permission.]

Instructions: Choose a single frame of reference for answering all fifteen items (e.g., work-related conflicts, family conflicts, or social conflicts) and keep that frame of reference in mind when answering the items.

Allocate ten points among the four alternative answers given for each of the fifteen items below.

Example: When the people I supervise become involved in a personal conflict, I usually:

Intervene to settle the dispute.	Call a meeting to talk over the problem.	Offer to help if I can.	Ignore the problem.
3	6	1	0

Be certain that your answers add up to 10.

1. When someone *I care about* is actively hostile toward me, i.e., yelling, threatening, abusive, etc., I tend to:

Respond in a hostile manner.	Try to persuade the person to give up his/her actively hostile behavior.	Stay and listen as long as possible.	Walk away.

2. When someone *who is relatively unimportant to me* is actively hostile toward me, i.e., yelling, threatening, abusive, etc., I tend to:

Respond in a hostile manner.	Try to persuade the person to give up his/her actively hostile behavior.	Stay and listen as long as possible.	Walk away.

3. When I observe people in conflicts in which anger, threats, hostility, and strong opinions are present, I tend to:

Become involved and take a position.	Attempt to mediate.	Observe to see what happens.	Leave as quickly as possible.

4. When I perceive another person as meeting his/her needs at my expense, I am apt to:

Work to do anything I can to change that person.	Rely on persuasion and "facts" when attempting to have that person change.	Work hard at changing how I relate to that person.	Accept the situation as it is.
_____	_____	_____	_____

5. When involved in an interpersonal dispute, my general pattern is to:

Draw the other person into seeing the problem as I do.	Examine the issues between us as logically as possible.	Look hard for a workable compromise.	Let time take its course and let the problem work itself out.
_____	_____	_____	_____

6. The quality that I value the most in dealing with conflict would be:

Emotional strength and security.	Intelligence.	Love and openness.	Patience.
_____	_____	_____	_____

7. Following a serious altercation with someone I care for deeply, I:

Strongly desire to go back and settle things my way.	Want to go back and work it out— whatever give-and-take is necessary.	Worry about it a lot but not plan to initiate further contact.	Let it lie and not plan to initiate further contact.
_____	_____	_____	_____

8. When I see a serious conflict developing between two people *I care about*, I tend to:

Express my disappointment that this had to happen.	Attempt to persuade them to resolve their differences.	Watch to see what develops.	Leave the scene.
_____	_____	_____	_____

9. When I see a serious conflict developing between two people who are *relatively unimportant to me,* I tend to:

Express my disappointment that this had to happen.	Attempt to persuade them to resolve their differences.	Watch to see what develops.	Leave the scene.
_____	_____	_____	_____

10. The feedback that I receive from most people about how I behave when faced with conflict and opposition indicates that I:

Try hard to get my way.	Try to work out differences cooperatively.	Am easygoing and take a soft or conciliatory position.	Usually avoid the conflict.
_____	_____	_____	_____

11. When communicating with someone with whom I am having a serious conflict, I:

Try to over-power the other person with my speech.	Talk a little bit more than I listen.	Am an active listener (feed-ing back words and feelings).	Am a passive listener (agreeing and apologizing).
_____	_____	_____	_____

12. When involved in an unpleasant conflict, I:

Use humor with the other party.	Make an occa-sional quip or joke about the situation or the rela-tionship.	Relate humor only to myself.	Suppress all attempts at humor.
_____	_____	_____	_____

13. When someone does something that irritates me (e.g., smokes in a nonsmoking area or crowds in line in front of me), my tendency in communicating with the offending person is to:

Insist that the person look me in the eye.	Look the person directly in the eye and maintain eye contact.	Maintain intermittent eye contact.	Avoid looking directly at the person.
_____	_____	_____	_____

14.

Stand close and make physical contact.	Use my hands and body to illustrate my points.	Stand close to the person without touching him or her.	Stand back and keep my hands to myself.
_____	_____	_____	_____

15.

Use strong direct language and tell the person to stop.	Try to persuade the person to stop.	Talk gently and tell the person what my feelings are.	Say and do nothing.
_____	_____	_____	_____

Scoring and Interpretation

Instructions: When you have completed all fifteen items, add your scores vertically, resulting in four column totals. Put these on the blanks below.

Totals: _____ _____ _____ _____

Column 1   Column 2   Column 3   Column 4

Using your total scores in each column, fill in the bar graph below.

	1	2	3	4
150				
125				
100				
75				
50				
25				
0				

Column 1. Aggressive/Confrontive. High scores (above 75) indicate a tendency toward "taking the bull by the horns" and a strong need to control situations and/or people. Those who use this style are often directive and judgmental.

Column 2. Assertive/Persuasive. High scores indicate a tendency to stand up for oneself without being pushy, a proactive approach to conflict, and a willingness to collaborate. People who use this style depend heavily on their verbal skills.

Column 3. Observant/Introspective. High scores indicate a tendency to observe others and examine oneself analytically in response to conflict situations as well as a need to adopt counseling and listening modes of behavior. Those who use this style are likely to be cooperative, even conciliatory.

Column 4. Avoiding Reactive. High scores indicate a tendency toward passivity or withdrawal in conflict situations and a need to avoid confrontation. Those who use this style are usually accepting and patient, often suppressing their strong feelings.

Now total your scores for Columns 1 and 2 and Columns 3 and 4.

Column 1 + Column 2 = _____ (A)
Column 3 + Column 4 = _____ (B)

If Score A is significantly higher than Score B (25 points or more), it may indicate a tendency toward aggressive/assertive conflict management. A significantly higher B score signals a more conciliatory approach.

CHAPTER 11

Epilogue

As discussed in the previous chapters, managing diversity is an organizational process by which human resources are identified, allocated, and expanded in ways that make them more efficient. Successful diversity initiatives allow an organization to improve its productivity. Another basic objective is to create self-renewing, self-correcting systems of employees who learn to organize themselves in various ways according to the nature of their tasks and their cultural conditioning. In order to be optimally effective, a diversity initiative must be (1) *planned,* (2) *organization-wide,* and (3) *coordinated from the top* through (4) *planned activities and interventions.* Individuals responsible for human resources in organizations recognize this focus as an organizational development (OD) approach (Hersey & Blanchard, 1982; Tichy & DeVanna, 1986). And, similar to any effective OD program, successful diversity programs:

1. Work with all employees who are affected by the changes.
2. Create linkage with all employees who can influence the outcome of diversity initiatives.
3. Establish specific, measurable goals.
4. Change the quality of work group relationships from destructive intragroup competition toward collaboration and healthy intergroup competition by encouraging direct and open communication.
5. Build active feedback loops among all employees.

FROM THEORY TO PRACTICE

When the workforce is successfully diversified, employers realize the optimum potentials of employees previously denied equal employment opportunities. Leadership qualities related to cultural diversity are continually reassessed. Even so, the beliefs that managers and supervisors initially hold about diversity outcomes are greatly determined by their own cultural conditioning (Henderson, 1989). Since a large number of interpersonal and intergroup problems are related in some way to job maladjustments, culturally successful organizations provide an environment conducive to identifying and utilizing different ways of doing things. For example, assertiveness, which characterizes traditional Anglo-American managers, is not the only way to accomplish organizational objectives. Many companies are utilizing diverse employee qualities that they believe can provide desirable job outcomes. Along with such redefinitions is a concurrent movement among employers to be more inclusive of cultural coping styles.

An excellent example of a company that has benefited from this flexible approach is General Motors. Coordination of a crucial $40 million marketing campaign was assigned to Shirley Young, an Asian American. As vice president of consumer market development, she got the job done. But paraphrasing a once popular song, "she did it her way." Her talents probably would have been overlooked had GM persisted in holding to the traditional male-dominated executive paradigm (Kennedy & Everest, 1991). Ms. Young's genteel demeanor did not fit the paradigm. Likewise, if other companies are to benefit from the intelligence and talents of high-context employees, they too must understand and value cultural differences. A growing number of organizations are learning to blend employees who have a propensity for individualism and self-expression with those who prefer group harmony and personal relationships. This requires most organizations to recruit new leaders. In many instances this is akin to a corporate culture revolution in which the "old guard"—defenders of the status quo—are being replaced or retrained.

Several U.S. companies have been pioneers in managing diversity. And in doing so they are leaders in the multicultural movement of this decade. Jim Kennedy and Anna Everest (1991) noted that companies such as Delta Air Lines, IBM, Kodak, McDonald's, and Procter & Gamble exhibited the following common characteristics. They implemented successful diversity programs. When an idea pertaining to diversity appeared to be promising, executives in those organizations designed a plan and carried it out. (See Table 11.1) They did not get bogged down in endless speculation or negative prognostication. They were well aware that countless diversity ideas have been talked to death. Further, they had consistent concern for their employees—they built on individual differences. The importance of each employee was underscored; each was viewed as a unique family member. Consequently, the companies studied developed a shared organization culture that synergistically bound its employees together. In a similar vein, *Black Enterprise* (1993) cited AT&T, Avon, IBM, J P Morgan, Miller Brewing, Philip Morris, Reebok, Ryder System, SmithKline Beecham, and

Table 11.1
Technical Training versus Diversity Training

Variable	Technical Training	Diversity Training
Unit of focus	Individual Employees	Groups—teams or work units
Areas of focus	Technical and administrative skills	Interpersonal and intergroup competence
Trainees	Managers and supervisors	All employees
Learning process	Cognitive	Cognitive, affective and emotional
Training style	Trainer-subject centered	Trainee-subject centered
Training goal	Job effeciency	Cultural awareness
Payoff	Greater individual productivity	Systemwide culture change

the U.S. Postal Service for outstanding diversity programs: They celebrated diversity and rewarded administrators who successfully managed it. A growing number of other organizations have learned to successfully manage diversity.

Employees in a model organization see themselves as important people, and they do not have to reject other employees to feel that way. On the contrary, their feelings are dependent upon accepting and being accepted by their co-workers and supervisors. The consensus is that other employees are significant. Even those who look and dress differently or speak another language are valued members of the organization. Nor are dual standards used by supervisors. All employees are expected to perform to the maximum of their abilities. The common standard sought is excellence. Because they know that excellence can be achieved in many ways, diversity literate managers and supervisors encourage and support employee creativity. Sometimes this leads to conflict.

There are four basic ways managers and supervisors respond in conflict situations growing out of diverse lifestyles. Some people *withdraw,* shutting out the world around them. They day dream about the "good old days" when there were no affirmative action plans, or the time when they worked in a homogeneous organization. These administrators feel powerless to resolve diversity conflicts, believing that it is too late to do anything. Other administrators send memorandums and then *ignore* the conflict. They believe that all problems can be solved by ordering the conflicting parties to cease and desist. Besides, they believe, the problems will eventually work themselves out. Some managers *attack* individuals or groups whom they believe are troublemakers—usually "liberals," "conservatives," "women libbers," or "political demagogues." And other managers—the more effective ones—*seek constructive solutions*. They are not immobilized by self-pity, despair, or anger. Instead, they opt to see conflict and actively try to improve the work environment.

There is a bit of the skeptic in more effective managers. They do not believe that time will take care of things or that most employees would be unprejudiced if left alone. Time, they know, is a neutral concept and it takes care of nothing; *people take care of things*. And unless taught to accept diversity, most employees will reject co-workers who are culturally different. "I wasn't trained to be a social worker," a senior executive said during an in-service diversity workshop. "It takes too much time to ferret out the different ways people do things," another agreed. They both missed the point of the workshop. Whether or not they learned it, there are culturally different ways employees react to assignments. This knowledge is not social work, it is management work.

RECORDS AND REPUTATIONS

Every employee has an academic record, an employment record, and a social reputation, all of which precede and follow him or her. Academic records mainly consist of school grades, while employment records chronicle the jobs and positions one has held. Social reputations are an imprecise mixture of anecdotal records and rumors. Seldom do records or reputations acknowledge unequal opportunities, cultural myths and stereotypes, and other circumstances beyond the control of the employee. Depending on a job applicant's record and reputation, managers will be either horrified or pleased at the mere thought of supervising certain individuals.

Some of the people described in this book are handicapped by their supervisors' and co-workers' low expectations of them. Despite numerous volumes detailing discrimination encountered by protected-class employees, a large number of supervisors cling to the pernicious myth that as a group minorities, women, and older employees are inferior employees. They succumb to the records or reputations as gospel. By so doing, they are relieved of the tiresome burden of individualizing their behavior. It is of utmost importance that individuals involved in diversity activities always keep in mind the injunction to avoid labeling, stereotyping, generalizing, categorizing, and rationalizing unique human beings who defy the reduction and simplification provided by their records and reputations. Quantified data certainly have their place and can provide employers with varied and invaluable heuristic tools to use in recruitment, but managers must be willing and prepared to discard these tools when they do not fit or when they cease to lend understanding of their subordinates.

The best way to learn what culturally diverse employees are like is to observe their behaviors, listen to their conversations, and let them tell about themselves. It is a rare experience for an ethnic minority or woman, for example, to talk with a supervisor who, instead of criticizing, listens without judging. It is even rarer for workers in trouble to talk with administrators who do not admonish them but instead listen in an effort to better understand and help. The major difference between an effective manager and an ineffective one is that the former listens with a sensitive ear and the latter with a deaf ear. When an employee asks for help, he or she usually needs to be assured of being understood and respected.

Being Understood

It seems easier for some managers to apply basic principles of career counseling with strangers than with their colleagues and subordinates. For example, federal and state civil rights organizations tend to have racist and sexist behaviors unchecked, chemical dependency agencies work more effectively with alcoholic clients than with alcoholic colleagues, and mental institutions diagnose and rehabilitate clients who walk in from the street but seem impotent to abate the maladjustment among their own staff. In the same vein, some organizations provide effective out-reach community services but provide few effective services for their own employees.

When discriminated against or harassed workers need assistance, they want their manager or supervisor to show friendly, warm interest. They want to be seen as persons. They do not want to be analyzed and intellectualized. The career counseling encounter is most effective between *people* rather than between *concepts* and *theories*. Distressed workers want to be able to tell their story in their own way and in their own time. Equally important, they want to be heard. True, they may ramble, digress, seem to be incoherent, and at times bring in extraneous details, but they want to tell it. They do not want supervisors to put words in their mouths.

Distressed workers can be helped to tell their stories by thoughtful questions. Rules of thumb for asking questions are: (1) determine what is needed to understand the problem; (2) ask questions that show the other person you are interested in him or her; (3) if a question can wait for another time, don't ask it; and (4) ask only questions necessary in offering the help that is needed. Carefully worded and timely questions can let an individual know that his or her situation is appreciated. Employees seeking relief from discrimination or harassment should not be judged as good or bad persons. Whatever their situation, supervisors should suspend value judgment. Useful help is not likely to come from administrators with negative beliefs about an employee's ethnicity. For example, a white racist should not counsel a minority worker complaining about job discrimination. Nor should a sexual harasser counsel a harassed employee.

Survival Needs

Beyond the noble injunctions for managers and supervisors to be non-judgmental and empathic, there are several reasons it is difficult for them to behave that way:

1. The actions of supervisors, co-workers, and subordinates sometimes make it difficult to resolve conflicts.
2. It is not easy or natural for some managers and supervisors to be culturally sensitive persons.
3. There are times when everyone in an organization is offended by the behavior of a complaining employee.

The more effective managers and supervisors seek to understand their own values, prejudices, and aspirations in order to cope with diversity-related problems in a constructive manner. It is imperative that whatever change strategy is employed, it should not result in either party losing their identity:

> To incorporate another person is to swallow him up, to overwhelm him, and to destroy him; and thus to treat him ultimately as less than a whole person. To identify with another person is to lose oneself, to submerge one's own identity in that of the other, to be overwhelmed, and hence to treat oneself ultimately as less than a whole person. To pass judgment, in Jung's sense, is to place oneself in an attitude of superiority; to agree offhandedly is to place oneself in an attitude of inferiority. . . . The personality can cease to exist in two ways—either by destroying the other, or being absorbed by the other—and maturity in interpersonal relationships demands that neither oneself nor the other shall disappear, but that each shall contribute to the affirmation and realization of the other's personality. (Storr, 1961, pp. 41–43)

It is not uncommon for minorities and women to maintain job-related anxieties that are not easily pinpointed. Such employees are plagued with pervasive apprehensions of impending disasters. Sometimes the mere thought of going to work is enough to produce physiological states of anxiety—rapid heartbeat, upset stomach, sweating, and trembling. Fear is one of the most troublesome of all emotion reactions. From the point of view of the individuals experiencing it, fear disables them at a time they most need to remain calm. Often the source of fear is unknown, has been forgotten or repressed.

A seminal study of cultural diversity in the workplace conducted by Fine and associates (1990) concluded that the white men, women, and minority respondents did not share a common culture of organizational life. White males experienced the organization culture in totality; women experienced it from the bottom; minority employees—few in number—shared it in isolation. Further, each individual was most comfortable communicating within his or her own group. That is, women more easily shared information with other women, white men with white men, and minorities with minorities. Consequently, different groups received differential information, which greatly restricted the knowledge base of women and minorities. While Fine's study was limited to a federal agency that employed five hundred people, the data provide strong evidence that gender and race are significant factors in managing diversity within any organization.

EMPLOYEE NEEDS RELATED TO SURVIVAL

Major obstacles to achieving diversity are delusions and phobias. The *maladjusted employee delusion* and the *maladjusted employee phobia* may be the most pervasive factors causing and perpetuating inadequate adjustments to culturally diverse workers. A delusion is a false judgment, while a phobia is an unreasonable and persistent fear of some object or situation and an attempt to avoid it. Both words are used by psychologists to indicate disorders in the cognitive processes of individuals. However, the terms are used in text to designate sociopsychological disorders that affect not only individuals but also groups. In addition, unlike psychological usages, the terms imply highly contagious social conditions transmitted to the organization culture through the process of socialization.

The maladjusted employee delusion is a false belief that people who deviate from organization norms because of gender, ethnic identity, age, or other cultural conditions are inferior. The maladjusted employee phobia is an unsubstantiated and persistent fear of individuals who are culturally different from majority-group employees, and an effort is made to avoid contact with them. The viable options for maladjusted employees are as follows: (1) change their jobs, (2) change their attitudes and behaviors, (3) change their co-workers' attitudes and behaviors, or (4) do nothing. Some combination of the first three options is the most helpful course of action.

Extremely neurotic or psychotic workers foster job aspirations that have little or no relation to reality. Excluding the extremely maladjusted, there does appear to be a significant relationship among actual job situations, defense mechanisms, and problem resolution. Most ethnic minority employees are not extremely maladjusted but often are treated as though they are. Sooner or later, their behavior reflects the initially erroneous perceptions of them. Much of the plight of distressed employees stems from the inability of their supervisors and co-workers to understand and accept them. Many managers think that distressed female and minority employees are alien people having needs unlike "normal" people. A closer analysis of corporate adjustment patterns of distressed female and minority employees shows that it is not their behavior that is abnormal but their opportunities to behave as normal people. They have the following needs.

The Need Not to Be Loved to Death

Distressed employees do not need misplaced kindness; instead, they need empathetic, fair supervisors. In some instances, supervisors try to make up for subordinates' debilitating ethnicity, gender, age, or physical conditions by giving them unearned rewards. No matter how well intended, unearned promotions and busy work jobs cause additional problems. With much emphasis currently being placed on understanding and assisting culturally diverse people, it is easy for supervisors to engage in overcompensatory actions. However, when this is done, it may lead to the *distressed employee syndrome.*

The distressed employee syndrome refers to the process by which people use their points of distress (e.g., gender, age, ethnicity, race, physical disability) to beat the system. "When I want to get out of doing an assignment," a female worker confided, "I just tell my male supervisor that I'm having 'female problems.' " This is beating the system by not doing the required work. Using their personal distress as a crutch, they hobble through work, manipulating their perceived oppressors (other personnel). Another individual said, "If I want to leave early and beat the traffic, I tell my boss that we old folks need to get on the road before the kids get out there." Few individuals in this category are seeking to optimize their contributions to their employers. Instead, they only seek to minimize complications during their employment.

To the worker who knows that he or she is not putting forth the required effort but is receiving positive sanctions, success based on merit is a meaningless concept. Yet using the old maxim that the shortest distance between two points is a straight line, many workers—well adjusted and maladjusted—are content to "slide by" with minimum effort. Making it easy for ethnic minorities, women, older workers, or any other workers to slide by also makes it easy to deny them promotions.

Rather than being loved to death, most minorities and women are typically denied opportunities to advance in the organization. It is common for managers to make what they believe are fair, objective evaluations. Upon review, it is evident that, compared with white workers, black, Hispanic, and women employees' evaluations are consistently lower—particularly those of black employees. Instead of having a normal evaluation curve, the evaluations of minorities and women cluster at the lower end of the scale. Those who succeed are more likely to be "super" workers—often heads and shoulders above their peers in ability.

The Need to Receive Consistent Treatment

As noted earlier, supervisors and co-workers often assume that culturally different employees are of lower intelligence. Along with this assumption goes the belief that culturally different people do not know the difference between properly executed and improperly executed job assignments. As a result, they frequently are talked to as if they were children. Furthermore, rewards and punishments are capriciously given to them. Unlike loving employees to death, supervisors and co-workers who use this technique thwart the recipient's desire to compete for success. "Why bother?" a dejected Hatian employee frowned. "When they feel like giving me praise, they will. When they don't, they won't." He was referring to his supervisor who had praised him the previous week for a similar report that he was criticized for this time. Feeling confused and powerless, many culturally different workers give up and sink deeper into the mire of mediocrity; others retire on the job. If enough supervisors respond this way, minorities and women do not drop out of the workplace; they are pushed out!

Managing diversity requires fair, not preferential, treatment. Nor should employers succumb to pressure to hire or promote protected class people to any positions that are available in order to fill quotas (Haro, 1990). That kind of behavior is offensive to the recipients of such charity ("tokens"), and it is detrimental to the organization. After people are fairly hired, the process of managing diversity can occur if the suggestions that follow are heeded.

MAKE A PLAN

First, an organization must agree that one of its goals is to increase organizational effectiveness and enhance self-renewal through diversity. Although specific objectives of a diversity effort will vary according to an organization's resources, the most successful organizations incorporate strategies:

1. To build trust among all employees.
2. To create an open, problem-solving climate in which diversity-related problems are confronted and differences are clarified, both within and between groups.
3. To assign decision-making and problem-solving responsibilities.
4. To increase the sense of sharing in diversity goals and objectives.
5. To increase each employee's awareness of the diversity "process" and its consequences for organization effectiveness.

Clearly, these objectives have a better chance of being achieved through carefully planned interventions. Drawing upon research studies and behavioral sciences principles, some of the basic assumptions underlying a diversity initiative should be the following:

1. The basic building blocks of any organization are people, and the most effective units of change are work groups, not individuals.

2. The attitudes most employees hold toward peoples of other cultures and working with them tend to reflect how culturally different people are treated by the organization. Therefore, if necessary, efforts should be made to improve the way out-group employees are treated rather than attempting to change the out-group employees.

3. Most employees are not motivated to achieve cultural diversity through tight control and threats of punishment. Rather, they respond best when challenged to accomplish organizational objectives to which they are committed.

4. The culture of most organizations tends to suppress the open expression of feeling that people have about each other and about cultural differences. Suppression of feelings adversely affects solving diversity-related problems. The expression of feelings is an important part of becoming committed to cultural diversity. But this must be done in a manner that does not result in psychological damage to individual employees. Nor should it foster group divisiveness.

5. Most employees will be committed to and care about diversity programs they help create. When change is introduced, it will be most effectively implemented if the groups and individuals involved have a sense of ownership in the process. Commitment is most likely to be attained where there is active employee participation in the design and implementation of diversity activities.

6. Employees who learn to work together in a constructively open way by providing feedback to each other become better able to profit from their own experiences and also to utilize more fully the resources of their co-workers. Further, the cultural growth of individual employees is facilitated by relationships that are open, supportive, and trusting.

Diversity Strategies

A popular strategy in diversity initiatives is the use of an *action-research model* of intervention. There are three processes in an action-research approach, all of which involve extensive collaboration between a consultant and the organization: (1) data gathering from individual employees and members of work units, (2) feedback to key personnel in the organization, and (3) joint action planning based on the feedback. Succinctly, this consists of conducting a comprehensive needs assessment by asking employees at all levels questions about how diversity currently is being implemented. Written questionnaires or oral interviews may be used. When correctly done, action research will help an organization evaluate the demographics of its workforce and devise strategies for better utilizing all employees. Proven building blocks for a diversity program include team building, intergroup problem solving, confrontation meetings, goal-setting and planning, third-party facilitation, and consulting pairs.

Team building focuses on early identification and solution of a work group's problems, particularly interpersonal and intergroup roadblocks that stand in the way of collaborative, cooperative, and creative functioning. Work procedures can be made more effective by using different approaches and by viewing leadership as a shared function to be performed by all members of the group. Interpersonal and intergroup relationships can be improved by working on communication skills and conflict management.

Intergroup problem solving focuses on bringing culturally diverse employees together for the purpose of reducing destructive competitiveness and resolving intergroup conflict centering on such matters as individual beliefs that discrimination is occurring in favor of minorities and women to the detriment of white workers and vice versa.

Confrontation meetings bring together the entire management team to focus on ways to solve specific diversity-related problems. Team members identify problems, establish priorities, and assign responsibilities for problem resolution.

Goal-setting and planning involve supervisor-subordinate pairs and teams throughout the organization. The goal is systematic job performance improvement through target-setting with mutual commitment and review.

Third-party facilitation involves skilled third parties (management/diversity consultants) helping executive officers diagnose, understand, and resolve difficult diversity problems.

Consulting pairs consist of a manager and a consultant analyzing day-to-day diversity activities. The consultant can be within the organization (human resource/diversity specialist) or without.

A major feature of these approaches is a heavy reliance on experience-based learning, especially to develop the competence needed to successfully manage diversity. Managers and supervisors accustomed to solving technical problems are often struck by the sharp contrast between technical problems and diversity problems:

- Technical problems tend to be clear and precise. Diversity problems tend to be difficult to isolate and state precisely.

- Technical problems tend to be specific and dependent on objective details. Diversity problems tend to evolve around feelings, personal opinions, and personalities.

- Technical problems are easily quantified and measured. Diversity problems, while measurable, often involve many subjective variables and this makes precise measurement difficult.

- Technical problems can be directly traced to human error or equipment failure. Diversity problems frequently resist clear cause and effect relations. This often leads to blaming innocent people.

- Solutions to technical problems are easier to implement. Resolution of diversity problems is often resisted because individuals are reluctant to share power, discard erroneous attitudes and beliefs, and alter the corporate culture.

- The assignment of responsibility for solving technical problems tends to be clear and precise. The complexity of diversity problems often crosses administrative lines of authority and thus makes assignment of responsibility and follow-up troublesome.

A common error made by managers and supervisors is to assume that all employees are talking the same diversity language. Stan Kossen (1987) provided valuable advice to individuals responsible for managing diversity: "(1) Do not assume everyone knows what you are talking about. (2) Do not assume that you know what others are talking about without asking them questions to make certain" (p. 63).

Goodwin Watson (1969) recommended certain critical factors and questions that can be adopted for analyzing an organization's diversity situation: (1) What is the history of the difficulty—when was it noticed? (2) What has been done in the past to deal with it? (3) Where and when does it occur? (4) Is the problem found in other work units? (5) What is the attitude of the people involved? Herbert Thelen (1969) provided additional advice: "To me, the most important conditions to understand are those that I can control, and they include my own behavior, the topic or task, and the organization (individual, self-selected small group, committee, large group, society, and so on) which provides the milieu for individual effort" (pp. 44–45).

OVERCOMING INERTIA

The best diversity plans evolve from creative individuals and team efforts initiated from within the organization. Whatever plan is adopted, however, the employees are likely to play one of three roles.

Cynics operate on the basis that diversity activities are naturally conflictual and competitive. They play a win-lose game in which some of the employees must lose—and they pray that it will not be them. They are willing to succeed at the expense of other employees.

Guileless ones assume that all they need is "a little help from their friends." And, everyone is their friend. They play a win-win game in which all employees will win. That is, they do not try to succeed at the expense of other employees.

Pragmatists play win-win and win-lose games of organization survival. They will embrace diversity, especially if it will earn them promotions, prestige, or additional salary. Or they will resist it if doing so is believed to be in their best interests.

The actors in the situation are not mere *tabulae rasae* to be coerced into new performance. Rather, they are human energy systems which provide the motive power as well as the specific behaviors of change. . . . Explicitly consider the conditions that must be set up in order to facilitate the proposed action; who must be involved, how, in what kinds of grouping. In short, define the roles of each person to be involved and decide who is going to communicate what to whom and when. (Thelen, 1969, pp. 44–46)

As noted earlier, a diversity program is not likely to succeed without support from the CEO. And repeating the requisite conditions cited earlier, the success of a diversity initiative will depend upon being well planned, organization-wide, and managed from the top. CEOs have the power not only to influence what goes on throughout their organizations but they can also set up functional diversity structures and appropriate reward systems that will determine such matters as who communicates with whom, who will cooperate and who will compete, how motivated subordinates will be, and so on. Robert Blake and Jane Mouton (1964) summed it up: "The character of a company, whether dynamic, forceful, initiating, and risk-taking, or mechanical, repetitive, conservative, dull, aimless, or backward-looking, is established at the top" (p. 35).

Structures must be devised to provide opportunities for continual feedback and evaluation in the change process. Without open channels of communication, managers and supervisors cannot know the outcome of their efforts; they are neither confronted with failure nor rewarded for success. Criteria that measure success in achieving diversity should be part of the annual evaluation of all managers and supervisors. Relatedly, cultural diversity topics must be incorporated into all training programs.

FINAL WORDS

In addition to the morality of treating all people fairly, there are laws against discriminatory behavior. This is not a "political correctness"; it is the law. Violation of these laws makes the individual perpetrators as well as their organization liable for damages. When hiring employees, evaluate each applicant based on the job description. And each job description must contain only the requirements needed to carry it out. Unnecessary education, physical abilities, experiences, or skills should be omitted. When interviewing job applicants, it is inappropriate to ask questions—or base hiring decisions—on race, national origin, religion, age, sex, family, or marital status. All employees must be informed of promotional opportunities. Nor should separate lines of job progression be based on race or sex. Also, all employees must have an equal opportunity to be selected for training.

Too many organizations are led by individuals obsessed with determining *who ought not to be hired and promoted* rather than *who needs to be hired and promoted*. Managers and supervisors should not engage in behaviors that can be construed as perpetuating racism, sexism, ageism, or handicappism. Nor should they allow such behavior to be carried out by their subordinates. When discipline is necessary, it should be based on objective standards with penalties being consistent among all employees. *All groups and individuals should be treated equitably.* Nothing should be done to create or perpetuate race, color, nationality, religion, sex, age, or disability stereotypes. Effective managers and supervisors show personal concern for all their subordinates. They budget time to talk with and listen to them. Trust and respect are the essential characteristics of successful managers and supervisors. In summary, they teach diversity by living it.

Working with culturally different people is not always easy. Nor is it always understood and appreciated by employees. There will be failures. But, as illustrated throughout this book, managing diversity is not only good human relations; it is good business. Survival in the workplace often requires extraordinary effort from minorities, women, and the other protected class people. The American workplace does not reflect *e pluribus unum* (from many, one). It is comprised of many peoples trying to become one cohesive, interrelated workforce. When artificial discriminators are removed and culturally different employees are judged and treated on their merit, diversity becomes the rule in an organization instead of the exception. During this transition, it is important for managers and supervisors, as well as their subordinates, to remember that progress has been made. While in most organizations much more remains to be done, an old slave saying puts situations like this in proper perspective.

> We ain't what we ought to be.
> We ain't what we gonna be.
> We ain't what we wanta be.
> But, thank God,
> We ain't what we was.

Appendix

ANSWERS TO THE SEXUAL HARASSMENT QUIZ

All of the behaviors on the list have been cited in court cases. The defendants were found guilty when their behaviors were deemed unwelcome sexual advances, requests for sexual favors, or other verbal or physical contact of a sexual nature. Sexual harassment (1) implicitly or explicitly pertains to the complainant's condition of employment, (2) requires submission to or rejection of the behavior that affects the complainant's employment conditions, and (3) the behavior unreasonably interferes with the complainant's job performance or creates an intimidating, hostile, or offensive work environment.

INTERPRETATION OF BEHAVIOR STYLE QUESTIONNAIRE SCORES

The longest bar represents your foremost concern in work-related situations. For example, some people are more concerned with their own individual growth and integrity than that of their colleagues or the organization (employer). The shortest bar indicates the area you may tend to overlook. People who are least concerned with group relationships may have difficulty effectively working with culturally different people.

References

Abbasi, S. M., & Hollman, K. W. (1991). Managing cultural diversity: The challenge of the 90s. *Records Management Quarterly, 25,* 24–32.

Abowd, J. M., & Freeman, R. B. (1991). *Immigration, trade and the labor market.* Chicago: University of Chicago Press.

Adler, N. J. (1986). *International dimensions of organizational behavior.* Boston: Kent.

Aiello, J. R., & Jones, S. E. (1971). Field study of the proxemic behavior of young school children in three subcultural groups. *Journal of Personality and Social Psychology, 27,* 351–356.

Albemarle Paper Co. v. Moody, 422 U.S. 405 (1975).

Albert, S., & Dobbs, J. M. Jr. (1970). Physical distance and persuasion. *Journal of Personality and Social Psychology, 15,* 265–270.

Allan, J. (Ed.). (1987). Counseling with expressive arts. [Symposium]. *Elementary School Guidance and Counseling, 21,* 251–323.

Allen, I. L. (1983). *The language of ethnic conflict.* New York: Columbia University Press.

Allen, V. L., & Wilder, D. A. (1979). Group categorization and attribution: A belief similarity. *Small Group Behavior, 10,* 73–80.

Allport, G. W. (1954). *The nature of prejudice.* New York: Doubleday.

Amott, T. L., & Matthaei, J. (1991). *Race, gender, and work.* Boston: South End Press.

Anderson, C. M., & Stewart, S. (1983). *Mastering resistance: A practical guide to family therapy.* New York: Guilford Press.

Anderson, J. A. (1993). Thinking about diversity. *Training & Development, 47,* 59–60.

Anderson, R. O. (1981). Off the shelf: New opportunity for older Americans. *Aging and Work, 4,* 203–207.

Anderson, S., & Weagant, R. (Eds.). (1972). *Retention of older persons in the labor force.* Chicago: The Forum Series.

Anderson, W. T. (1990). *Reality isn't what it used to be: Theatrical politics, ready-to-wear religion, global myths and other wonders of the postmodern world.* New York: HarperCollins.

Apostle, R. A., & Glock, C. Y. (1983). *The anatomy of racial attitudes.* Los Angeles: University of California Press.

Arrendo-Dowd, P. M., & Gonsalves, J. (1980). Preparing culturally effective counselors. *Personnel and Guidance Journal, 58,* 657–662.

Asher, R., & Stephenson, C. (Eds.). (1990). *Labor divided: Race and ethnicity in United States labor struggles, 1835–1960.* New York: State University of New York Press.

Asuncion-Lande, N. (1983). Language theory and linguistic principles. In W. B. Gudykunst (Ed.), *Intercultural communication theory: Current perspectives.* Beverly Hills, CA: Sage.

Atchley, R. C. (1980). *The social forces in later life.* Belmont, CA: Wadsworth.

Atkinson, D., Morten, G., & Sue, D. W. (1979). *Counseling minorities: A cross-cultural perspective.* Springfield, IL: Charles C. Thomas.

Bailey, T. R. (1987). *Immigrant and native workers.* Boulder, CO: Westview Press.

Banerji, S. (1987). *Deferred hopes: Blacks in contemporary America.* New York: Advent.

Barcorn, C. N., & Dixon, D. (1984). The effects of touch on depressed and vocationally undecided clients. *Journal of Counseling Psychology, 31,* 489–497.

Barkin, A. C. (1986). *A supervisor's guide to the employee counseling service program.* Washington, DC: U.S. Department of Health and Human Services.

Barna, L. M. (1976). Intercultural communication stumblingblocks. In L. A. Samovar & R. E. Porter (Eds.), *Intercultural communication: A reader* (pp. 291–297). 2d ed. Belmont, CA: Wadsworth.

Barnlund, D. C. (1989). *Communicative styles of Japanese and Americans: Images and realities.* Belmont, CA: Wadsworth.

Bateson, G. (1966). Readings in the codes of human interaction. In A. Smith (Ed.), *Communication and culture* (pp. 417–422). New York: Holt, Rinehart & Winston.

Baxter, J. C. (1970). Interpersonal spacing in natural settings. *Sociometry, 33,* 444–456.

Beach, M. H. (1981). Business and the graying of America. *Aging and Work, 4,* 190–200.

Beamer, L. (1992). Learning intercultural communication competence. *Journal of Business Communication, 29,* 285–303.

Beauvoir, S. D. (1952). *The second sex.* Trans. by E. M. Parshley. New York: Alfred A. Knopf.

Beck, M., Hager, M., Dentworth, L., & Carroll, G. (1991). Old enough to get fired. *Newsweek,* December, 64–66.

Beckett, S. (1965). *Proust.* London: J. Calder.

Beckhard, R. (1969). *Organization development: Strategies and methods.* Reading, MA: Addison-Wesley.

Bennett, C. I. (1990). *Comprehensive multicultural education: Theory and practice.* 2d ed. Boston: Allyn & Bacon.

Benokrantis, N. V., & Feagin, J. R. (1986). *Modern sexism: Subtle and covert discrimination.* Englewood Cliffs, NJ: Prentice-Hall.

Biles, G. E., & Pryatel, H. A. (1978). Myths, management, and women. *Personnel Journal, 57,* 572–578.

Birdwhistell, R. L. (1970). *Kinesics and content.* Philadelphia: University of Pennsylvania Press.

Bitter, J. A. (1979). *Introduction to rehabilitation.* St. Louis: C. V. Mosby.

Bittle, L. R. (1985). *What every supervisor should know.* 5th ed. New York: McGraw-Hill.

Black Enterprise. (1993). The challenge of managing diversity in the workplace. *Author, 23,* 79–90.

Blackwell, J. E. (1991). *The black community.* New York: HarperCollins.

Blake, R. R., & Mouton, J. S. (1964). *Building a dynamic corporation through grid organization development.* Reading, MA: Addison-Wesley.

Blanchard, F. A., & Crosby, F. J. (1989). *Affirmative action in perspective.* New York: Springer-Verlag.

Bohren, J. (1993). Six myths of sexual harassment. *Management Review, 82,* 61–63.

Bohrer v. Hanes Corp., 715 F.2d 213 (5th Cir. 1985).

Bolman, L. G., & Deal, T. E. (1984). *Modern approaches to understanding and managing organizations.* San Francisco: Jossey-Bass.

Bowe, F. (1980). *Rehabilitating America.* New York: Harper & Row.

Bowie, N. E. (Ed.). (1988). *Equal opportunity.* Boulder, CO: Westview Press.

Bowman, G. (1968). Quoted in C. Bird. *Born female.* New York: Simon & Schuster.

Brantman, M. (1978). What happens to insurance rates when handicapped people come to work? *Disabled USA.* Washington, DC: President's Committee on Employment of the Handicapped.

Brenner, M. (1972). Management development for women. *Personnel Journal, 51,* 165–167.

Brimmer, A. F. (1993). The economic discrimination. *Black Enterprise, 23,* 2.

Brislin, R. W. (1981). *Cross-cultural encounters.* New York: Pergamon Press.

Brislin, R. W., Cushner, K., Cherrie, C., & Yong, M. (1986). *Intercultural interactions: A practical guide.* Beverly Hills, CA: Sage.

Broadnax, W. (1992). From civil rights to valuing differences. *The Bureaucrat, 19,* 9–13.

Broverman, I. K., Vogel, S. R., Boverman, D. M., Clarkston, F. E., & Rosenkrantz, P. S. (1972). Sex-role stereotypes: A current appraisal. *Journal of Social Issues, 28,* 59–78.

Brown, I. C. (1973). *Understanding race relations.* Englewood Cliffs, NJ: Prentice-Hall.

Burdett, M., & Frohlich, B. (1977). *The effect of disability on unit income.* Washington, DC: Social Security Administration.

Burgen, M. (1977). The problem of women bosses. *Ebony, 3,* 94–100.

Butler, R. N. (1969). *The effects of medical and health progress on the social and economic aspects of the life cycle.* Paper delivered at the National Institute of Industrial Gerontology, Washington, DC, March 12.

Butler, R. N. (1974). Successful aging. *Mental Health, 58,* 1–12.

Butler, R. N. (1975). *Why survive? Being old in America.* New York: Harper & Row.

Calabrese, R. L. (1990). The public school: A source of alienation for minority parents. *Journal of Negro Education, 59,* 154.

Campbell, K. (1991). Factoring culture into the women in management equation. *Equal Opportunities International, 10,* 53–60.

Carnegie Foundation. (1988). *An imperiled generation: Saving urban schools.* Princeton, NJ: Author.

Carroll, L. (1982). *Through the looking glass.* New York: Oxford University Press.

Carter v. Bennett, 840 F.2d 63 (D.C. Cir. 1988).

Cashmore, E. E. (1986). *The logic of racism.* New York: Unwin Hyman.

Combs, M. W., & Gruhl, J. (1986). *Affirmative action: Theory, analysis, and prospects.* Jefferson, NC: McFarland.

Comer, R. C., & Pillavin, J. A. (1975). As others see us: Attitudes of physically handicapped and normals toward own and other groups. *Rehabilitation Literature, 36,* 206–221.

Condon, J. C. (1985). *Good neighbors: Communicating with Mexicans.* Yarmouth, ME: Intercultural Press.

Condon, J. C., & Yousef, F. (1985). *An introduction to intercultural communication.* New York: Macmillan.

Connecticut v. Teal, 102 S.Ct. 2525 (1982).

Cornell v. Sparrow Hospital Assn., 377 N.W. 2d, 755 (Mich. 1985).

Coupland, N., Giles, H., & Wiemann, J. M. (1991). *"Miscommunication" and problematic talk.* Beverly Hills, CA: Sage.

Cova v. Coca-Cola Bottling Co. of St. Louis, 574 F.2d 958 (8th Cir. 1978).

Cox, R. H., & Blake, S. (1991). Managing cultural diversity: Implications for organizational competitiveness. *Academy of Management Executives, 5,* (3), 45–54.

Cox, T. H. Jr. (1991). Managing diversity: Implications for organizational effectiveness. *Academy of Management Executives, 5,* (3), 45–54.

Crigler, P. (1973). Quoted in H. Call. Why does activist feminine role attract or repel some women? *San Diego Union,* October 21.

Crosby, F., Broomely, S., & Saxe, L. (1980). Recent unobtrusive studies of black and white discrimination and prejudice: A literature review. *Psychological Bulletin, 87,* 546–563.

Cull, J. G., & Hardy, R. E. (1973). *Adjustment to work.* Springfield, IL: Charles C. Thomas.

Cummings, T. G., & Huse, E. F. (1989). *Organization development and change.* 4th ed. Chicago: West.

Curt, C.J.N. (1980). *Hispanic-Anglo conflicts in nonverbal communication.* Second Annual Conference of the Institute of Nonverbal Research, Teachers College, Columbia University, March.

Curtis, D., Windsor, J., & Stephen, R. (1989). Preferences in business and communication education. *Communication Education, 38,* 6–14.

Cushman, D., & King, S. (1986). The role of communication rules in explaining intergroup interaction. In W. B. Gudykunst (Ed.), *Intergroup communication* (pp. 39–50). London: Edward Arnold.

Davis, M., & Skupier, J. (1982). *Body movement and nonverbal communication: An annotated bibliography, 1971–1980.* Bloomington: Indiana University Press.

Deloria, V., Jr. (1973). *God is red.* New York: Grosset & Dunlap.

Dewart, J. (Ed.). (1991). *The state of black America.* New York: Urban League.

Dickens, F. Jr., & Dickens, J. B. (1991). *The black manager: Making it in the corporate world.* Rev. ed. New York: American Management Association.

Disraeli, B. (1849). Address. British House of Commons, February 1.

DiStefano, J. (1979). Cited in M. Asante et al. (Eds.), *Handbook of intercultural communication.* Beverly Hills, CA: Sage.

Dominguez, C. (1992). The challenge of Workforce 2000. *The Bureaucrat, 21,* 15–19.

Donaldson, S., Geneva, W., & Van Dyk, R. A. (1988). *Discourse and discrimination.* Detroit: Wayne State University Press.

Dorenkamp, A. G., McClymer, J. F., Moynihan, M. M., & Vadum, A. C. (Eds.). (1985). *Images of women in American popular culture.* New York: Harcourt Brace Jovanovich.

Dubinskas, F. A. (1988). *Making time: Ethnographies of high-technology organizations.* Philadelphia: Temple University Press.

Duleep, H. O., & Sanders, S. (1992). Discrimination at the top: American-born Asian and white men. *Industrial Relations, 31,* 416–432.

The Economist. (1960). April 12.

Edwards, A. (1991). The enlightened manager: How to treat all employees fairly. *Working Woman, 16,* 45–51.

Ehrlich, H. (1992). National Institute Against Prejudice and Violence. *Personnel Journal, 71,* 30–36.

Eisenberg, M. G., Griggins, C., & Duval, R. J. (1982). *Disabled people as second-class citizens.* New York: Springer-Verlag.

Eisner, R. J. (1987). *The expression of attitude.* New York: Springer-Verlag.

Ekman, P., & Friesen, W. V. (1986). A new pan-cultural expression of emotions. *Motivation and Emotion, 20,* 288–298.

Ekman, P., et al. (1987). Universals and cultural differences in judgments of facial expressions of emotion. *Journal of Personality and Social Psychology, 43,* 712–717.

Endo, R., Sue, S., & Wagner, N. (Eds.). (1980). *Asian Americans: Social and psychological perspectives.* Palto Alto, CA: Science & Behavior Books.

Equal Employment Opportunity Commission. (1991). Work and workers in the year 2000. *Indicators of equal employment opportunity status and trends.* Washington, DC: U.S. Government Printing Office.

Esponoza v. Farah Mfg. Co., 414 U.S. 811 (1973).

Evans, S. (1992). Conflict can be positive. *HR Magazine, 37,* 49–51.

Fabian, J. J. (1972). The hazards of being a professional woman. *Professional Psychology, 3,* 324–326.

Farb, P. (1973). *Word play.* New York: Alfred A. Knopf.

Farley, J. (1979). *Affirmative action and the woman worker.* New York: AMACOM.

Farley, R., & Allen, W. A. (1987). *The color line and the quality of life in America.* New York: Russell Sage Foundation.

Feagin, J. R., & Feagin, C. B. (1993). *Discrimination American style.* Englewood Cliffs, NJ: Prentice-Hall.

Fernandez, J. P. (1991). *Managing a diverse work force: Regaining the competitive edge.* Lexington, MA: Lexington Books.

Festinger, L. (1950). Informal social communication. *Psychological Review, 57,* 271–282.

Filipczak, B. (1994). Is it getting chilly in here? Men and women at work. *Training, 31,* 25–30.

Fillmore, A. (Ed.). (1987). *Women MBAs: A foot in the door.* Boston: G. K. Hall.

Fine, M. G., & Asch, A. (1981). Disabled women. *Journal of Social Welfare, 8,* 233–248.

Fine, M. G., Johnson, F. L., & Ryan, M. S. (1990). Cultural diversity in the workplace. *Public Personnel Management, 19,* 505–519.

Fisher, S. (1982). *From margin to mainstream: The social progress of black Americans.* New York: Praeger.

Fixico, D. L. (1986). *Termination and relocation.* Albuquerque: University of New Mexico Press.

Flanders, J. (1976). *Practical psychology.* New York: Harper & Row.

Flanigan v. Prudential Federal Savings & Loan Assn., 720 P.2d (Mont. 1986).

Fletcher, B. R. (1990). *Organization transformation theorists and practitioners: Profiles and themes.* Westport, CT: Praeger.

Florian, V. (1978). Employees opinions of the disabled person as a worker. *Rehabilitation Counselor, 22,* 38–43.

Flower, J. (1989). Differences make a difference. *Healthcare Forum, 35,* 62–69.

Flynn, K. (1992). How to avoid hostility in the workplace. *Personnel Journal, 17,* 32

Follman, J. F. (1978). *Helping the troubled employee.* New York: AMACOM.

Foster, C. R. (1953). *Psychology for life and adjustment.* Chicago: American Technical Society.

Fountain v. Safeway Stores, 555 F.2d 753 (9th Cir. 1977).

Foxman, L. D., & Polsky, W. L. (1989). Cross-cultural understanding. *Personnel Journal, 68,* 12–14.

Frame, R. M., Nielson, W. R., & Pate, L. E. (1989). Creating excellence of crisis: Organizational transformation. *Journal of Applied Behavioral Sciences, 25,* 109–122.

Franklin, P. A. (1977). Impact of disability on the family structure. *Social Security Bulletin, 40,* 3–18.

Freud, S. (1967). Quoted in G. Selder (Ed.), *Great quotations.* New York: Pocket Books.

Frideres, J. (1989). *Multiculturalism and intergroup relations.* New York: Greenwood Press.

Friedan, B. (1963). *The feminine mystique.* New York: W. W. Norton.

Frink, S. (1992). Job stress: $ down the drain. *New Mexico Business Journal, 16,* 31–33.

Fritz, N. R. (1989). Sexual harassment and the working woman. *Journal of Personnel, 66,* 4–10.

Frontera v. Sindell, 522 F.2d 1215 (6th Cir. 1975).

Furnco Construction Co. v. Waters, 438 U.S. 567 (1978).

Galen, M., & Palmer, T. (1994). White, male, and worried. *Business Week,* January 31, 50–55.

Garcia v. Gloor, 609 F.2d 156 (5th Cir. 1980).

Gbekobu, K. N. (1984). Counseling African children in the United States. *Elementary School Guidance and Counseling Journal, 18,* 225–230.

Gemson, C. (1991). How to cultivate today's multicultural work force. *Employment Relations Today, 18,* 157–160.

Giles, H., & Edwards, J. R. (Eds.). (1983). Language in multicultural settings. [Symposium]. *Journal of Multilingual and Multicultural Development, 4.*

Glasgow, D. (1980). *The black underclass: Poverty, unemployment, and entrapment of ghetto youth.* San Francisco: Jossey-Bass.

Glasser, W. (1965). *Reality therapy.* New York: Harper & Row.

Gold, S. J. (1992). *Refugee communities: A comparative field study.* Newbury Park, CA: Sage.

Goldberg, D. (Ed.). (1990). *The anatomy of racism.* Minneapolis: University of Minnesota Press.

Goldberg, P. (1967). *Misogyny and the college girl.* Paper presented at the annual meeting of the Eastern Psychological Association, April.

Goldstein, J., & Leopold, M. (1990). Corporate culture vs. ethnic culture. *Personnel Journal, 69,* 83–92.

Gordon, J. (1992). Rethinking diversity. *Training, 29,* 23–30.

Gordon, J. E. (1963). *Personality and behavior.* New York: Macmillan.

Greenberg, J., & Pysczynski, T. The effects of an overheard ethnic slur on evaluations of the target: How to spread a social disease. *Journal of Experimental Social Psychology, 21,* 61–72.

Greenblum, J. (1977). Effect of vocational rehabilitation on employment and earnings of the disabled: State variations. *Social Security Bulletin, 40,* 3–16.

Greenwald, A. (1988). *Psychological foundations of attitudes.* New York: L. Erlbaum Associates.

Greiff, J. (1989). When an employee's performance slumps. *Nation's Business, 77,* 44–45.

Grier, W. H., & Cobbs, P. M. (1968). *Black rage.* New York: Basic Books.

Griggs v. Duke Power, 401 U.S. 424 (1971).

Gross, B. R. (1978). *Discrimination in reverse: Is turnabout fair play?* New York: New York University Press.

Gudykunst, W. B., & Ting-Toomey, S. (1988). Culture and affective communication. *The American Behavioral Scientist, 31,* 384–400.

Gunsch, D., & Filipowski, D. (1991). The government's view of the "glass ceiling." *Personnel Journal, 70,* 28.

Guthrie, R. V. (1976). *Even the rat was white: A historical view of psychology.* New York: Harper & Row.

Gutteridge, T. G., & Otte, F. L. (1983). Organizational career development: What's going on out there? *Training & Development, 37,* 22–26.

Hafner, M., & Marcus, N. (1979). Information and attitude toward disability. *Rehabilitation Counselor Bulletin, 23*, 95–102.

Haines, D. W. (Ed.). (1989). *Refugees as immigrants: Cambodians, Laotians, and Vietnamese in America.* Totowa, NJ: Rowman & Littlefield.

Halford, W. K., Hahlweg, K., & Dunne, M. (1990). The cross-cultural consistency of marital communication associated with marital distress: Germany and Australia. *Journal of Marriage and the Family, 52*, 487–500.

Hall, E. T. (1959). *The silent language.* New York: Doubleday.

Hall, E. T. (1966). *The hidden dimensions.* New York: Doubleday.

Hall, E. T. (1976). *Beyond culture.* New York: Doubleday.

Hall, E. T. (1987). *Hidden differences: Doing business with the Japanese.* New York: Doubleday.

Hall, J. A. (1980). Voicetone and persuasion. *Journal of Personality and Social Psychology, 27*, 924–934.

Hamilton v. Rodgers, 783 F.2d 1306 (5th Cir. 1986).

Hammond, T., & Kleiner, B. (1992). Managing multicultural environments. *Equal Opportunities International, 11*, 6–9.

Handy, C. (1981). Building smaller fires. *Modern Maturity, 34*, 35–39.

Hanna, J. L. (1984). Black, white nonverbal differences, dance and dissonance: Implications for desegregation. In A. Wolfgang (Ed.), *Nonverbal behavior, perspectives, applications, and intercultural insights* (pp. 349–385). Toronto: C. J. Hogrefe.

Hardiman, R. (1982). White identity development: A process oriented model for describing the racial consciousness of white Americans. *Dissertation Abstracts International, 43*, 104A. University Microfilms No. 82-10330.

Harman, W. (1988). *Global mind change.* Indianapolis, IN: Institute of Noetic Sciences.

Haro, R. P. (1990). Latinos and executive positions in higher education. *Educational Record, 71*, 39–42.

Harris, L. (1987). *Inside America.* New York: Vintage Books.

Harris, P. R., & Moran, R. T. (1986). *Managing cultural differences.* 2d ed. Houston, TX: Gulf.

Harty, S. J. (1992). Etiquette tips fight discrimination. *Business Insurance, 26*, 16.

Hasan, J. (1992). Human resource management in a new era of globalism. *Business Forum, 17*, 56–59.

Hasazi, S., Brody, G., & Roe, C. A. (1985). Factors associated with the employment status of handicapped youth exiting high school from 1979–1983. *Exceptional Children, 51*, 445–469.

Hayakawa, S. I. (1941). *Language in action.* New York: Harcourt, Brace.

Heikal, M. (1980). Communication across cultural barriers. *Editors and Publishers, 113*, 120.

Helms, J. E. (1984). Toward a theoretical model of the effectiveness of race on counseling: A black and white model. *The Counseling Psychologist, 12*, 153–165.

Henderson, G. (Ed.). (1979). *Understanding and counseling ethnic minorities.* Springfield, IL: Charles C. Thomas.

Henderson, G. (1983). *The human rights of professional helpers.* Springfield, IL: Charles C. Thomas.

Henderson, G. (1989). *Understanding indigenous and foreign cultures.* Springfield, IL: Charles C. Thomas.

Henning, M., & Jardin, A. (1977). *The managerial woman.* New York: Doubleday.

Hersey, P., & Blanchard, K. H. (1982). Leadership style: Attitudes and behaviors. *Training & Development, 36,* 50–52.

Hersey, P., & Blanchard, K. H. (1993). *Management of organizational behavior: Utilizing human resources.* Englewood Cliffs, NJ: Prentice-Hall.

Heslin, R., & Patterson, M. L. (1982). *Nonverbal behavior and social psychology.* New York: Plenum Press.

Hill, N. C. (1981). *Counseling at the workplace.* New York: McGraw-Hill.

Hofstede, G., & Bond, M. (1986). Hofstede's culture dimensions: An independent validation using Rokeach's Value Survey. *Journal of Cross-Cultural Psychology, 15,* 417–433.

Holmes, S. A. (1994). Survey finds minorities resent each other almost as much as they do whites. *New York Times,* March 3, A9.

Hooton, E. A. (1938). *Apes, men and morons.* London: G. Allen & Unwin.

Horowitz, E. L., & Horowitz, R. E. (1938). Development of social attitudes in children. *Sociometry, 1,* 301–338.

Horton, P. B. (1965). *Sociology and the health sciences.* New York: McGraw-Hill.

Huber, G., & Williams, J. (1986). *Human behavior in organizations.* 3d ed. Cincinnati: South-Western.

Hudson Institute. (1987). *Workforce 2000.* Indianapolis, IN: Author.

Hughey, A., & Gelman, E. (1986). Managing the women's way. *Newsweek,* March 17.

Huhn v. Koehring Co., 718 F.2d 239 (7th Cir. 1983).

International Association of Business Communicators (IABC). (1982). *Without bias: A guide book for nondiscriminatory communication.* New York: John Wiley & Sons.

Issacs, H. R. (1963). *The new world of Negro Americans.* New York: John Day.

Jaimes, M. A. (Ed.). (1992). *The state of Native America.* Boston: South End Press.

Jakobson, R. (1972). Non-verbal signs for "Yes" and "No." *Language in Society, 1,* 91–96.

Jennings, E. (1970). Mobicentric man. *Psychology Today, 4,* 35–36, 70–72.

Johnson, J. R., & Szcupakiewicz, N. (1987). The public speaking course: Is it preparing students with work-related speaking skills? *Communication Education, 36,* 131–137.

Johnson, K. R. (1971). Black kinesics: Some non-verbal communication patterns in the black culture. *Florida Reporter, 57,* 17–20.

Jones, E. W., Jr. (1986). Black managers: The dream deferred. *Harvard Business Review, 64,* 84–93.

Jones, R. L. (1980). *Black psychology.* New York: Harper & Row.

Jones, R. T. (1989). Four by four: How do you manage a diverse workforce? *Training & Development, 43,* 13–21.

Jones, S. E. (1971). A comparative proxemics analysis of dyadic interaction in selected subcultures of New York City. *Journal of Social Psychology, 84,* 35–44.

Jones-Wilson, F. C. (1990). Race, realities, and American education: Two sides of the coin. *Journal of Human Education, 59,* 119–128.

Josselson, R. (1992). *The space between us: Exploring the dimensions of human relationships.* San Francisco: Jossey-Bass.

Jung, C. G. (1968). *The collected works of Carl Jung.* Vol. 10. Edited by G. Adler et al. Princeton, NJ: Princeton University Press.

Kahn, H., & Wiener, A. (1967). *The year 2000.* New York: Macmillan.

Kalish, R. A. (1982). *Late childhood: Perspectives on human development.* Monterey, CA: Brooks/Cole.

Kameda, N. (1992). "Englishes" in cross-cultural communication. *Bulletin of the Association for Business Communication, 55,* 3–8.

Kanter, R. M. (1977). *Men and women of the corporation.* New York: Basic Books.

Kanter, R. M. (1983). *The change masters: Innovations for productivity in the American corporation.* New York: Simon & Schuster.

Katz, D. (1960). The functional approach to the study of attitudes. *Public Opinion Quarterly, 24,* 163–204.

Katz, J. H. (1978). *White awareness: Handbook for anti-racism training.* Norman: University of Oklahoma Press.

Kelly, E. W., Jr., & True, J. H. (1980). Eye contact and communication of facilitative conditions. *Perceptual and Motor Skills, 51,* 815–820.

Kelly, J. L. (1990). Employers must recognize that older people want to work. *Personnel Journal, 69,* 44–47.

Kennedy, J., & Everest, A. (1991). Put diversity in context. *Personnel Journal, 70,* 50–54.

Kiernan, W. E., & Brinkman, L. (1985). Barriers to employment for adults with developmental disabilities. In W. E. Kiernan & J. A. Stark (Eds.) *Employment options for adults with developmental disabilities* (pp. 21–29). Logan: Utah State University Affiliated Facility.

Kiernan, W. E., & Schalock, R. L. (1989). *Economics, industry and disability: A look ahead.* Baltimore: Paul H. Brooks.

Kiesler, C. A. (1983). *Attitude change: A critical analysis of theoretical approaches.* Melbourne, FL: Krieger.

Kim, Y. Y. (1984). Searching for creative integration. In W. G. Gudykunst & Y. Y. Kim (Eds.), *International communication annual.,* Vol. 7 (pp. 13–30). Beverly Hills, CA: Sage.

King, S. W. (1982). Taxonomy for the classification of language studies in intercultural communication. In L. Samovar & R. Porter (Eds.), *Approaches to intercultural communication* (pp. 201–207). Belmont, CA: Wadsworth.

Kiplinger, A. H., & Kiplinger, K. A. (1989). *America in the global 90s.* Washington, DC: Kiplinger.

Klopf, D. W., et al. (1991). Nonverbal immediacy differences among Japanese, Finnish, and American university students. *Perceptual and Motor Skills, 73,* 209–210.

Kluckholm, F. R., & Strodtbeck, F. L. (1961). *Variations in value orientations.* New York: Harper & Row.

Kochman, T. (1981). *Black and white styles in conflict.* Chicago: University of Chicago Press.

Koestler, F. A. (1980). *Jobs for handicapped persons.* New York: The Public Affairs Committee.

Koshel, J. J., & Granger, C. V. (1978). Rehabilitation terminology: Who is serving the disabled? *Rehabilitation Literature, 39,* 102–106.

Kossen, S. (1987). *The human side of organizations.* 4th ed. New York: Harper & Row.

Kovel, J. (1984). *White racism.* New York: Columbia University Press.

Krantz, R. (1992). *Straight talk with prejudice.* New York: Facts on File.

Krech, D., Crutchfield, R. S., & Ballachy, E. L. (1962). *Individual in society.* New York: McGraw-Hill.

Kutch, M.J.E. (1992). *Comprehending and teaching humor in a second language.* Norman: Master's Thesis, University of Oklahoma.

Lacey, D. (1992). *Your rights in the workplace.* San Francisco: Nolo Press.

Landes, D., & Brislin, R. W. (1983). *Handbook for intercultural training.* New York: Pergamon Press.

Landry, B. (1987). *The new black middle class.* Berkeley: University of California Press.

Lasker, B. (1929). *Race attitudes in children.* New York: Holt.

Lawrie, J. (1990). Subtle discrimination pervades corporate America. *Personnel Journal, 69,* 53–55.

Leigh, D. E. (1978). *An analysis of occupational upgrading.* New York: Academic Press.

Leonard, B. (1991). Ways to make diversity programs work. *HR Magazine, 36,* 37–39, 98.

Levesque, J. D. (1988). *Manual of personnel policies, procedures and operations.* New York: McGraw-Hill.

Levin, G. N., & Rhodes, C. (1981). *Japanese American community.* New York: Praeger Press.

Levin, J., & Levin, W. C. (1980). *Ageism: Prejudice and discrimination against the elderly.* Belmont, CA: Wadsworth.

Levinson, H. (1973). Employee counseling in industry: Observations on three programs. In R. L. Nolan (Ed.), *Industrial mental health and employee counseling.* New York: Behavioral Books.

Lewin, K. (1951). *A dynamic theory of personality.* New York: McGraw-Hill.

Lewis, J. A., & Lewis, M. D. (1986). *Counseling programs for employees in the workplace.* Monterey, CA: Brooks/Cole.

Lewis v. Metropolitan Transit Comm., 320 N.W.2d 426 (Minn. 1982).

Likert, R. (1967). *The human organization: Its management and value.* New York: McGraw-Hill.

Lindesmith, A. R., & Strauss, A. L. (1950). *Social psychology.* New York: Columbia University Press.

Livingston, A. (1991). Twelve companies that do the right thing. *Working Woman, 16,* 57–60.

Loden, M., & Loeser, R. (1991). Working diversity: Managing the difference. *Bureaucrat, 20,* 21–25.

Longstreet, W. S. (1978). *Aspects of ethnicity: Understanding differences in pluralistic classrooms.* New York: Teachers College Press.

Maccoby, M. (1977). *The gamesman.* New York: Simon & Schuster.

Maggio, R. (1988). *The nonsexist word finder*. Boston: Beacon Press.

Maine Human Rights Comm. v. Canadian Pacific Ltd., 458 A.2d 1125 (Me. Sup. Ct. 1983).

Malcolm, S. H., Hall, P. Q., & Brown, J. W. (1976). *The double bind: The price of being a minority woman in science*. Washington, DC: American Association for the Advancement of Science.

Maldonado-Denis, M. (1972). *Puerto Rico: A socio-historic interpretation*. New York: Viking Books.

Mangum, C. S. Jr. (1940). *The legal status of the Negro*. Chapel Hill: University of North Carolina Press.

Maril, R. L. (1989). *Poorest of the Americans*. South Bend, IN: University of Notre Dame Press.

Marshall, D. (1979). Implications for intercultural counseling. *Multiculturalism, 3*, 9–13.

Maruyama, M. (1974). Paradigmatology and its application to cross-disciplinary, cross-professional, and cross-cultural communication. *Dialectica, 28*, 135–196.

Masi, D. A. (1984). *Designing employee assistance programs*. New York: AMACOM.

Masud-Piloto, F. R. (1988). *With open arms: Cuban migration to the U.S.* Totowa, NJ: Rowman & Littlefield.

Mauer, R. A. (1979). Young children's response to physically disabled storybook hero. *Exceptional Children, 45*, 326–330.

Maurer, D. W. (1950). The argot of the dice gambler. *Annals of the American Academy of Political and Social Sciences, 269*, 119.

Maxwell, R. B. (1992). A silver jubilee for the ADEA. *Modern Maturity, 35*, 2–8.

Maxwell-Hanley, C., Rusch, F. R., Chadsey-Rusch, J., & Renzaglia, A. (1986). Reported factors contributing to job terminations of individuals with severe disabilities. *Journal of the Association for the Severely Handicapped, 11*, 45–52.

May, R. (1953). *Man's search for himself*. New York: W. W. Norton.

McCarthy, C. (1988). Rethinking liberal and radical perspectives on racial inequality in schooling: Making the case for nonsynchrony. *Harvard Education Review, 58*, 265–279.

McCarthy, J., & Hoge, D. (1987). The social construction of school punishment: Racial disadvantage out of universalistic process. *Social Forces, 65*, 1101–1120.

McCoy, F. (1994). Rethinking the cost of discrimination. *Black Enterprise, 25*, 54–59.

McCready, W. (Ed.). (1983). *Culture, ethnicity, and identity*. New York: Academic Press.

McDaniel, J. W. (1970). *Physical disability and human behavior*. New York: Pergamon Press.

McGinley, H., Blau, G. L., & Takai, M. (1984). Attraction effects of smiling and body position: A cultural comparison. *Perceptual and Motor Skills, 58*, 915–922.

McTavish, D. G. (1971). Perceptions of old people: A review of research methodologies and findings. *The Gerontologist, 11*, 90–102.

Mehrabian, A. (1972). *Nonverbal communication*. Chicago: Aldine.

Mehrabian, A., & Wiener, M. (1967). Decoding inconsistent messages. *Journal of Personality and Social Psychology, 6,* 109–114.

Meniendez, E., Rodriguez, C., & Figueroa, J. B. (1991). *Hispanics in the labor force: Issues and policies.* New York: Plenum Press.

Menninger, K. (1930). *The human mind.* New York: Alfred A. Knopf.

Menninger, K. (1942). *Love against hate.* New York: Harcourt, Brace.

Meritor Savings Bank, FSB v. Vinson, 106 S.Ct. 2399 (1986).

Mill, J. (1970). *The subjection of women.* Cambridge, MA: MIT Press.

Miller, C., & Swift, K. (1976). *Words and women.* Garden City, NY: Anchor Press.

Miller, F. A. (1988). Moving a team to multiculturalism. In W. B. Reddy & K. Jamison, (Eds.), *Team building: Blueprints for productivity and satisfaction.* San Diego, CA: University Associates.

Miller v. Missouri Pacific Railway, 410 F.Supp. 533 (D.C. Mo. 1976).

Mizell, L. (1992). *Think about racism.* New York: Walker.

Mobley, M., & Payne, T. (1992). Backlash! The challenge to diversity training. *Training & Development, 46,* 45–52.

Morbach, H. (1973). Aspects of nonverbal communication in Japan. *Journal of Nervous and Mental Disease, 6,* 157.

Morris, D. (1981). *Gestures.* Yarmouth, ME: Intercultural Press.

Morrison, A. M. (1992). Developing diversity in organizations. *Business Quarterly, 57,* 42–48.

Morrison, A. M., White, R. P., & Velsor, E. V. (1982). *Breaking the glass ceiling.* Reading, MA: Addison-Wesley.

Murray, F. (Ed.). (1958). *The Negro handbook.* New York: Doubleday.

Nathanson, R. B. (1979). The disabled employee: Separating myth from fact. *Harvard Business Review, 57,* 101–110.

Nation's Business. (1988) Should you have a language policy? July, 21.

Nehru, J. (1950). *Visit to America.* New York: John Day.

Nelson, J. A. (1985). *Counseling and development in a multicultural society.* Monterey, CA: Brooks/Cole.

Nelson, P. A. (1962). The stolen identity of the so-called American Negro. *Negro History Bulletin, 26,* 40–88.

Nelton, S. (1991). Men, women, and leadership. *Nation's Business, 79,* 16–22.

Nelton, S. (1992). Winning with diversity. *Nation's Business, 88,* 18–24.

Nicoll, M. (1964). *Psychological commentaries.* London: Vincent Stuart & John M. Watkins.

Obermann, C. E. (1965). *A history of vocational rehabilitation in America.* Minneapolis: T. S. Denison.

O'Conner, B. W. (1991). Age bias at work. *New Choices, 18,* 36.

Ogden, C. K., & Richard, I. A. (1963). *The meaning of meanings.* New York: John Day.

Okun, B. F. (1992). *Effective helping: Interviewing and counseling techniques.* Pacific Grove, CA: Brooks/Cole.

Olson, J. S., & Wilson, R. (1984). *Native Americans in the twentieth century.* Albuquerque: University of New Mexico Press.

Palmore, E. B. (1990). *Ageism: Negative and positive.* New York: Springer-Verlag.

Pasteur, A. B., & Toldson, I. L. (1982). *Roots of soul: The psychology of black experience.* Garden City, NY: Doubleday.

Patten, T. H. Jr. (Ed.). (1988). *Fair play.* San Francisco: Jossey-Bass.

Pearce, W. B., & Conklin, F. (1971). Nonverbal vocalic communication and perceptions of a speaker. *Speech Monographs, 30,* 235–241.

Pennar, K. (1988). It's time to put our money where our future is. *Business Week,* September 19, 140–141.

Perdue, C. W., & Gurtman, M. B. (1990). Evidence for the automaticity of ageism. *Journal of Experimental Social Psychology, 26,* 199–216.

Perlman, H. H. (1957). *Social casework: A problem-solving process.* Chicago: University of Chicago Press.

Peter, L. J. (1977). *Peter's quotations: ideas for our time.* New York: Bantam Books.

Peters, T. J., & Waterman, R. H. Jr. (1982). *In search of excellence: Lessons from America's best-run companies.* New York: Harper & Row.

Peterson, K. S. (1993). Many women say their place is in the home. *USA Today,* September 20, D1.

Peterson, K. S. (1994). Harassment issue keeps men wary. *USA Today,* September 24, D1.

Petrini, C. M. (1993). The language of diversity. *Training & Development, 47,* 35–37.

Petry, A. (1971). *Miss Muriel and other stories.* Boston: Houghton Mifflin.

Pfordresher, J. (1991). How will cultural diversity affect teaching? *Education Digest, 57,* 49–51.

Phillips v. Martin Marietta Corp., 400 U.S. 542 (1971).

Pickney, A. (1984). *The myth of black progress.* New York: Cambridge University Press.

Pollack, E., & Menacker, J. (1971). *Spanish-speaking students and guidance.* Boston: Houghton Mifflin.

Ponterotto, J. G. (1988). Racial consciousness development among white counselor trainees: A stage model. *Journal of Multicultural Counseling and Development, 16,* 146–156.

Porter, R. E. (1972). An overview of intercultural communication. In L. A. Samovar & R. E. Porter (Eds.), *Intercultural communication: A reader.* Belmont, CA: Wadsworth.

President's Committee on Employment of the Handicapped. (1982). *Affirmative action for disabled people: A pocket guide.* Washington, DC: U.S. Government Printing Office.

Quattrone, G., & Jones, E. E. (1980). The perception of variability within ingroups and out-groups: Implications for the law of small numbers. *Journal of Personality and Gestalt Social Psychology, 38,* 141–152.

Rajecki, D. W. (1990). *Attitudes.* 2d ed. New York: Sinauer Associates.

Rawson v. Sears, Roebuck and Co., 615 F.Supp. 1546 (D.C. Colo. 1985).

Ray, D., & Poonwassie, D. H. (1992). *Education and cultural differences.* New York: Garland.

Reynolds, A. L., & Pope, R. L. (1991). The complexities of diversity: Exploring multiple oppression. *Journal of Counseling & Development, 70,* 174–178.

Rhine, S. H. (1978). *Older workers and retirement.* New York: The Conference Board.

Rich, A. L. (1974). *Interracial communication.* New York: Harper & Row.

Riche, M. (1991). We're all minorities now. *American Demographics, 13,* 26–34.

Richie, J. (1971). Church, caste and women. In M. E. Marty & D. G. Peerman (Eds.), *New theology No. 8: Our cultural revolution.* New York: Macmillan.

Riesman, D. (1973). Quoted in C. Bird. *Born female.* New York: Simon & Schuster.

Robbins, S. (1988). *Essentials of organizational behavior.* 2d ed. Englewood Cliffs, NJ: Prentice-Hall.

Roe, A. (1956). *The psychology of occupations.* New York: John Wiley & Sons.

Rogler, L. H., & Cooney, R. B. (1984). *Puerto Rican families in New York City: Intergenerational processes.* Maplewood, NJ: Waterfront Press.

Rosen, B., & Jerdee, T. H. (1976). Influence of age stereotype on management decisions. *Journal of Applied Psychology, 6,* 428–432.

Rosenberg, M. J. (1960). *Attitude organization and change: An analysis among attitude components.* New York: Greenwood Press.

Ross, S. R., & Weintraub, S. (1982). *"Temporary" alien workers in the United States.* Boulder, CO: Westview Press.

Sabnani, H. B., Ponterotto, J. G., & Borodovsky, L. G. (1991). White racial identity development and cross-cultural counselor training: A stage model. *The Counseling Psychologist, 19,* 76–102.

Sachs, C. (1937). *World history of dance.* New York: W. W. Norton.

Saltzman, A. (1991). Trouble at the top. *U.S. News & World Report,* June 17, 40–48.

Samora, J. (Ed.). (1966). *La Raza: Forgotten Americans.* South Bend, IN: University of Notre Dame Press.

Samovar, L. A., & Porter, R. E. (Eds.). (1972). *Intercultural communication: A reader.* Belmont, CA: Wadsworth.

Samovar, L. A., Porter, R. E., & Jain, N. C. (1981). *Understanding intercultural communication.* Belmont, CA: Wadsworth.

Saporta, S. (1988). Linguistic taboos: Code-words and women's use of sexist language: A double bind. *Maledicta, 10,* 163–166.

Sarbaugh, L. E., & Asuncion-Lande, N. (1983). Theory building in intercultural communication: Synthesizing the action caucus. In W. B. Gudykunst (Ed.), *Intercultural communication theory: Current perspectives* (pp. 45–60). Beverly Hills, CA: Sage.

Schein, E. H. (1992). *Organization culture and leadership.* 2d ed. San Francisco: Jossey-Bass.

Schellenbarger, S. (1993). Work-force study finds loyalty is weak, divisions of race and gender are deep. *The Wall Street Journal,* September 1, B1, B8.

Scherer, K. R., London, H., & Wolf, J. J. (1973). The voice of confidence: Paralinguistic cues and audience evaluation. *Journal of Research in Personality, 7,* 31–44.

Schroeder, D. G., & Ibrahim, F. A. (1982). *Cross-cultural couple counseling.* Paper presented at the annual meeting of the American Association for Marriage and Family Therapy, Dallas, TX.

Schulman, S., & Darity, W. Jr. (Eds.). (1989). *The question of discrimination: Racial inequality in the U.S. labor market.* Middletown, CT: Wesleyan University Press.

Schuman, H., Steeth, C., & Bobo, L. (1985). *Racial attitudes in America.* Cambridge, MA: Harvard University Press.

Schweitzer, A. (1961). *Pilgrimage to humanity.* Trans. by W. E. Stuerman, New York: Philosophical Library.

Shaheen, J. G. (1984). *The TV Arab.* Bowling Green, OH: Bowling Green State University Press.

Shein, E. H. (1992). *Organization culture and leadership.* 2d ed. San Francisco: Jossey-Bass.

Shepherd, G. W. Jr., & Penna, D. (1991). *Racism and the underclass.* New York: Westport.

Sherif, C. W. (1982). *Attitude and attitude change: The social judgment approach.* Westport, CT: Greenwood Press.

Sherif, M., & Sherif, C. W. (1953). *Groups in harmony and tension.* New York: Harper & Row.

Shute, S. (1981). *Sexist language and sexism.* New York: Harper & Row.

Shuy, R. W. (1976). The medical interview: Problems in communication. *Primary Case, 3,* 365–386.

Sidlo, R. (1992). Discrimination in employment by race. *Equal Opportunity International, 11,* 1–5.

Sigelman, L., & Welch, S. (1991). *Black Americans' views of racial inequality.* Cambridge: Cambridge University Press.

Sikkema, M., & Niyekawa, A. (1987). *Design for cross-cultural learning.* Yarmouth, ME: Intercultural Press.

Siller, J. (1963). Reactions to physical disability. *Rehabilitation Counselor Bulletin, 7,* 12–16.

Simons, G. (1989). *Working together: How to become more effective in a multicultural organization.* Los Altos, CA: Crisp.

Siperstein, G. N., Bak, J. J., & Gottlieb, J. (1977). Effects of group discussion on children's attitudes toward handicapped persons. *Journal of Educational Research, 70,* 131–134.

Smitherman, G. (1977). *Talking and testifying: The language of black Americans.* Boston: Houghton Mifflin.

Snell, B. (1953). *The discovery of the mind.* Oxford: Basil Blackwell.

Snipp, C. M. (1989). *American Indians: The first of this kind.* New York: Russell Sage Foundation.

Snow, K. M. (1973). My liberated mind has a Wuthering Heights heart. *Harper's,* July.

Solomon, C. (1992). Keeping hate out of the workplace. *Personnel Journal, 71,* 30–36.

Sonnenstuhl, W. J., & O'Donnell, J. E. (1980). EAPs: The why's and how's of planning them. *Personnel Administrator, 25,* 35–38.

Southeastern Community College v. Davis, 422 U.S. 397 (1979).

Steinmetz, L. L. (1969). *Managing the marginal and unsatisfactory performer.* Reading, MA: Addison-Wesley.

Stephens, J. (1945). *The crock of gold.* New York: Macmillan.

Stewart, E. C. (1971). *American culture patterns: A cross-cultural perspective.* Pittsburgh, PA: The Regional Council for International Education.

Stewart, E. C., & Bennett, M. J. (1991). *American cultural patterns: A cross-cultural perspective.* Yarmouth, ME: Intercultural Press.

Stoddard, E. R. (1973). *Hispanics in the United States.* Englewood Cliffs, NJ: Prentice-Hall.

Stolz, B. A. (Ed.). (1985). *Still struggling: America's low-income working women confronting the 1980's.* Lexington, MA: D. C. Heath.

Storr, A. (1961). *The integrity of the personality.* New York: Atheneum.

Strathie v. Department of Transportation, 716 F.2d 227 (3rd. Cir. 1983).

Stuart, P. (1992). What does the glass ceiling cost you? *Personnel Journal, 70,* 99–105.

Sue, D. W. (1991). A model for cultural diversity training. *Journal of Counseling and Development, 70,* 99–105.

Sue, S., & Sue, D. W. (1973). Understanding Asian-Americans: The neglected minority. *Personnel and Guidance Journal, 5,* 387–389.

Suiter, R. L., & Goodyear, R. K. (1985). Male and female counselor and client perceptions of four levels of counselor touch. *Journal of Counseling Psychology, 32,* 645–648.

Sundberg, N. D. (1981). Cross-cultural counseling and psychotherapy: A research overview. In A. J. Marsella & P. B. Pedersen (Eds.), *Cross-cultural counseling and psychotherapy* (pp. 28–62). New York: Pergamon Press.

Swerdloff, P. (1975). *Men and women.* New York: Time-Life Books.

Swingle, C. (1993). Study: Women attribute past of success to luck. *USA Today,* June 30, 4 B.

Syfers, J. (1973). Quoted in F. Klagsbrun (Ed.), *The first Ms. reader.* New York: Simon & Schuster.

Takai, R. (1989). *Strangers from a different shore: A history of Asian Americans.* New York: Penguin.

Tanner, D. (1991). *You just don't understand.* New York: Ballantine.

Texas Department of Community Affairs v. Burdine, 450 U.S. 248 (1981).

Thelen, H. A. (1969). Concepts for collaborative action-inquiry. In G. Watson (Ed.), *Concepts for social change* (pp. 37–46). Washington, DC: National Training Laboratories Institute for Applied Behavioral Science.

Thiederman, S. (1991). *Bridging cultural barriers for corporate success.* Lexington, MA: Lexington Books.

Thomas, R. R., Jr. (1990). From affirmative action to affirming diversity. *Harvard Business Review, 68,* 107–117.

Thomas, R. R., Jr. (1991). *Beyond race and gender.* New York: AMACOM.

Thompson, T. (1992). Experience not wanted. *U.S. News & World Report,* December, 59.

Thurer, S. L. (1982). Women and rehabilitation. *Rehabilitation Literature, 43,* 194–197.

Tibbitts, C. (1950). Quoted in *Living in the latter years: A conference on old age.* Huntington, WV: Marshall University.

Tichy, N. M. (1983). *Managing strategic change.* New York: John Wiley & Sons.

Tichy, N. M., & DeVanna, M. A. (1986). *The transformational leader.* New York: John Wiley & Sons.

Torrance, E. P. (1970). What it means to become human. In M. Scobery & G. Graham (Eds.), *To nurture humanness: Commitment for the 70's* (pp. 1–10). Washington, DC: Association for Supervision and Curriculum Development.

Tournier, P. (1957). *The meaning of persons.* New York: Harper & Row.

Triandis, H. C., & Lonner, W. (Eds.). (1980). *Handbook of cross-cultural psychology: Basic processes.* Vol. 3. Boston: Allyn & Bacon.

Trotter, J. R. (1979). The other hemisphere. *Science News, 109,* 218.

Tumin, M. N. (1958). *Desegregation.* Princeton, NJ: Princeton University Press.

Turner, M. A., Fix, M., & Struyk, R. (1991). *Opportunities denied: Discrimination in hiring.* Washington, DC: Urban Institute.

Turner, V. (1969). *The ritual process.* Chicago: Aldine.

United States Commission on Civil Rights. (1980). *The tarnished golden door: Civil rights issues in immigration.* Washington, DC: U.S. Government Printing Office.

United States Commission on Civil Rights. (1983). *Accommodating the spectrum of individual abilities.* Washington, DC: U.S. Government Printing Office.

United States Commission on Civil Rights. (1986). *Recent activities against citizens and residents of Asian descent.* Washington, DC: U.S. Government Printing Office.

United States Department of Commerce. (1992). *Statistical abstract of the United States.* Washington, DC: U.S. Government Printing Office.

United States Department of Labor. (1981). *Employment and training.* Washington DC: U.S. Government Printing Office.

United States Department of Labor. (1991). *Employer sanctions and U.S. labor markets: First report.* Washington, DC: U.S. Government Printing Office.

United States General Accounting Office (GAO). (1992). *Immigration and the labor market.* Washington, DC: U.S. Government Printing Office.

United States Merit Systems Protection Board. (1988). *Sexual harassment in the federal government: An update.* Washington, DC: U.S. Government Printing Office.

Upmeyer, A. (Ed.). (1988). *Attitudes and behavioral decisions.* New York: Springer-Verlag.

Valdes, J. M. (Ed.). (1986). *Culture bound: Language teaching from a curriculum perspective.* New York: Cambridge University Press.

Van Dijk, T. A. (1984). *Prejudice and discourse.* Englewood Cliffs, NJ: Prentice-Hall.

Van Horn, W. A. (Ed.). (1985). *Ethnicity and the work force.* Madison: University of Wisconsin Press.

Van Horn, W. A., Winston, A., & Tonnesen, T. V. (Eds.). (1989). *Ethnicity and language.* Vol. 6. Milwaukee: University of Wisconsin Institute on Race and Ethnicity.

Vash, C. L. (1981). *The psychology of disability.* New York: Springer-Verlag.

Vash, C. L. (1982). Employment issues for women with disabilities. *Rehabilitation Literature, 43,* 198–207.

Vogel, V. J. (Ed.). (1968). *This country was ours.* New York: Harper & Row.

Wagner, E. J. (1992). *Sexual harassment in the workplace: How to prevent, investigate and solve problems in your organization.* New York: AMACOM.

Wall, E. (Ed.). (1992). *Sexual harassment: Confrontation and decision.* New York: Prometheus Books.

Watson, G. (Ed.). (1969). *Concepts for social change.* Washington, DC: National Training Laboratories Institute for Applied Behavioral Science.

Watzlawick, P., Beavin, A. B., & Jackson, M. D. (1967). *Pragmatics of human communication.* New York: W. W. Norton.

Weaver, C. L. (1991). *Disability and work.* Washington, DC: AEI Press.

Webb, S. L. (1981). *Sexual harassment: Guidelines for supervisors and managers.* Seattle, WA: Pacific Resource Development Group.

Weeks v. Southern Bell Telephone and Telegraph Co., 408 F. 2d 228 Cir. (5th Cir. 1959).

Wehman, P., & Moon, M. S. (1988). *Vocational rehabilitation and supported employment.* Baltimore: Paul H. Brooks.

Weissman, H. (1965). Absenteeism and accidents of rehabilitation workers. *Rehabilitation Record, 6,* 15–17.

Wells, T. (1973). Equalizing advancement between women and men. *Training & Development, 27,* 20–24.

White, J. L. (1984). *The psychology of blacks: An Afro-American perspective.* Englewood Cliffs, NJ: Prentice-Hall.

Wierzbicka, A. (1992). *Semantics, culture, and cognition: Universal human concepts in culture-specific configurations.* New York: Oxford University Press.

Will, M. (1984). *OSERS programming for the transition of youth with disabilities: Bridges from school to working life.* Washington, DC: U.S. Department of Education.

Williams v. Saxbe, 413 F.Supp. 654 (D.C. 1976).

Willison, B. G., & Masson, R. L. (1988). The role of touch in therapy: An adjunct to communication. *Journal of Counseling and Development, 64,* 497–500.

Wilson, E. O., & Alcorn, D. (1969). Simulation and development of attitudes toward the exceptional. *Journal of Speech Education, 3,* 303–307.

Wilson, H. (1962). *Counseling employees.* Deerfield, IL: Administrative Research Associates.

Wilson, W. J. (1987). *The truly disadvantaged: The inner city, the underclass, and public policy.* Chicago: University of Chicago Press.

Wolfgang, A. (1985). The function and importance of nonverbal behavior in intercultural counseling. In P. B. Pedersen (Ed.), *Handbook of cross-cultural counseling and therapy.* Westport, CT: Greenwood Press.

Woods, G. (1989). *Affirmative action.* New York: Moffa Press.

Work, J. W. (1984). *Race, economics, and corporate America.* Wilmington, DE: Scholarly Resources.

Wright, B. A. (1960). *Physical disability: A psychological approach.* New York: Harper & Row.

Wright, R. (1940). *Native son.* New York: Modern Library.

Young, W. M. Jr. (1969). *Beyond racism: Building an open society.* New York: McGraw-Hill.

Yuker, H. E. (1982). *Disability hierarchies.* Unpublished manuscript. Hempstead, NY: Center for the Study of Attitudes Towards Persons with Disabilities, Hofstra University.

Yuker, H. E. (1988). *Attitudes toward persons with disabilities*. New York: Springer-Verlag.

Yuker, H. E., Cambell, W., & Brock, J. (1960). Selection and placement of the handicapped worker. *Industrial Medical Surgery, 29*, 419–421.

Zander, A. (1950). Resistance to change: Its analysis and prevention. *Advanced Management, 15*, 10.

Zellman, G. (1976). The role of structural factors in limiting women's institutional participation. *Journal of Social Issues, 32*, 33–46.

Zimbardo, P., & Ebbeson, E. B. (1969). *Influencing attitudes and changing behaviors*. Reading, MA: Addison-Wesley.

Zola, I. K. (1982). *Missing pieces*. Philadelphia, PA: Temple University Press.

Zunker, V. G. (1990). *Career counseling: Applied concepts of life planning*. Pacific Grove, CA: Brooks/Cole.

Index

AARP (American Association for Retired Persons), 83, 88

Absenteeism, 8, 31, 53, 96, 211

Accents, 153, 179, 180, 197

Acceptance, 10, 43, 97, 134

Accidents, 8, 9, 93

Accomodations for individuals with disabilities, 97, 105, 107–8

Action/activity, orientation to, 25, 65, 127, 166, 168

Action-research model, 226–28

ADEA. *See* Age Discrimination in Employment Act

Administrators. *See* Managers/supervisors

Affirmative action, 6–7, 15, 34, 140, 192, 193; conflict triggered by perception of, 198–99; directed toward women, 64–65; covered in 1974 Rehabilitation Act, 104

African Americans (Blacks), 5, 22–23, 25–27, 29, 133, 183–88; body language, 158–59, 160, 163; with disabilities, 99, 102; employment, 3, 6, 36–37; Hispanics erroneously labeled as, 22–23, 30; in management positions, 5–6, 206; multiple identities, 196; myths and stereotypes, 23–24, 135–36, 198; new immigrants' separation from, 119; "silent mind" at work in dealing with, 170; use of term "nigger," 190; women in workforce, 53, 56. *See also* Ethnic minorities

Africans, 22–23, 28, 30, 154, 158, 160; culture, 114, 126, 127, 153, 163, 165–69; as 20th-century immigrants, 112, 113

Age and aging, 29, 32, 55, 73–74, 126, 198; attitudes quiz, 88–90; discrimination on basis of, 59, 80–88; of retirement, 77, 81. *See also* Ageism; Older people/workers

Age Discrimination in Employment Act (ADEA) (1967), 80–81, 82–83; 1978 and 1986 amendments, 81

Ageism, 75–77, 101, 137, 170, 197, 209, 230. *See also* Age and aging

Aggressiveness, 30, 53, 181–82, 219–20

Agricultural workers, 28, 111

Alaskan natives, 23, 25, 31, 36

Albermarle Paper Co. v. Moody (1975), 38

Alienation, 11–12, 59, 178, 196

Allport, Gordon, 184, 189

American Association for Retired Persons (AARP), 83, 88
American English, 179–80, 181
American Indians, use of term, 23. *See also* Native Americans
Americans with Disabilities Act (1990), 105
Anderson, Carl, 201
Anderson, James A., 10, 153–54
Anglo-Saxon culture, as low-context, 165–69
Anthropologists, on race, 20, 183–84
Anti-Defamation League, 187, 210
Anti-Semitism, 187–88
Anxiety, 78–79, 152, 197, 222–23
Apple Computer, Inc., 44, 195
Apprenticeship programs, under Title VII, 34–35
Arabs, 117–18, 159, 160, 161–62, 188
Architectural and Transportation Barriers Compliance Board, 104, 108
Argots, as communication barriers, 155–57
Arts, use in communication, 163
Asher, Robert, 112
Asian Americans, 22, 25, 33–34, 133; in workforce, 3, 5–6, 36–37
Asian and Pacific Islanders, 3, 22, 25, 33, 36
Asians, 22–23, 181, 198, 206; body language, 117, 158, 160, 161–62; culture, 122–24, 127–28, 153, 163–69; as 20th-century immigrants, 25, 112–13
Assertiveness, 53, 218
Assessment of comprehensive needs, in intervention, 226–27
Assimilation, 6–8, 10, 19, 34, 202
Association, 24, 91. *See also* Comfort zones; Interpersonal relations
Asuncion-Lande, Nobleza, 153
Atchley, Robert, 101
AT&T, 218
Attitudes, 21, 65, 68, 134–39, 178–79, 187–88, 226; argots as key to, 156; changes in, 137–39, 191, 207; not major problem for managers and supervisors, 19, 133; sexism expressed in, 48; in symbolic racism, 182–83; toward foreigners, 113–14
Australians, 181
Authoritarianism, in management, 205
Authority, 15, 27, 48, 69, 162, 165; attitudes toward, 43, 116, 128, 158; respect for, 33, 126
Avoidance, in conflict situations, 200, 210
Avon Products, Inc., 44, 218

Ballachy, Egerton, 185
Barden-LaFollette Act (1943). *See* Vocational Rehabilitation Act (1943)
Barkin, Amy, 200
Barna, LaRay, 156
Barnlund, Dean, 152
Beauvoir, Simone de, 49
Beckhard, Richard, 4
Behaviors, 4, 19, 114, 137, 143, 204, 222; business styles, 122–28; changes in, 39, 139, 191, 204; changing paradigms effect, 179; as communication, 151; conflict triggered by, 198–99; cultural differences, 115–17, 170; determination by gender, myth of, 49, 51–55; focus on in conflict resolution, 205, 207, 209; high- and low-context, 163–69; patterns among African American children, 27; relationship to attitudes, 133–35, 191; relationship to language, 182, 185, 192; role in racism, 20–21; sexist, 48; in sexual harassment, 60–63; social class effects, 24–25
Beliefs, cultural, 19, 115–17, 143, 146, 154, 163; effect on language, 180; high- and low-context, 163–69; role in managing diversity, 4–5, 10
Bennett, Christine, 164
Biles, George, 53
Bilingualism, 29, 31, 120, 129
Bismarck, Otto von, 81
Bitter, James, 92
Black Enterprise (periodical), 218–19
Black History Week, 29

Blacks: ancient names for, 183; use of term, 23, 184, 186. *See also* African Americans; Africans
Blake, Robert, 229
Blind, the. *See* Vision impairment
Body language, 117, 122–26, 157–63, 170
Bohren, Jan, 63
Bohrer v. Hanes Corp. (1985), 82–83
Bona fide occupational qualification (BFOQ), 61, 106
Bowe, Frank, 98
Bowman, Garda, 51
"Boy," use for adult males, 66, 191
Braceros, 28
Brainstorming, 143
Brazil, 114
Brimmer, Andrew, 6
Brown, Corinne, 21
Business and industry, 9, 36, 38, 48, 57, 115, 177; cultural diversity, 122–28, 163–64; English language usage, 179–80. *See also* Culture, organization; Organization, business
Butler, Robert, 75

Career counseling. *See* Counseling of employees
Carroll, Lewis, 66
Carter v. Bennett (1988), 106
Caucasoid classification, 183
Cautious (C style) managers, 206
Census, U.S. Bureau of, 31, 33, 73, 100–101, 184
CEOs. *See* Executives
Chaucer, Geoffrey, 186
Chicanos, use of term, 22, 28. *See also* Mexican Americans
Children, 26, 50, 65, 93, 135, 196; African American, 26–27; Asian American, 33; language learning, 154
China, 114–15
Chinatowns, California, 33
Chinese, 122, 129, 192
Chinese-Americans, 22, 33–34
Chinese language, 181
Citizenship, U.S., 28, 30, 113, 184

Civil Rights Act of 1964, 184; Title VII, 34–35, 38, 61–63, 119–20
Civil Rights Act of 1991, 35
Class, social, 21, 24–25, 47, 153
"Club," the, getting into, 10, 44
Coca-Cola Co., 114
Codes: linguistic, 154, 156–57; restricted and elaborate, 165
Collectivistic cultures, 153, 163, 165–69
College education. *See* Higher education
Color, skin. *See* Skin color
Comfort zones, 11–12, 117, 159–60, 165, 166, 167, 172; personal boundaries, 159, 181
Communication, 4, 151–57, 163–69, 179, 192, 197; in cross-national interaction, 114–15, 121–22; DELs as powerful device for, 190; of feelings, 208; with female employees, 68–69; habits, quiz on, 172–75; with immigrant workers, 128–29; with individuals with disabilities, 108; in Japanese management style, 180; between managers/supervisors and employees, 14, 17, 21, 39–44, 151–62; nonverbal, 40, 109, 152, 157–64, 179, 197; with older workers, 87–88; role in change process, 138–39, 229; role in conflict resolution, 199–203; in team building approach, 227. *See also* Cross-cultural communication; Languages
Compadrazgo, 29, 30
Company men, as style of manager, 205–6
Compensation. *See* Salaries/wages
Competence: communication of, 42–43; gender difference myths, 51–52
Competition, 4–6, 19, 119, 136–37, 187, 206; in conflict resolution, 210; women's motivation toward, 53
Complaint procedures, 40, 41–42
Condon, John, 167–68
ConEd, 95
Conferences, participation in, 68

Conflict, 13, 15, 39–44, 181, 187, 195–99; action-research model strategies for resolution, 226–28; between Indians and non-Indians, 31–32; defined, 202; problem solving techniques, 205, 206–9; resolution, 199–211, 219–23; style survey, 211–16. *See also* Discrimination; Prejudices; Violence

Connecticut v. Teal (1982), 38

Consultants, role in action-research model of intervention, 226–28

"Contact" cultures, 117, 160

Control, 65, 115, 182, 226

Cooperation, 4, 32, 52, 202, 209–10

Cornell v. Sparrow Hospital Assn. (1985), 61–62

Corning, Inc., 44, 195

Corporate cultures. *See* Culture, organization

Counseling of employees, 67, 145, 199–203, 221; conflict resolution, 203–5

Court cases, 192, 204; against individuals with disabilities, 105–6; discrimination, 35, 38, 61–62; discrimination on basis of age, 82–84; discrimination on basis of national origin, 119–20, 129; sexual harassment, 61–63

Cova v. Coca-Cola Bottling Co. of St. Louis (1978), 82

Craftsmen, as style of manager, 205

Crigler, Pat, 50

Crock of Gold, The (Stephens), 40

Cross-cultural communication, 40–44, 153–57, 169–72, 178–79; barriers to, 156–57, 179–80, 197–98; cross-national, 112–15, 121–22, 152. *See also* Communication

Crutchfield, Richard, 185

C style (Cautious) managers, 206

Cubans, 22, 135; as immigrants, 28, 118

Cultures, 5, 20–22, 25–34, 91, 135, 178; adoption of subcultures' argot, 156–57; business style differences, 122–28; relationship to language,

152–57, 154, 197; role in cross-national interaction, 112–14

Culture, organization, 4–5, 39, 139, 178–79, 218, 222–26; adjustment of employees to, 120; changes in, 12–13, 180–81; communication to minority employees, 41, 44; diversity problems rooted in, 15–17; role in workplace conflicts, 200, 204, 210

Cynicism, 178, 228

Damages: compensatory, 35; punitive, 35, 83

Deafness. *See* Hearing impairment

Decision-making, 4, 8, 127, 195, 197, 225

Defense mechanisms, 10, 43, 181, 223

Deficiency/deficit, differences equated with, 5, 6, 94

DELs (derogatory ethnic labels), 188–90, 193

Delta Air Lines, 218

Delusions, as obstacle to achieving diversity, 223–25

Demographics: ethnic minorities, 25–26, 28, 30; immigrants, 117–18; individuals with disabilities, 98–99; workforce, 77, 195, 226–27. *See also* Age; Life expectancy

Derogatory ethnic labels (DELs), 188–89

Developmental Evaluation Clinic, 99

Dialects, 29, 156

Diet, cultural and religious restrictions on, 123, 129

Differences, 7–8, 20, 23–25, 48, 94; emphasized by group labels, 189–90; equated with deficit, 5, 6, 94. *See also* Diversity, cultural

Digital Equipment Corp., 44

Dignity, 23, 30, 31

Disabilities. *See* Individuals with disabilities

Disability liability, 95–96

Discharge. *See* Firing

Discipline, 27, 67, 204

Discrimination, 19, 118–19, 182; court cases, 8–9, 35, 38; curtailment and prevention, 34, 38–44, 191–93; laws against, 34–35, 61–62, 64, 133; 1990 Americans with Disabilities Act, 105; 1991 Civil Rights Act, 35. *See also* Age and aging; Racial discrimination; Sex

Discussions: in conflict resolution, 200, 210; in diversity training, 141, 142–44

Disparate impact, 35, 38

Disparate treatment, 38

Disraeli, Benjamin, 20

Distance. *See* Comfort zones

DiStefano, Joseph, 115

Distressed employee syndrome, 224

Diversity, cultural, 3, 8–13, 113–19, 151–52, 192, 196; achievement of, 169–72, 225–29; attitudes related to, 134–39; barriers to, 133–34, 223–25; among diversity trainers, 140; in social interaction, 163–69. *See also* Affirmative action; Conflict; Diversity training; Managing diversity; Valuing diversity

Diversity training, 133–34, 139–46, 156, 203–4, 218–19; job training accompanied by, 195–96

Doby's Girl (Petry), 190

Domestic role for women, 47–48, 56

Dominance, 48, 65

Dominant (D style) managers, 206

Downsizing, organizational, 6, 14

Dress, 48, 61–62, 120, 126

"Drug language," 156

D style (Dominant) managers, 206

DuPont Co., 44, 92, 94–96

Early retirement, 8, 13–14, 77–78, 81–82

Earnings. *See* Economics; Salaries/wages

Economics, 47, 56, 136–37, 187; and older workers, 78, 82; in *quid pro quo* sexual harassment, 62; status of African Americans, 26–27; status of Asian Americans, 33; status of individuals with disabilities, 98, 102; status of Native Americans, 31; status

of older people, 75, 77–78. *See also* Salaries/wages

Education, 8, 9, 48, 115, 119, 177; academic records for employees, 220; authority roles, 48; gender differences in performance, 50; for individuals with disabilities, 100, 106, 108; levels, 6, 26, 31, 33, 50, 53–54, 56; place in Japanese culture, 124; public, 26, 86, 196; Smith-Hughes Act, 102. *See also* Higher education; Vocational rehabilitation and training

Edwards, Audrey, 206

EEOC (Equal Employment Opportunity Commission), 34–35, 38, 55, 60, 82, 83

Ekman, P. et al., 158

Elderly, the. *See* Age and aging; Ageism; Older people/workers

E-mail, use for hate mail, 188

Emotions, 53, 154–56, 190, 192, 208, 222–23; expression of, 126, 158, 159, 161–62, 226; influence on quality of work, 65, 68; place in diversity training, 141, 145–46

Empathy, 42–43, 52, 75, 145, 162, 207–8

Employee Retirement Income Security Act (ERISA) (1974), 81

Enclaves, ethnic, 113

English language, 26, 121–22, 155, 179–80, 181, 197–98

Equal employment opportunities, 6–7, 38–44, 82, 133, 139, 217–18; adjustment to by minority groups, 79; corporate guidelines for, 11, 210; for women, 54, 56, 64–65, 191

Equal Employment Opportunity Act of 1972, 34–35, 38

Equal Employment Opportunity Commission (EEOC), 34–35, 38, 55, 60, 82, 83

Equality: in Japanese management style, 180; for women, attitudes toward, 50–51, 56, 64. *See also* Rights

Equal Pay Act of 1963, 61

Equal protection clause, of 14th Amendment, 64

Equity adjustments, treatment of employees needing, 13–14
ERISA (Employee Retirement Income Security Act) (1974), 81
Eskimos. *See* Alaskan natives
Espononza v. Farah Mfg. Co. (1973), 120
Ethnicity: appropriate identification of people by, 191–92; confusion with race, 22–23
Ethnic minorities, 3, 19, 25–34, 58–59, 94, 211; competition with new immigrants, 119; definitions, 19–23; DELs, 188–90; with disabilities, 99, 102; distressed employee syndrome use, 224; employment, 36–37, 57–58; in management, 5–12; multiple identities, 75, 136, 196–97; myths and stereotypes, 23–25, 220; opportunities under Title II of Civil Rights Act of 1991, 35, 38; treated as being maladjusted, 223–24. *See also individual ethnic and national groups*
Ethnocentrism, 20, 113–14, 116, 185
Euro-Americans, 22, 36–37, 133, 185, 206; cultural value preferences, 25, 32, 160, 163. *See also* Men
Europeans: northern, 117, 160; southern (Latin), 117, 160, 163, 167
Evaluations, 67, 156, 197, 224, 229
Everest, Ann, 218
Excellence, as a standard, 206, 219
Executive Order 11246, As Amended (Oct. 14, 1968), 34
Executives, 9, 13–14, 63, 119, 127, 136; role in combating job discrimination, 65; use of racial epithets, 182; women as, 5, 10, 35, 48, 51, 54, 56, 59
Extended family, 27, 32, 125
Eye contact, as nonverbal communication, 117, 160–61, 162

Facial expressions, 158, 161, 170
Facts: in conflict resolution, 200, 207; in corrective action for equal opportunity problems, 39–40

Fair Labor Standards Act (FLSA), amendment to, 61
Families, 47–48, 50, 52, 68, 77, 126, 168; African American, 26–27; Asian American, 33; Japanese, 123; Mexican, 125; Mexican American, 29; Native American, 32
Fatalism, in Third World cultures, 33, 115, 126, 127, 168
Faxes, use for derogatory messages, 187
Federal Board for Vocational Education, 106
Federal buildings, accessibility, 104
Federal Contract Compliance, U.S. Office of, 34
Feedback, 226–27, 229
Feminism, 50–51, 54, 64
Filipczak, Bob, 65–66
Fine, M. G. et al., 222–23
Firing, 13–14, 81–82, 204, 211; under Title VII, 34–35
Flanigan v. Prudential Federal Savings and Loan Assn. (1986), 83
Fletcher, Beverly, 178
Folk medicine, 27, 29, 31, 32, 33–34
Follman, Joseph, 8–9, 201
Ford Motor Co., 114
Foreign workers, 111–13, 119, 120–22, 128–30, 133, 188. *See also* Immigrants
Formal attitude-change approach, 138–39
Fortune 500 corporations, 5, 11, 44, 60, 64
Fountain v. Safeway Stores (1977), 120
Fourteenth Amendment, 64, 105
Franklin, Paula, 100
Freud, Sigmund, 49
Friedan, Betty, 49
Friendships, cultural diversity, 116, 168–69
Fringe benefits, under Title VII, 35
Frink, S., 9
Fritz, Norma, 60
Frontera v. Sindell (1975), 120
Furnco Construction Co. v. Waters (1978), 38

Future, the, orientation to, 25, 32, 115

Gamesmen, as style of manager, 205–6
Garcia v. Gloor (1980), 120
Gay people, 187–88, 196
Gbekobu, Kofi, 163
Gemson, C., 139–40
Gender. *See* Roles; Sex
General Motors (GM) Corp., 9, 114, 218
Genetics, definition of race based on, 20, 183
Germans, 165–69, 181
Gestures, 157–59
"Girl," use for adult females, 66–67, 191
"Giving face," issue of, 164
"Glass ceiling," 5, 10
"Glass Ceiling Act" (Title II) (1991), 35
"Glass Ceiling Initiative" (Labor Dept. program), 10
Glasser, William, 208–9
GM (General Motors) Corp., 9, 114, 218
Goals, 4, 48; for diversity programs, 6–8, 140, 227
Goldstein, Jeffrey, 170, 210
Gordon, Jack, 9
Government, 38, 48; employment in, 37, 58; federal, 31, 60–61, 84; state and local, 84, 95–96. *See also* Laws, federal; *individual agencies*
"Government Employee Rights Act" (Title III) (1991), 35
Granger, Carl, 92
Greeks, body language, 159, 163
Greetings, cultural customs, 122, 124–25, 126
Greiff, James, 8–9
Griggs v. Duke Power (1971), 35, 38
Group dynamics approach to attitude change, 138–39
Guam, people from, 22, 33

Haitians, as immigrants, 118
Hall, Edward, 152

Hamilton v. Rogers (1986), 63
Handicaps and handicappism, 91, 92–93, 170, 230. *See also* Individuals with disabilities
Handshaking, cultural practices, 122, 124, 125, 126, 162
Harassment, 35, 63, 162. *See also* DELs; Sexual harassment
Harris, Philip, 153
Hate crimes, 187–88
Hawaiians, 22, 33
Hayakawa, S. I., 184–85
Heads of household, individuals with disabilities as, 100, 102
Health care, 8, 13–14, 75, 81, 177. *See also* Folk medicine
Hearing impairment, 79, 93, 94, 99, 106
Henderson, George, 197
Heredity, racial characteristics due to, 20, 183
Hewlett Packard Co., 44
Higher education, 8, 9, 54, 56, 113, 196
Hindus, 123
Hiring, discrimination in, 9, 82, 182; legislation on, 34–35, 80–81, 104–5, 229–30
Hispanics (Hispanic Americans), 25–26, 118, 133, 160, 192, 206; classifications, 22–23, 184; culture, 25, 28–30, 165–69; employment, 3, 5–6, 36–37, 56; myths and stereotypes, 23–24, 198; names, 42; as targets of hate crimes, 187
"Hoboes," argot, 156
Holiday customs of foreign workers, workplace adaptations to, 129
Homosexuals, 187–88, 196
Honeywell, Inc., 44
Hostility, 62–63, 178, 187–89, 200, 211. *See also* Conflict
Housing, 26–27, 31, 74, 108, 113, 182
Huhn v. Koehrnig Co. (1983), 83
Human nature, cultural assumptions on, 25, 166, 167–68

Human relations. *See* Interpersonal relations

Human relations approach: in conflict resolution, 204; in diversity-related management style, 15

Human relations commission, in Los Angeles County, 187

Human resources, 8; approach to managing diversity, 4–5; development of in corporate cultures, 181, 217; utilization, 177, 196

IBM Corp., 95, 218

Identity, 15, 22, 116, 153, 163, 168; defined by work, 91; ethnic, 19, 28–29, 197; loss in conflict resolution, 222; multiple, 196–97; of Native Americans, 31; relationship to language, 153, 197; in workplace, 196, 206

Idioms, as communication barrier, 156

Immigrants, 3, 25, 111–13, 117–19, 187, 197; appropriate interaction techniques, 120–22, 128–30; assimilation, 19, 34; from Latin America, 28. *See also individual nationalities*

Immigration and Naturalization Service (INS), 119, 129

Immigration and the Labor Market (GAO report), 111

Immigration Reform and Control Act of 1986, 119–20

Impairment, definitions, 92, 93

Implication of attitudes, 20, 21, 182–83, 191–92

Income. *See* Economics; Salaries/wages

Independence: gender differences in views on, 53; services for individuals with disabilities, 105

Indians, East, 22, 117, 122–23, 160

Individualism/individuality, 30, 165–69, 181, 196, 198, 218; as value, 65, 205

Individuals with disabilities, 91, 98–102, 133, 192, 198; court cases, 105–6; federal legislation, 102–5; myths and stereotypes, 91, 92–98; as workers, 11–12, 106–10

Industry. *See* Business and industry

Infant mortality, 26, 31

Inferiority, 198, 222, 223; connotation of, 184; feelings of among individuals with disabilities, 97–98; implied, 191, 192

Influencers (I style managers), 206

Information: in attempt to change attitudes, 137–38, 139, 146; barriers confronting individuals with disabilities, 108; communication of among Japanese, 159; in conflict resolution, 200–202, 207

In-groups versus out-groups, 135, 181–82, 189–90

INS (Immigration and Naturalization Service), 119, 129

Insurance, for workers with disabilities, 95

Integration, 28, 186. *See also* Assimilation

Intelligence, 50; assumptions about, 108–9, 113, 197–98, 225

Intent, 39, 63

Interagency Committee on Handicapped Employees, 104

International Center for the Disabled, 99

International Telephone and Telegraph Co. (ITT), 94, 96, 97

Interpersonal (Human) relations, 21, 65, 112–13, 152, 218, 227; behavior style quiz, 147–50, 231; changes in, 177, 178–79; cultural diversity in, 25, 116, 127, 163–69, 195; in diversity training sessions, 141; as task of managers and supervisors, 39–44. *See also* Conflict

Interviews, 189, 226, 229; between managers/supervisors and employees, 67, 162, 199–203

Issacs, Harold, 186

I style managers (Influencers), 206

ITT (International Telephone and Telegraph Co.), 94, 96, 97

Japanese, 22, 158, 159, 161, 190; customs, 123–24, 127–28, 163–64; management style, 180–81

Japanese language, 153, 154, 181

Jargon, 157, 179
Jews, as targets of hate crimes, 187–88
Job Accommodation Network (JAN), 107–8
Job performance, 14, 63, 91, 203, 211, 219; ADEA applicability in cases of, 82–83; evaluations, 67, 197
Job procedures, communication on, 40–42
Job sharing, 84, 86
Job skills, 10–11, 13, 40–42; of workers with disabilities, 96, 106
Job training. See Training; Vocational rehabilitation and training
Johnson, Kenneth, 158
Jones, Edward, 8
Jones Act of 1917, 30
Josselson, Ruthellen, 153, 155
J P Morgan, 218
Jung, Carl, 135
Jungle fighters, as style of manager, 205–6

Kahn, Herman, 178
Kaiser Aluminum Co., 97
Kanter, Rosabeth, 9, 59
Katz, Judy, 21–22
Keller, Helen, 92
Kennedy, Jim, 218
Khadafy, Moammar, 188
Kindness, misplaced, 224
Kinesics. See Body language; Nonverbal communication
K Mart Corp., 9
Kochman, Thomas, 6
Kodak Co., 218
Koreans, 22, 124
Koshel, Jeffrey, 92
Kossen, Stan, 228
Krech, David, 185
Kutch, Mary, 155

Labels, ethnic. See DELs
Labor, division of: sexual, 47–48; in work groups, 144
Labor, U.S. Dept. of, 11, 54, 56, 74–75
Labor organizations, under Title VII, 34–35

Languages, 26, 114, 120, 121–22, 129, 152–57; as barrier to accurate communication, 119, 152; learning, 153–54, 179–80; links to discrimination and racism or sexism, 181–91; preservation by immigrants, 113; restricted and elaborate codes, 165; spoken by Native Americans, 31; in verbal sexual harassment, 60, 62–63, 65–67; as workplace conflict cause, 197–98. See also English language; Spanish language
Latin Americans, 117, 160–63; as immigrants, 25, 28, 112
Latin (southern) Europeans, 117, 160, 163, 167
Latinos, 22, 158. See also Hispanics; Latin Americans
Law, personalized and procedural, 165
Lawrie, J., 86
Laws, federal: on alien workers' rights, 119; on discrimination, 34–35, 61–62, 64, 80–84, 129, 133, 229–30; on immigration, 111; on individuals with disabilities, 102–5
Laws, state, 84, 95–96
League of Women Voters, 50
Learning, 140, 227; of languages, 153–54, 179–80
Legislation. See Laws
Leopold, Marjorie, 170, 210
"Let's Get Rid of 'The Girl'" (United Technologies Corp.), 66–67
Lewin, Kurt, 138
Liability, myths concerning workers with disabilities, 95–96
Life expectancy, 31, 73, 74, 75, 78, 100
Lindesmith, Alfred, 185
Line positions, women and minorities rarely found in, 11, 59
Listening, 40, 141; role in communication, 69, 87, 109, 162, 170, 221; role in conflict resolution, 201–2, 210
Livingston, Abby, 44
Logic, 137–38, 165
Longstreet, Wilma, 163
Lose-lose situation, 209

Lose-win situation, 209. *See also* Win-lose situation
Loved to death, need not to be, 224

Maccoby, Michael, 205–6
McConnell, John, 10
Machismo, 29, 30
"Made in Japan," connotations, 178–79
Maine Human Rights Comm. v. Canadian Pacific Ltd. (1983), 106
Maladjusted employee delusion and phobia, 223–25
Management, 4, 42, 203–4; styles, 180–81, 205–6. *See also* Managers/supervisors
Managers/supervisors, 4–15, 30, 36, 38, 157, 160; in action-research model of intervention, 226–28; combating ageism, techniques for, 86–88; conflict resolution methods, 203–5, 219–20; counseling of employees, 67, 145, 199–203, 221; cross-cultural communication, 8–17, 42–44, 169–72, 203–11; interaction with foreign workers, 120–22, 128–30; interaction with individuals with disabilities, 108–10; older workers' perception of, 79; perceptions of gender differences in, 51–55; program for learning Spanish, 211; provision of equal treatment and opportunities, methods for, 39–44, 69, 191–93; sexual harassment, methods for dealing with, 63, 69–71; sexual harassment by, 60–61; tendency toward ethnocentrism, 116; women and minorities as, 5–12, 35, 56, 59–60, 206. *See also* Management; Managing diversity
Managing diversity, 3–10, 140, 152, 195–96, 217–23, 230; barriers to, 133–39; conflict resolution, 203–11. *See also* Conflict
Mangum, Charles, 184
Marginality, of minorities, 28–29
Masi, Dale, 8

Mauer, Ruth, 100
Maurer, D. W., 156
McDonald's Corp., 218
Meanings, 152–55, 166, 180, 185, 197. *See also* Body language
Media, influence of, 182, 188, 198
Mediation, 14, 210
Men, 47, 48, 55, 59, 77, 160; competition, 5–6, 37; with disabilities, 100, 101–2; superiority implied in sexism, 191; white, 8, 10, 65, 77, 145–46. *See also* Ethnic minorities
Menninger, Karl, 207–8
Mental disabilities, 8, 99, 103
Mental illness, 75, 103
Mentoring, 59, 68, 206
Meritor Savings Bank, FSB v. Vinson (1986), 61–62
Mexican Americans, 22, 25, 28–30, 136, 160. *See also* Hispanics
Mexicans, 112, 114, 117, 124–25, 162, 192
Middle class, 25, 47, 49
Middle Easterners, 158, 161, 166–67
Mill, John Stuart, 49
Miller Brewing Co., 218
Miller v. Missouri Pacific Railway (1976), 120
Milton, John, 186
Minorities. *See* Ethnic minorities; Individuals with disabilities; *individual ethnic and national groups*
Mobility, 177, 186
Mobley, Michael, 140
Mongoloid classification, 183
Monochronic culture, 165, 166–67
Montana Supreme Court, 83
Morale: affected by sexual harassment, 60, 63; employee counseling for, 67
Moran, Robert, 153
Mouton, Jane, 229
Movement, body, as nonverbal communication, 157–59, 161–63, 170
Multiculturalism, 178. *See also* Diversity, cultural
Muslims, 117–18, 123, 126, 129
"Myths, Management, and Women" (Biles and Pryatel), 53

Namaste gesture, 122–23

Names, appropriate use of, 41, 42, 121–22, 126, 171

Namesakes, among Native Americans, 32

National Association of Manufacturers, 95

National Center for Health Statistics, 100

National Conference of Christians and Jews, 133

National Institute of Handicapped Research, 107

National Opinion Research Center, 23

National Organization for Women (NOW), 50

National origin: discrimination on basis of, 34–35, 38–44, 119–20; stereotypes, 198

Native Americans (American Indians), 3, 23, 25–26, 31–32, 192, 197, 206; appropriate use of names, 41; culture, 25, 31–32, 163, 165–69; definition used by Census Bureau, 184; employment, 36–37; stereotypes, 198

Nativism, 111, 112

Nature/environment, relationship with, 25, 27, 32, 115, 167–68

Nature of Prejudice, The (Allport), 189

Negroes, derivation and historical usage of term, 183–84. *See also* African Americans; Africans

Negroid classification, 183

Nehru, Jawaharlal, 169

Nelson, Phobena, 183

Neo-Ricans, 30

New Deal, 81

Nigerians, 126, 137, 154, 192

"Nigger," use as term, 188, 190

"Noncontact" cultures, 117, 160

Nonverbal communication, 109, 152, 157–64, 179, 197

Nonzero-sum (Win-win) situation, 198, 209, 211, 228–29

"Normal" person, in definition of impairment or handicap, 94

Northwest Airlines, 9

Nurses, dress code case, 61–62

O'Donnell, J. E., 200

Ogden, Charles, 185

Okun, Barbara, 200, 201

"Old boy network," 59

Older people/workers, 3, 73–75, 77–82, 86–88, 100–101; prejudice against, 133; stereotypes, 75–77, 220. *See also* Age and aging; Ageism

Older Workers Benefits Protection Act (OWBPA), 81–82

Organization, business, 4–5, 152, 202; conflict resolution, 203–5; diversity programs, 7, 8, 217–20; racist behavior within, 187–89. *See also* Culture, organization; Executives; Managers/supervisors

Organizational development (OD) approach, 217

Organization Transformation: A New Paradigm (Fletcher), 178

Out-groups versus in-groups, 135, 181–82, 189–90

Overcompensation, 43, 224

Pacific Bell, 44

Pacific Islanders, 3, 22, 25, 33, 36

Pakistanis, 22, 117, 160

Paradigms of cross-cultural relations, new, 178–79; barriers to, 180–81

Paraplegia, 108. *See also* Physical disabilities

Part-time work, for older workers, 78, 84–85

Passivity, seen as feminine behavior, 48, 50, 52, 65

Past, the, orientation to, 25, 115

Pay. *See* Salaries/wages

Payne, Tamara, 140

Pension plans, 78, 81, 85–86

People of color, use of term, 23

Pepsi Cola Co., 114–15

Perlman, H. H., 200

Personal problems, supervisors' understanding of, 52, 68–69

Personal relationships. *See* Interpersonal relations

Peters, Thomas, 9

Peterson, Karen, 54

Petry, Ann, 190

Philip Morris Co., 218

Phillips v. Martin Marietta Case (1971), 61

Phobias, as obstacle to achieving diversity, 223–25

Physical disabilities, 91, 99, 106, 108. *See also* Individuals with disabilities

Physical sexual harassment, 60, 62

Pigmentation, skin. *See* Skin color/pigmentation

Pillsbury Co., 9

Polish language, 154

Polychronic culture, 165, 167

Pope, Rachelle, 196–97

Portuguese, 126–27

Portuguese Americans, 184

Postindustrial society, 177–78

Power, 15, 21–22, 48, 162, 182, 198

Power flow interaction process, 199

Pregnancy, 35, 56

Prejudice(s), 19–21, 23, 48, 91, 133, 135; awareness of during diversity training, 146; displayed in symbolic racism, 182–83; effect on provision of equal treatment and opportunity, 38–39; ethnic, 30, 113–14, 179, 189; perpetuated by media stories, 182; toward new immigrants, 118–19

Present, the, orientation to, 25, 29, 32, 115

President's Committee on Employment of the Handicapped, 94–95, 96

Problem solving, 144, 145, 205, 206–9, 225, 227–28

Procter & Gamble Co., 44, 218

Productivity, 7, 8–9, 153, 217; myths on, 86, 96, 101; sexual harassment effects, 60, 63–64

Professionals, 36, 56, 59

Profits, corporate, 7, 8, 9

Promotions, 6, 13, 44, 53, 65, 81; double standards, 79–80; lawful practices, 229–30

Prostheses, 101–2, 103, 106

Protected class. *See* Ethnic minorities; Individuals with disabilities; Women

Prototypical workers, men seen as, 53

Proxemics. *See* Comfort zones

Pryatel, Holly, 53

Psychosocial adjustment patterns, of white males to diversity training, 145–46

Public Employees Retirement System (Kansas), 86

Public Law 95-256 (1978 Amendments to ADEA), 81

Public Law 102-166. *See* Civil Rights Act of 1991

Public Law 236 (Smith-Fess Act) (1920), 102–3

Public schools, 26, 196

Public School System (Wichita, Kansas), 86

Public services, under 1990 Americans with Disabilities Act, 105

Puerto Ricans, 22, 28, 30–31, 160, 170

Punishment, use of, 225, 226

Quaker Oats Co., 195

Quid pro quo sexual harassment, 62

Race, 3, 19–23, 28, 116, 183–87, 198; appropriate identification of people by, 191–92; employment figures by, 36. *See also* Racial discrimination; *individual groups*

Race, The (La Raza), 22, 29

Racial discrimination, 20–21, 23, 59, 204, 211; court cases, 35, 38; prevention of, 38–44; prohibited by executive order and laws, 34–35; racist language as form of, 181–82. *See also* Discrimination

Racism, 20–25, 137, 170, 185, 187–89, 230; among administrators, 16; as a cause of cross-cultural conflict, 197, 210; demonstrated by racial ha-

rassment, 9, 63; as focus in problem solving, 209; institutional, 20–22, 39, 190; language of, 181–87; sexism compared with, 48–49
Randall, Iris, 206
Randolph-Shepard Act (1936), 104
Rapport, 42–44, 151
Rationalization, 43, 135
Rawson v. Sears, Roebuck and Co. (1985), 83
Raza, La (The Race), 22, 29
Reality: cultural differences on, 115–16, 154, 166; objective, 207
Reasoning, comprehensive and linear logic, 165, 167
Recessions, economic, 47, 187
Recognition, need for, 80, 91
Recreation, 74, 108
Recruitment, 9, 11, 13, 38, 129; role in equal opportunity, 6, 64
Reebok Intl. Ltd., 218
Regard, unconditional positive, 16, 210
Rehabilitation Act (1973), 103–5; 1974 and 1978 amendments, 104–5
Rehabilitation Institute of Chicago, 97
Rehabilitation services, 92–93, 96, 100, 102–5, 106
Rehabilitation Services Administration, 107
Reinforcement of attitudes, 136–37
Religion, 27, 29, 32, 33–34; diet restrictions, 123, 129; discrimination on basis of, 21, 34–35, 38–44; foreign workers' holidays, 129
Remediation, 6–7, 140
Reservations, Indian, 31
Resistance, 134; to disclosure of conflict information, 200–201; to diversity management, 6–8
Respect, 43, 80, 91, 126, 230; in conflict resolution, 202, 210; in Third World cultures, 29, 32, 33
Responsibility: attitudes toward, 195; diversity climate measured by, 14
Retirement, 75–76, 84, 85–86; early, 8, 13–14, 77–78, 81–82

"Reverse discrimination," 6, 7, 68, 100, 139
Rewards, organization, 13–14, 134, 138, 224–25
Reynolds, Amy, 196–97
Richard, Ivor, 185
Riesman, David, 51
Rights, equal: under Civil Rights Act of 1991, 35; of individuals with disabilities, 106; myths on, 23–24; for women workers, 54, 56. *See also* Civil Rights Act of 1964
Roe, Anna, 106
Role models, 11, 68, 86, 140, 170
Role-playing, in diversity training, 144–45
Roles, 48, 91, 165, 195, 205–6; gender, 47–48, 53, 56, 68, 77, 100, 154
Roman Catholic Church, 29, 30, 196
Roosevelt, Franklin Delano, 93
Ryder System, Inc., 218

Sabnani, Haresh et al., 145–46
Sachs, Curt, 163
Safety, occupational, 94–95, 106
Salaries/wages, 11, 37, 100; federal legislation covering, 35, 61; for foreign workers, 111, 112; for older workers, 80–81, 85–86; for women workers, 47, 54, 56, 59. *See also* Economics
Samoans, 22, 33
Samovar, Larry et al., 155, 156
"San Francisco drug language," 156
Sarbaugh, L. E., 153
Schellenbarger, Sue, 5, 52
Schweitzer, Albert, 15
Science, 48, 185
Scientific racism, 20
Sears, Roebuck and Co., 95, 97
Second Injury Funds, 95–96
Second Sex, The (Beauvoir), 49
Security Pacific Bank, 44
Segregation, housing, 26–27, 113
Self, 13, 16, 168, 169, 190; acceptance, 146; control, 33; paradigms of, 179

Self-defense, argots as aid to subculture's, 156
Self-esteem, 47, 91, 101, 202
Self-expression, 91, 218
Sensitivity, 16, 66, 68–69, 207
Separatism, 28, 202
Service workers, 36, 111
Sex (Gender), 29, 36, 191–92; discrimination on basis of, 34–35, 38–44, 48–49, 55–56, 59–60, 64–69. See also Men; Roles; Sexism; Women
Sexism, 48–49, 64, 137, 170, 182, 207; among minority men, 59; as a cause of cross-cultural conflict, 197, 210; in children's books, 65; as focus in problem solving, 209; in language, 190–91; sexual harassment as outgrowth of, 61; in the workplace, 16, 51–55, 65–66, 187, 230. See also Sex
Sexual harassment, 8–9, 48, 60–64, 65–71, 204, 211; quiz on, 71–72, 231
Shakespeare, William, 75, 186
Sherif, Carolyn, 189
Sherif, Muzafer, 189
Shute, Sara, 191
Shuy, Roger, 120–21
Sick leaves, 8, 62, 64
Sign language, Native American, 31
Silence, 142, 163–64, 192–93
Silent mind, in cross-cultural communication, 170, 199
Siller, Jerome, 101–2
Simons, George, 169
Skin color/pigmentation, 19–20, 30, 183, 184, 191–92; discrimination on basis of, 34–35, 38–44
Slang, as communication barrier, 156, 179
Slavery, 51, 184, 197
Small Business Administration, 105
Smitherman, Geneva, 190
Smith-Fess Act (Public Law 236) (1920), 102–3
Smith-Hughes Act (1917), 102
SmithKline Beecham Co., 218
Smith-Sears Veterans' Rehabilitation Act (Soldier Rehabilitation Act) (1918), 102
Snow, Kathleen, 50
Social insurance programs, 78. See also Social Security system
Social interventions, 22
Socialization, 48, 163, 180, 185, 223–25; of women, 49–51, 53
Social Security system, 58, 78, 84, 103
Social status, 119, 163, 195
Society, 33, 68, 156, 165, 177–78
Sojourner immigrants, 113
Soldier Rehabilitation Act (Smith-Sears Veterans' Rehabilitation Act) (1918), 102
Sonnenstuhl, W. J., 200
Southeastern Community College v. Davis (1979), 105–6
Southwestern Bell Corp., 195
Space. See Comfort zones
Spanish language, 26, 28–30, 129, 211
Special education in public schools, 98
Speech, 48, 159, 197; impairment of, 93, 94, 109
S style (Steady) managers, 206
Staff position, women and minorities in, 11, 59
State Farm Insurance, 9
Status. See Economics, status; Social status
Steady (S style) managers, 206
Stephens, James, 40
Stephenson, Charles, 112
Stereotypes, 41, 68, 138, 188, 198, 220, 230; awareness of during diversity training, 146; as barriers to communication, 152, 197; cultural, 10, 113–17; of ethnic minorities, 23–25; of individuals with disabilities, 91, 92–98, 100–101; of older workers, 75–77, 101; sexist, 49–51, 191
Stewart, Susan, 201
Storr, A., 222
Strathie v. Department of Transportation (1983), 106
Strauss, Anselm, 185
Stress, psychological, 43, 61, 68, 117, 145

Structure, 14; as source for change, 177–78

Subcultures, use of argots, 156–57

Subjection of Women, The (Mill), 49

Submissiveness. *See* Passivity

Superiority: attitude of in passing judgment, 222; implied, 20, 21, 191; legitimation of by oppressors, 198

"Super minority" theory, 41

Supervisors. *See* Managers/supervisors

Suspension, paradigm of, 204

Swahili language, 154

Swerdloff, Peter, 65

Syfers, Judy, 51

Symbolism, 152–55, 166, 178; linguistic, 153, 156–57, 185; racist, 183–87, 190

Taoism, 33–34

Teamwork, 30, 205–6, 227

Technical language, use by managers and supervisors, 157

Technology, 56, 177–78, 195

Territory, zones of. *See* Comfort zones

Texas Department of Community Affairs v. Burdine (1981), 38

Thelen, Herbert, 228

Thiederman, Sondra, 115–17, 128–29

Thinking, modes of, 116, 156

Third World peoples, 22, 113–14, 192; cultural perspectives, 115–17, 161, 163, 165–69; nonverbal communication, 158, 159–62; as 20th-century immigrants, 112, 117–19. *See also* Foreign workers; Immigrants; *individual groups*

Thoreau, Henry David, 110

Through the Looking Glass (Carroll), 66

Tibbitts, Clark, 74

Time, cultural assumptions on, 25, 116, 127–28, 165, 166–67, 195, 211; Chinese, 122; Mexican, 125; Mexican American, 29; Native American, 32; Portuguese, 126–27

Title I of Civil Rights Act of 1991, 35

Title II of Civil Rights Act ("Glass Ceiling Act") of 1991, 35

Title III of Civil Rights Act ("Government Employee Rights Act") of 1991, 35

Title VII, of Civil Rights Acts of 1964, 34–35, 38, 61–63, 119–20

Titles of respect, use by managers and supervisors, 171

"Tokenism," 6, 68

Tolerance, 110, 189, 210

Torrance, E. Paul, 109–10

Touching, as nonverbal communication, 161–62

Tournier, Paul, 201

Training, 6, 59, 67–68, 86, 219; in-service programs, 8, 9–10, 203–4; of job skills, 64, 96, 100, 107, 128–29, 195–96, 230. *See also* Diversity training; Vocational rehabilitation and training

"Tramps," argot, 156

Transfers, 39, 84–85

Translation, 129, 154, 180, 197

Transportation, 108, 178, 179

Trust, 4, 43, 169, 225, 230

Truth, concepts of, 125, 166

Tsukiai (Japanese interpersonal relationship), 168–69

Tumin, Melvin, 186–87

Turnover, employee, as result of sexual harassment, 60, 63

"Type A" personality cultures, 117

"Type B" personality cultures, 117

Underemployment: of individuals with disabilities, 100, 108; of women, 47, 100

Underground job market, 112

Understanding, communication of, 159, 221

Unemployment, 31, 56, 99–100, 108, 182, 187

Unions, labor, 111, 112, 120

United States Chamber of Commerce, 94

United Technologies Corp., 66–67

Urban areas, 25, 187, 196

U.S. Merit Systems Protection Board, 60–61, 63–64

U.S. Postal Service, 219
U.S. Supreme Court, decisions, 35, 38, 61–63
U.S. West Co., 44
USX Corporation, 9

Valdes, Joyce, 153–54
Values, 4–5, 19, 65, 68, 135, 201–2; in corporate cultures, 181; cultural, 10, 122–23; high- and low-context, 163–69; relationship to language, 154, 180; role in diversity training, 143
Valuing diversity, 6–8, 9, 13, 140, 143
Van Dijk, Teon, 189
Verbal communication, 152–57, 163, 165, 179; racist, 181–87; sexual harassment, 60, 62–63, 65–67. See also Communication; Languages
Vietnamese, 22, 26, 118
Violence, 118–19, 182, 188, 189
Vision impairment, 79, 93, 94, 104, 106
Vocational Education, Board for, 102
Vocational Rehabilitation Act (Barden-LaFollette Act) (1943), 103; 1954 and 1965 amendments, 103; replaced by 1973 Rehabilitation Act, 103–4
Vocational rehabilitation and training, 92–93, 96, 100, 102–5, 106

Wages. See Salaries/wages
Wagner, Ellen, 60, 63–64
Waiver of employment and retirement rights, OWBPA regulations on, 81–82
Waterman, Robert, 9
Watson, Goodwin, 228
Weeks v. Southern Bell Telephone and Telegraph Co. (1959), 106
Welfare, public, 23, 110
White House Conference on Aging (1981), 78
Whites. See Euro-Americans; Men
Wiener, Anthony, 178
Wierzbicka, Anna, 154
Williams v. Saxbe (1976), 63

Wilson, Woodrow, 102
Win-lose (Zero-sum) situation, 198, 206, 209, 228–29
Win-win (Nonzero-sum) situation, 198, 209, 211, 228–29
Withdrawal response, 141, 219
Women, 7–8, 47–49, 122–23, 126–27, 160; with disabilities, 99–100, 102; divorced, 56, 100; income of elderly, 77–78; in management positions, 5–12, 35, 206; prejudices against, 133, 146; stereotypes and myths, 49–55, 220; under Title II of Civil Rights Act of 1991, 35, 38; in workforce, 3, 11, 53, 55–60, 71, 211, 224; workforce adjustment, 64–69. See also Roles; Sex; Sexism; Sexual harassment
Women's liberation movement, 49–51, 54, 64
Women's organizations, efforts for women in the 1980s and 1990s, 56
Women's studies courses, 56
Workers' compensation insurance, 8, 95, 112
Workers with disabilities. See Individuals with disabilities
Work groups, use of, 144, 226–28
Working Woman (periodical), 60, 63
Wright, Beatrice, 92–93

Xerox Corp., 44

Year 2000, The (Kahn and Wiener), 178
Yiddish language, 156
Yin and yang, 34
Young, Shirley, 218
Young, Whitney, 20

Zander, Alvin, 139
Zen Buddhism, 163–64
Zero-sum (Win-lose) situation, 198, 206, 209, 228–29
Zola, Irving, 101–2
Zones, comfort (Zones of territory). See Comfort zones

About the Author

GEORGE HENDERSON, a pioneer among African American educators in Oklahoma, is chair of the Department of Human Relations and a Regents' Professor at the University of Oklahoma. Professor Henderson is the author or co-author of 22 books and numerous articles focusing on cultural diversity and multicultural education, including *Understanding Indigenous and Foreign Cultures* (1989).